❧ CONTENTS ❧

ACKNOWLEDGMENTS

This book is the result of over fifty years of work, interest, research, interviews, writing and rewriting, discussing, listening, traveling, and every other type of human endeavor. Gayle began researching the life of Robert Johnson in 1962 and Bruce in 1968. As we write this we are struck that it was exactly fifty years ago from this current writing that Gayle Dean first uncovered Robert Johnson's death certificate, providing previously unknown information and leading the way to much future research.

Because so much time has elapsed since we both began our journeys into the life and times of Robert Johnson there are literally hundreds of people we could thank; many have passed on, but a great number are still with us. Among those blues musicians and acquaintances of Robert Johnson who are now gone, but who provided Gayle Dean with amazing interviews, and whom he wishes he could thank are Henry Austin and Lillian Berry, Ishmon Bracey, Joe Calicott, Ledell Johnson, Hayes Mullin, Willie and Elizabeth Moore, H. C. Speir, Lula Mae Steps, Reverend and Mrs. Frank Howard, Otis Hopkins, Charlie Mullin, Willie Brown (from Arkansas), Sammy Watkins, Marvin "Smokey" Montgomery, Fred Morgan, Eula Mae Williams, Johnnie Temple, and Rosie Eskridge. Bruce similarly interviewed and wishes he could thank Robert Lockwood Jr., Johnny Shines, David "Honeyboy" Edwards, and Loretha Zimmerman-Smith. The late Mack McCormick, the first person to locate Robert's family in the form of his half sister Carrie Harris, was also the first to see the photos of Robert in her possession. Mack was one of the foremost Johnson scholars and it is a shame that his book about Robert, *Portrait of a Phantom*, never saw completion. Over several years both Gayle Dean and Bruce had many conversations with Mack and when he learned of this project he graciously provided comments and suggestions that allowed us to do additional research that would add to our body of knowledge. The late Steven LaVere was likewise a great source of information on Robert, and his published work, while occasionally incomplete, served as another great resource. We also thank the company he founded, Delta Haze Corporation, for permission to use so many wonderful photos from his collection. Tremendous thanks go to Lawrence Cohn, friend and supporter who won a Grammy for his 1990 work *Robert Johnson, the Complete Recordings* (Columbia). Lawrence, a record collector, historian, music scholar, ex-music executive, and so much more, provided a great deal of information about Robert that he had personally gleaned from Don Law, Frank Driggs, and so many others. His book *Nothing But the Blues: The Music and the Musicians* (Abbeville, 1993) is one of the finest overviews of the entire spectrum of the blues. Dan Handwerker, whose family owned the land on which Charley Dodds Spencer and family (including Robert) lived in Memphis was a generous and informative resource. Robert Hirsberg, whose parents owned Hirsberg's store in Friars Point, Mississippi, in front of which Robert used to play, was also a great source of information. Dr. Richard Taylor, director of the Tunica Museum, verified contextual information for us concerning Robert's early schooling and the cemetery in which his first wife, Virginia, is buried. John Tefteller of Blues Images was a great supporter of this project and supplied us with the only known photo of Charley Patton. Thanks to Steve Armitage for digitally cleaning Robert Johnson's death certificate. Lew Campbell graciously supplied us with a photo of Johnny Shines from his collection, and Jane Templin provided a rare photo of Marie and Ernie Oertle. John Paul Hammond, who has spent much of his life studying and performing Johnson's music, enthusiastically supported this project and has been a great friend. His brother, Jason Hammond, gave us a wonderful photo of their father, John Henry Hammond II, circa 1937. Jim O'Neal, Scott Barretta, Jas Obrecht, Barry Lee Pearson, Barry Mazor, Adam Gussow, David Evans, Mark Ari, Nicholas Gray, Paul Vernon, James Smith, Frank Matheis, Andy Cohen, Shelley Ritter of the Delta Blues Museum, Dr. John Hasse of Music at the National Museum of American History Smithsonian Institution, Brett Bonner and *Living Blues* magazine, Greg Johnson at the University of Mississippi Blues Archives, and all the contributors to Facebook's *Real Blues Forum* provided much needed and appreciated comments, critiques, and discussion. Elijah Wald and Alan Govenar provided excellent information, comments, and edits. Michael Malis of the University of Michigan School of Music did transcriptional analysis of Johnson's music. Thanks to Sony Music Entertainment; the Memphis Public Library Memphis and Shelby County Rooms; Leticia Vacek, city clerk of the City of San Antonio; the San Antonio Police Department; and the Mississippi Department of Archives and History.

We would be remiss if we did not acknowledge the scholars before us who attempted to write about Johnson's life: Stephen Calt, Samuel Charters, Bruce Cook, Francis Davis, David Evans, Julio Finn, Tom Freeland, Paul Garon, Ted Gioia, Peter Guralnick, Steve James, Edward Komara, Steve LaVere, Alan Lomax, Greil Marcus, Margaret Moser, Giles Oakley, Robert Palmer, Barry Lee Pearson and Bill McCulloh, Dave Rubin, Tony Sherman, Patricia Schroeder, John Michael Spencer, Elijah Wald, Pete Welding, Dick Waterman, and any others we might have missed.

Musicians or friends of Robert we never personally interviewed but who knew him and whose testimonies we researched included Son House, Henry Townsend, Calvin Frazier, Memphis Slim,

Willie Mae Powell Holmes, Willie Mason, Cedell Davis, Willie Coffee, Annye Anderson, Don Law, Marie Oertle, Virgie Cain, Israel "Wink" Clark, R. L. Windum, Nate Richardson, and others.

Steve Amos, chancery clerk of Hazelhurst, Mississippi; Randall Day, executive director of the Hazlehurst Area Chamber of Commerce; Dr. Jim Brewer, founder and chairman of the Board of the Mississippi Musicians Hall of Fame in Hazlehurst, Mississippi; and Mr. Hugh Jenkins of Hazlehurst, owner of the original shack in which Robert Johnson was born, are all owed inestimable thanks.

So many friends are still playing the music of Robert Johnson and have given us so much feedback and inspiration that they deserve special mention: John Paul Hammond was one of the first modern players to learn and perform Robert's incredible music, and his technique and approach set a high bar for all to follow. Rory Block early on began meticulously studying and performing Robert's songs. Her instruction books, dvds, and performances have influenced countless numbers of guitarists. These two ground-breakers helped open the doors to Robert's music. Scott Ainslie, Andy Cohen, Stefan Grossman, Erik Frandsen, Shari Kane, Woody Mann, and many others have been gracious and talented friends. Thanks to you all for keeping the tradition alive.

The family of Robert Johnson—his late son Claud Johnson and his grandsons Steven Johnson, director of the Robert Johnson Blues Foundation (who in 2006 invited Bruce to serve as an advisor on the foundation's executive board); Michael Johnson; and Greg Johnson have been good friends and supportive of every aspect of this work. We are, as we like to say, brothers from another mother.

We would like to give a big thank you to both our literary agent Russell Galen of Scovil, Galen, Ghosh Literary Agency, Inc., New York, and Larry Townsend, Esq. of San Francisco, our intellectual property lawyer, for working us through matters beyond our comprehension.

Any book is ultimately only as good as the editors and staff with whom the authors work, and Yuval Taylor, Michelle Williams, and the entire staff of Chicago Review Press have been among the very best. Their meticulous review of our work and clarifying and exciting edits and suggestions have made this work a far better book than we originally brought to Chicago Review Press. You, the reader, owe them, as do we, a great deal of appreciation.

Gayle would like to personally thank Jan Swanson, Wendell Cook, Christopher Smith, Steve Cushing, Jim DeCola, Ace Atkins, and Jas Obrecht. These friends were largely responsible for the successful competition of this joint effort.

Finally, Bruce would like to thank Pamela Peterson for helping him through some rough times and providing him with interest and musical inspiration, and to Emily Maria Marcil, whose daily love and encouragement continue to give him the strength and belief to go on.

With so many to thank it is possible we missed someone. If so we apologize, but know that this work would not have been possible without all of you. For those mentioned, this book is dedicated.

Bruce Conforth, Ann Arbor, Michigan
Gayle Dean Wardlow, Milton, Florida
2018

INTRODUCTION

Robert Johnson has occupied a unique place in the American musical psyche for almost sixty years. Until 1959 he was an interesting bluesman only to those few 78 rpm record collectors who were lucky enough to find one of his old recordings. But all that changed when Samuel Charters published his landmark book *The Country Blues*, the first scholarly text devoted solely to the blues.[1] Of Robert Johnson, Charters admitted, "Almost nothing is known about his life."

That sentence is still true today. Johnson is the subject of the most famous myth about the history of the blues: he allegedly sold his soul at the crossroads in exchange for his incredible talent, and this "deal" led to his tragic death at age twenty-seven. This notion can be recited by almost everyone who has heard of him, but the actual story of his life remains obscure save for a few inaccurate anecdotes.

Charters claimed, incorrectly, that Robert was poisoned by his common-law wife in San Antonio, Texas, shortly after finishing his last recording session. He added the apocryphal anecdote that some of his recordings were done in a pool hall and were broken during a billiard ball fight. He interpreted Robert's lyrics in a sensational manner. "The finest of Robert Johnson's blues," he wrote, "have a brooding sense of torment and despair. The blues has become a personified figure of despondency. . . . His singing becomes so disturbed it is almost impossible to understand the words."[2] Charters was well intentioned, but by publishing these words he inadvertently assisted in the creation of a mythic Robert Johnson with little relation to the real musician.

Robert's music was rereleased for the first time in 1959 on the companion album to Charters's book, which included "Preaching Blues." Then, in 1961, Columbia released the album *King of the Delta Blues Singers*, finally giving the public wide access to his recordings.[3] Producer Frank Driggs, in the liner notes to the album, drew upon Charters's book and the work of British blues scholar Paul Oliver. He admitted how little was known about Robert or his life: "Robert Johnson is little, very little more than a name on aging index cards and a few dusty master records in the files of a phonograph company that no longer exists. Efforts on the part of the world's foremost blues research specialists to trace Johnson's career and substantiate details of his life have provided only meager information." But he added to Robert's mythic proportions with erroneous information: "[He] was already a legend in 1938 when John Hammond was planning his 'Spirituals to Swing' concert for presentation in Carnegie Hall"; "Johnson's recordings became collectors' items almost as soon as they were released"; "Until his recording debut, Johnson had seldom, if ever, been away from the plantation in Robinsonville, Mississippi, where he was born and raised"; "It was obvious he wanted to get away, but never could."[4]

The album was produced largely through the instigation of the noted producer John Henry Hammond II, who had championed Johnson's work as early as the 1930s. *King of the Delta Blues Singers* was a landmark for several important reasons: It made Robert's music available to a new generation and audience—mostly young whites who were involved in the folk music revival. It boldly proclaimed Robert to be the king of the Delta blues singers—there was no one better. As the first major-label reissue of any of the guitar-oriented country blues artists from the 1920s or 1930s there was no other music to compare it to—Robert Johnson was it, the new generation's first experience in hearing the Delta blues. And it strongly influenced such future trendsetters as a young Bob Dylan,

Eric Clapton, and Keith Richards. They became Robert Johnson proselytizers.

That release created new interest in all things Robert Johnson. His legacy and life were already being researched by scholars similar in age to or slightly younger than Charters such as Mack McCormick and coauthor Gayle Dean Wardlow. But this release coincided with the launching of the blues revival. It sent young record collectors and fans seeking out bluesmen who recorded in the 1920s and '30s, and in the process they found Son House, Skip James, and others who actually knew Robert. Then, in 1968, Gayle Dean made a historical discovery, locating Robert's death certificate. He also conducted a number of interviews in the 1960s with people who knew Robert personally, providing the first factual information about his life.

In 1970 Columbia issued a second volume of Robert's songs with only three brief paragraphs of liner-note information. There, blues writer Pete Welding maintained and added to Robert's myth by proclaiming,

> No other blues are so apocalyptic in their life view. They are shot through with dark foreboding, and almost total disenchantment with the human condition [and] besetting, mindless terrors that haunted all his days and nights. . . . His songs are the diary of a wanderer through the tangle of the black underworld, the chronicle of a sensitive black Orpheus in his journey along the labyrinthine path of the human psyche. In his songs one hears the impassioned, unheeded cries of man, rootless and purposeless. The acrid stench of evil burns ever in his mind.[5]

In 1973, Mack McCormick, a folklorist from Houston, Texas, who had already revived the career of Sam "Lightnin'" Hopkins, located Robert's half sister Carrie Harris Thompson. She showed him two photos of Robert. One was the now famous Hooks Brothers studio portrait, and the other (unpublished and supposedly still in McCormick's collection) was a photo of Robert, his half sister Carrie, and her son Louis in his navy uniform. Finding Carrie launched McCormick into a decades-long search for additional factual information. Eventually he even found the man who had accidently murdered the bluesman. McCormick planned to use his information to write a definitive book about Johnson tentatively titled *Biography of a Phantom*. But the book never happened.

Sam Charters reentered the Robert Johnson universe in 1973 with a new book simply titled *Robert Johnson*. Charters used Robert's death certificate, found by Gayle Dean, to focus on his story. He questioned Robert's birthplace as listed on the certificate and argued that Robert had to have been born in the Delta "since Hazlehurst is south of Jackson, about thirty-five miles out of it on Route 51, in Copiah County, and everybody else who knew Robert had always said he was from the Delta, north of Jackson in Tunica County." Charters also relied on recollections of Robert's sometime traveling partner, Johnny Shines, providing some insights into Johnson's personality and musical ability. But Shines provided little actual information about his life.[6] The storyline was still missing.

That same year Bruce Cook published *Listen to the Blues*, describing Robert's importance to blues music and American culture:

> If Robert Johnson had not existed, they would have had to invent him. He is the most potent legend in all the blues— that of the gifted young artist, driven by his hunger for life and his passion for music to excesses that killed him at the age of twenty-four. . . . He is the Shelley, Keats, and Rimbaud of the blues all rolled into one. If any bluesman is assured of immortality it is this little drifter-with-a-guitar who may never have left the South.[7]

Actually Robert was accidently murdered when he was twenty-seven years old, not twenty-four. But misinformation was not Cook's only problem. His analysis is preterit, romantic hyperbole. It articulated one of the quintessential American myths: the gifted drifter "driven by his hunger for life"—the individual versus society and convention. Cook's comparison to Shelley, Keats, and Rimbaud furthered the image of a bright light burning itself out.

When Memphis blues researcher Stephen C. LaVere began tracing Robert's life, he used McCormick's lead to locate Robert's half sister Carrie Harris Thompson. In 1973, he convinced her to make a contractual agreement to assign him 50 percent of all royalties and other monies generated by his overseeing Robert's material. LaVere became, in essence, the overseer of Robert's life, music, and photos for the next several decades, fiercely protecting his own interests.

In 1982, using information that Mack McCormick shared with him, Peter Guralnick published "Searching for Robert Johnson" in *Living Blues* magazine. But this "biography" contained little hard data. Guralnick tried to document Robert's life, but his account is more widely known for one single sentence: "Son House was convinced that Robert Johnson had [sold his soul to the Devil at the crossroads], and undoubtedly, as Johnny Shines says, others were too." There is no evidence, however, that House ever made such a statement. The myth that had been a rumor now seemed to be fact.[8]

Guralnick expanded his article into a book released in 1989 under the same title, and that same year *Rolling Stone* magazine published the first photo of Robert.[9] One year later, *Living Blues* magazine dedicated an entire issue to "The Death of Robert Johnson," his legend, crossroads and hoodoo myths, and more. Using interviews from many of Robert's contemporaries, it attempted to produce a factual understanding of the man and his life.[10]

In 1991 Sony Music released a two-CD set of Johnson's recordings, *The Complete Recordings*. It marked the first time that all of

Robert's known recordings, including alternate takes, were issued in one package. Producer Lawrence Cohn, a former head of Epic Records, which was now part of Sony Music, had led the effort to create a roots music reissue program, but Sony kept refusing. After several years of persuasion they finally relented and approved the project. Cohn decided that Robert Johnson would be his first release. Sony expected the boxed set to sell no more than ten thousand copies over a five-year period and ran an initial pressing of four thousand. Immediately they were shocked. The set sold hundreds of thousands of copies in the first several weeks and today has sold more than fifty million copies in the United States alone. It also won a Grammy award.[11] The accompanying booklet by LaVere provided, arguably, the most complete information about Robert's life at that time. But it was still factually incomplete because it did not focus on certain periods of his life (Memphis, for example). It also provided erroneous information about persons in Robert's life. The most glaring errors concerned guitarist Ike Zimmerman and his role in Robert's musical development. LaVere's work was good, but far from complete.[12]

In 1992 Sony films released the British documentary *The Search for Robert Johnson* featuring blues guitarist/singer and Johnson disciple John Paul Hammond. The film introduced the world to Robert's former girlfriends and his boyhood pals, and used informants like Gayle Dean and McCormick.[13] In 1996, Gayle Dean found the back side of Johnson's death certificate and published its contents in *Guitar Player* magazine. Two years later he challenged the crossroads myth in his book *Chasin' That Devil Music*.

In 2003, Barry Lee Pearson and Bill McCulloch published *Robert Johnson Lost and Found*.[14] One year later Elijah Wald's *Escaping the Delta: Robert Johnson and the Invention of the Blues* was released.[15] While both are stellar books, neither claimed to be a biography of Robert. Pearson and McCulloch's work analyzed the genesis of myths surrounding his life. They claimed that these were created by contemporary popular culture, stereotyping, and a fascination with reconstructing history. Wald examined the myths surrounding Robert's life too, and tried to separate him from them.

The closest written biography produced in recent years is *Crossroads: The Life and Afterlife of Blues Legend Robert Johnson* by Tom Graves, which was published in 2008.[16] LaVere claimed that *Crossroads* contained "less hyperbole and more factual information about Johnson than any other book."[17] But Graves's writings fell far short of LaVere's claim. Fewer than thirty pages contained information about Johnson's life, and much of that was erroneous.[18]

Sony Records, who owned Johnson's recordings, recognized his strong marketability and decided to capitalize on his centennial year by releasing a special boxed set: the 2011 *Robert Johnson, The Complete Original Masters: Centennial Edition*. It was marketed as "the ultimate collector's vinyl piece." It re-created the historic look and feel of the original dozen ten-inch 78 rpm discs that were sold to record buyers in the 1930s. The limited edition sets were individually numbered from one to one thousand. Housed in a lavish ten-inch album book, each vinyl disc played at 45 rpm, and the set also reproduced the original record labels. Music historian Ted Gioia wrote a fifteen-hundred-word essay and LaVere contributed a five-page "new" biography.[19]

Robert's name and image were spawning many concerts, tributes, trinkets, and geegaws, including computer flash drives, guitar picks, and even a limited-edition Robert Johnson "Hellhound on My Ale" beer. Manufactured by Dogfish Head Brewery, it bore the claim: "To accentuate and magnify the citrusy notes of the centennial hops (and as a shout out to Robert Johnson's mentor Blind Lemon Jefferson) we add dried lemon peel and flesh to the whirlpool."[20] There is no evidence that Jefferson ever mentored Robert, but such factual information is unimportant when you're celebrating the birthday of a myth.

No book before this one has included all of the reminiscences of Johnson by the people who knew him personally. After more than fifty years of researching Robert's life and performing his music, we decided to correct that omission and bring together those resources in our comprehensive biography. We meticulously researched every article, book, video, or film by any author or producer, from academic scholar to lay blues fan; we transcribed every quote by anyone who ever knew Robert; and we grounded this all with quotations from our own research and every other resource we could find. Every census record, city directory, marriage license, funeral notice, and newspaper article was studied and referenced.

Herein you will find memories of Robert from his stepfamily, boyhood friends, neighbors, fellow musicians, girlfriends, and other acquaintances: everyone who ever committed a personal recollection to tape, page, or film. (The quotations have been lightly edited for clarity.) These sources helped us create a timeline of Johnson's life. What we produced is a book based not on conjecture about Robert Johnson, but on first-person accounts of who he actually was. By doing so we hope to free Johnson from being the sign and myth that blues fans created and return him to his human particulars.

Not only do we reveal Robert's real story, but also where other accounts were in error. Basically, we discovered that everything we, and everyone else, believed or thought about Robert Johnson was wrong in some respects. At this point, whatever remains unknown about Robert Johnson will probably remain unknown forever. Although this will almost certainly not be the last book about him, the possibility of any new revelations surfacing seems extremely remote.

His story, a human story of suffering and joy, extreme highs and devastating lows, has finally been told.

❦ 1 ❦

ROBERT JOHNSON IS IN TOWN

The summer of 1936 Robert Johnson stood in front of Walker's General Store and Gas Station adjoining the Martinsville train depot. He put down his bag made of blue-and-white bed ticking packed full of clothes, at least one notebook, and other belongings, and began playing his guitar. He was there to advertise his night-time performance at O'Malley's—a bootleg house not far from the old Damascus Church just north of neighboring Hazlehurst's city limits, up the railroad tracks on the east side of old Highway 51. Hazlehurst was a town of about three thousand souls sitting thirty-five miles south of Jackson, Mississippi. Robert had been born in Hazlehurst twenty-five years earlier, and now he was there to play his blues at one of the many juke joints he frequented throughout the area. A slight five foot eight, 140 pounds, Robert was well known for more than just his music.

Robert had already gotten one local girl pregnant—Virgie Jane Smith—and the men in and around Hazlehurst wanted to make sure that was not going to happen to their daughters. Rosa Redman was eleven years old that year. Later a short, plump history teacher, she lived most of her life on the old Mangold Plantation, near both the house where Robert was born and O'Malley's juke. She recalled

Martinsville train depot, Walker's General Store and Gas Station.
Mississippi Department of Archives and History

that Robert's presence would create a certain stir among the residents. "People would know when Robert was in town. The men would let people know, and if they saw him coming up the road, our mothers would make all the girls go inside. It was OK for our older brothers, uncles, or fathers to go see him play and get drunk, but it was off limits to us girls. They'd keep us inside and locked up!"[1]

His blues was the devil's music and could only lead to sin.

Throughout the Delta region and beyond, Robert's rambling had left a trail of drunken men and brokenhearted women. Whether he was playing a juke like O'Malley's, a picnic, or a party, Robert was always looking for a woman to satisfy his needs, financially or sexually. His songs were often a tool to seduce some woman he took a fancy to, and the human remnants he left behind were well known to locals. He even bragged about his conquests in one of his songs, "Traveling Riverside Blues": "I got womens in Vicksburg, clean on to Tennessee, but my Friars Point rider, now, hops all over me."

※

Robert Johnson was using his guitar abilities to forge the transition from the older blues of Charley Patton, Henry "Ragtime

Texas" Thomas, Lead Belly, or even Son House, to the more modern approach and sounds of Muddy Waters and the postwar blues players. He played blues, pop tunes, jazz, and ragtime; started to popularize the use of guitar riffs as signature elements of a song; and was one of the first to use a boogie beat for his rhythm accompaniment, copying the driving, rhythmic bass that barrelhouse pianists played with their left hand. His playing helped move blues guitar fretting out of the first position and into the use of the entirety of the fretboard, opening musical possibilities that had previously been reserved for jazz guitarists.

He was a dancer and harmonica player in ways that surprised his companions, and he used all his entertainment talents as vehicles to further his quest for fame and freedom from the burdens of sharecropping, and even, perhaps, from the Jim Crow racism of the South. Yet, in spite of his considerable talents, Robert displayed an untrusting and insecure personality. He refused to let you pay too close attention to how he was playing, turning his back on you or stopping his playing completely if he thought you were watching him too closely.

But Robert also had an unrelenting desire for a good time, and his personal exploits would eventually lead to myth and speculation. He did little to make his world clear, for he refused to speak about his family and life, and he never—if he ever knew about them—did anything to either validate or disavow the ideas about him that circulated among his listeners and acquaintances. He was a chameleon who was perhaps on his own search for his true identity.

By the time Rosa Redman saw him, Robert's rambling had become both his main way of traveling from one musical job to the next and his way to satisfy his need to just "get up and go." His travels on both sides of the Mississippi River took him on circuitous journeys throughout Mississippi and parts of Louisiana and Arkansas. He followed Highway 1, which ran alongside the Mississippi

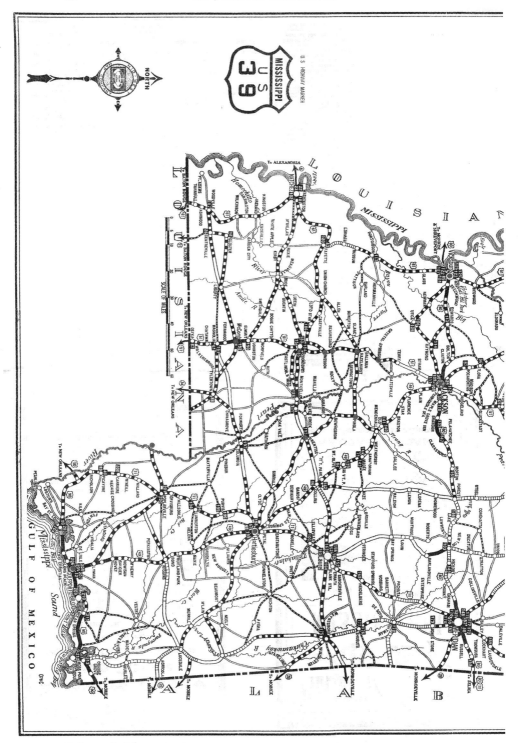

Robert Johnson's Mississippi. *Bruce Conforth*

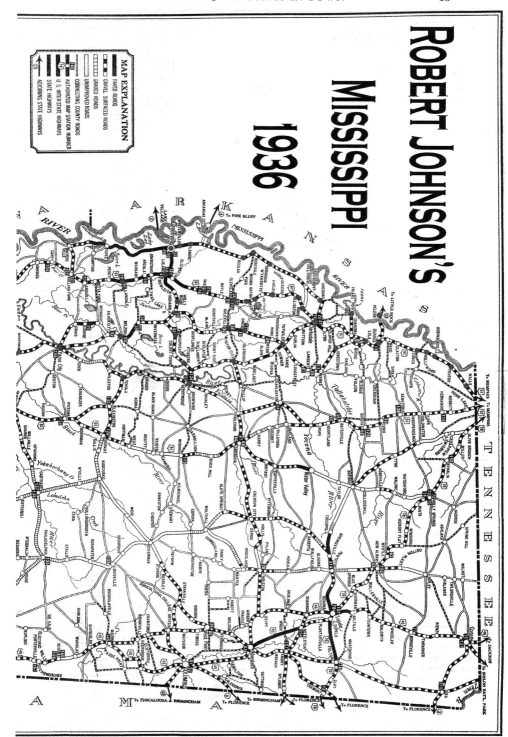

River, Highways 61 and 49, which went north and south through the center of the Delta, and Highway 82, which ran east and west.

Robert found places to play and sing in Greenwood, Itta Bena, Moorhead ("where the Southern cross the Dog"), Indianola, Holly Ridge, Leland, and Greenville, all located on Highway 82. From Greenville, Robert traveled north on Highway 1, stopping at Winterville, Lamont, Beulah, Rosedale, Gunnison, Sherard, and then into Clarksdale. From Clarksdale he had several options.

He could continue north on Highway 61 and stop at Jonestown (with a detour west to Friars Point), Lula (onetime home of Charley Patton), Tunica, Robinsonville (where his mother lived), Walls, and then his Memphis home. Memphis was where he spent his seminal childhood years, the home of the family he considered his true kin, headed by Charles Dodds Spencer, his mother's ex-husband. He would go back there as often as he could throughout his life. From Memphis he could easily cross into Arkansas to reach West Memphis with its freewheeling base of jukes and party houses, then go to Marianna, Helena, and West Helena—wide-open towns for black blues singers—which Robert could also reach via the Friars Point ferry.

If he went south from Clarksdale on Highway 61 he hit Alligator, Shelby, Mound Bayou, Merigold, Cleveland, and Shaw. Conversely, if he headed south on Highway 49 West he stopped at Tutwiler, Drew, and Ruleville. Highway 49 East took him to Minter City, Greenwood, Tchula, Yazoo City, Bentonia (where Skip James had lived and played), and finally into Jackson.

From Jackson south on Highway 51 Robert stopped at Crystal Springs (home of Tommy Johnson), Hazlehurst (where his Aunt Clara lived), Beauregard and Wesson, and from there to Bogalusa, Louisiana, and over to Gulfport, Mississippi.

Of the locations Robert frequented, Friars Point was particularly important—a ferry ran between there and Arkansas. Mississippi

Friars Point, ca. 1935, levees to the left with Mississippi River behind.
Mississippi Department of Archives and History

was still a dry state even after Prohibition ended in 1933, so liquor was transported into Friars Point by way of that ferry. That Delta river town was full of jukes, black lodges, and clubs. Robert loved playing in Friars Point for all those reasons and more.

Elizabeth Moore ran a Friars Point juke and recalled that her husband used to bring Robert, before he had recorded, to play there on Saturday nights. She had moved there from Robinsonville, where Johnson had first played for her. "He was staying over there in West Stover [a small sawmill community] cross the river and my husband went over there and got him. Brought him cross the river [on a ferry] and he played over here for 'bout two or three months. He had three or four songs he did then [his originals]."[2]

In downtown Friars Point, Hirsberg's store carried every item that the local residents needed: drugs, farm supplies, clothing, food. They extended credit too, an important consideration during the Depression. As a main meeting place for area residents, Hirsberg's was the perfect location for Robert to play during the day, both to make extra money and to advertise where he would be that night. He would sit on one of the red wooden benches Hirsberg had placed on either side of the front door, and his afternoon appearances drew

Hirsberg's store. *Bruce Conforth*

such enormous crowds that they created a bottleneck, making it hard for anyone to get to the door. The owners found a simple solution: they would climb to the roof of their one-story building and throw vegetables down onto the entertained assembly to get them to disperse.[3] Robert was used to drawing such crowds, however, and they just made the possibility of his making a decent night's pay and going home with the woman of his fancy more probable.

The night in Hazlehurst that Rosa Redman remembered was filled with men and women dancing and drinking, whooping and hollering, pairing up for a night of partying and sex. They frolicked until Robert either went home with one of the women or collapsed drunk on the floor of the store to sleep it off.

In a few short months Robert would be a recording artist, and the next time they saw him they might have even purchased his

"Terraplane Blues"—a modest hit—and "Kind Hearted Woman Blues" for their own home Victrolas.

But on this particular night the audience had no inkling of what was to come, and neither did Robert. They only knew that Robert Johnson was in town: a good-guitar-playing, hard-drinking, woman-loving little man who kept them entertained.

So who was this Robert Johnson?

To find that out we need to go back to the beginning.

2

BEFORE THE BEGINNING

Saturday afternoon, February 2, 1889, in Hazlehurst, Mississippi, was a clear and cool day. The temperature was in the sixties, the sun was shining, and the air was full of the expectation that spring was not far away. It was a good day for a wedding. Reverend H. Brown had driven his horse and buggy ten miles from his home in Crystal Springs to perform several marriages, and now nineteen-year-old Julia Ann Majors and twenty-two-year-old Charles C. Dodds stood before him ready to take their vows. Around them were family and friends all joined in anticipation of the ceremony and the party that would follow. Julia was a short, fair-skinned young lady, and Charles was a slightly taller, lanky young man. It was almost inevitable that they would meet and marry, for both their families had been residents in the Hazlehurst area for decades—and both the bride's and groom's mixed-race heritage went as far back as records existed.

Julia was born in Hazlehurst in October 1870, the daughter of Gabriel (b. 1850) and Lucinda Brown Majors (b. 1853). Gabriel's father, Wiatt Majors, was born in Virginia in 1814, as was Lucinda's father. All Julia's family dating back to the eighteenth century identified as mulattoes, not as Negroes. This meant more social, legal, and cultural acceptance; mulattoes had greater freedom to own personal

19

Julia Majors.
© Delta Haze Corporation

property and could "acquire . . . and . . . dispose of the same in the same manner and to the same extent that white persons may." Cohabitating mulattoes were considered legally married, and mulattoes were even considered to be "by law competent witnesses . . . in civil cases, and in criminal cases where they are the victims." These were rights that blacks in the Mississippi Delta simply did not enjoy.[1]

Charles C. Dodds was born in Hazlehurst around 1867. His father, Charles Dodds Sr., was born in 1831 in North Carolina, and his mother, Harriet (last name unknown), was born in 1846. She also listed herself as a mulatto.

On that Saturday the young couple was starting a new life together, and this would have been a time for celebrating. As an increasingly prosperous carpenter and maker of wicker furniture, Charles would have had the ability to provide a pleasant time for his new wife and

Charles Dodds.
© *Delta Haze Corporation*

anyone else in attendance. One can imagine the crisp afternoon air becoming full of the smell of barbecue or a fish fry, both Mississippi culinary standards, and possibly the sounds of music makers: perhaps a fiddle and guitar. There was little that would not have made the prospects seem bright for the newly married pair. With Charles able to provide comfortably for his wife and family-to-be and Julia a hard-working housekeeper, the freedom they found in Hazlehurst seemed welcoming, as it had to their parents and grandparents.

Even in those early years, according to a 1907 Sanborn Fire Insurance map, the nine blocks that comprised the town proper contained at least seven general merchandise stores, five grocery stores, three drugstores, two hardware stores, at least two restaurants, three livery stables and harness shops, two women's clothing and notions stores, three churches, a Masonic Hall, a bank, carpentry shop, three hotels, a dentist/doctor's office, a barber, a courthouse, a jail, a train station, a cotton gin, and a school. Blacks and whites at least appeared to peacefully coexist. It was everything that a new family could want.

Although not in the Delta proper (Hazlehurst is some thirty-five miles south of the state's capital, Jackson, fifty miles southeast of Vicksburg—generally regarded as the southern tip of the region—and two hundred miles south of Clarksdale, considered the "heart" of the Delta), the town is still in the alluvial plain created by thousands of years of regular flooding of the Mississippi and Yazoo Rivers, a plain that boasts some of the most fertile soil in the world. European settlers in the eighteenth century grew sugarcane and rice at first, but the invention of the cotton gin at the end of the century made the cultivation of cotton more profitable, and an increased demand for labor drove the domestic slave trade, forcing more than one million slaves to fill that need. After the Civil War the need for labor to farm this rich land attracted thousands of migrants who traded their labor for the opportunity to purchase some of its acreage. Somewhat surprisingly, by the late 1800s two-thirds of the independent farmers were African American. Economic conditions changed, however, and the price of cotton fell, causing many black landowners to sell their property and become sharecroppers, laborers for white landowners. Between 1910 and 1920, the first and second generations of African Americans after slavery lost almost all of their stake in the land.

Although sharecropping and tenant farming replaced the slave system, there was little actual difference in social and working conditions, and since many black families were illiterate, they were often horribly exploited by plantation owners. The number of lynchings of black men rose dramatically, and due to its harsh and tenacious brand of oppression, the Delta became known as "the most Southern place on earth."[2] But Hazlehurst, though still within

February 2, 1889, marriage license of Julia Majors and Charles Dodds.
Marriage Certificates, Recorder of Deeds, City of Hazlehurst, Copiah County, Mississippi

a state whose racist history was considerably worse than that of its neighbors, developed a culture that was far more liberal in its treatment of African Americans, especially those who were biracial, such as Robert's ancestors.

Of the approximately twelve million Africans brought to the Americas, as few as 350,000 came directly to the territories that would become the United States.[3] Virtually all of those slaves were brought to the East Coast, primarily to Virginia and the Carolinas. Among them were the ancestors of Wiatt Majors and Charles Dodds, who were given their freedom in their respective states prior to the Civil War and moved from Virginia and North Carolina to Mississippi as free men. There are no records that they settled anywhere else in between, and there is no indication that members of either side of the family were enslaved in Mississippi.

Free blacks in the South were not uncommon. In 1810, there had been 108,265 free black persons there, representing "the fastest-growing element in the Southern population." By 1860, more free blacks lived in the South (261,918) than in the North (226,152). Forty percent were mulattoes, and for the most part they had been released from slavery through manumission (formal acts of emacipation by their slaveowners). After receiving their freedom they often moved, as did Robert's ancestors, from the Upper South (Delaware, Maryland, Virginia, North Carolina, Kentucky, Missouri, and Tennessee) to the Lower South (Alabama, Arkansas, Florida, Louisiana, Mississippi, and Texas). For the most part, such movement was instigated by the possibility of money to be made in the Lower South's cotton industry.[4]

Because of their status as free black persons before the Civil War, and as mulattoes after, the Dodds and Majors families enjoyed

1900 Hazlehurst Census for Dodds family. *Department of Commerce, Bureau of the Census. State: Mississippi; County: Copiah; Hazlehurst West; Precinct: Part of Beat One; Enumeration District 31, Sheet 2-B. June 1, 1900.*

ha___ Granted, Bargained, Sold and Conveyed, and by these presents do____ Grant, Bargain, Sell, Alien and Convey to the said party of the second part, a certain tract or parcel of land, situated in the County of Copiah and the State of Mississippi, and more particularly described as follows, to-wit: *Lot. 2, Square, 12,*

Sec 33. T. 1. R. 2 West as per map of Damascus land recorded in book W. W. pages 28 & 29, in the office of the Clerk of the Chancery Court for the County of Copiah and State of Miss. Containing eight acres more or less.

TO HAVE AND TO HOLD the above described premises, together with all and singular the improvements and appurtenances thereunto belonging or in anywise appertaining, to the party of the second part, *his* heirs and assigns, forever.

AND the part__ of the first part covenant___ with the party of the second part, that *they* will warrant and forever defend the title to the above described premises to the party of the second part, *his* heirs and assigns, free from and against the right, title or claims of the part___of the first part, and *his* heirs, and from all and every person or persons whomsoever, both at law and in equity.

IN WITNESS WHEREOF, The said part___ of the first part hereunto set *their* hand3 and seal3, the day and year first above written.

A Mangold (seal)
I F Mangold (Seal)
M F Mangold (Seal)
Magdalena Faler (Seal)
A B Guynes Receiver (x3)

STATE OF MISSISSIPPI, } ss.
COPIAH COUNTY.   PERSONALLY appeared before me, *Clerk of the Circuit Court* in and for the County and State aforesaid, the within named *A Mangold, I F* *Mangold, M F Mangold, & Magdalena Faler, A B Guynes Receiver* who acknowledged that *they* signed, sealed and delivered the foregoing Deed on the day and year therein mentioned, as *their* act and deed.

GIVEN under my hand and seal, this 4th day of *Dec* A.D. 190*1* (Seal) *D.C. Woods Clk* (Seal)

Filed for Record the 4th day of *Dec* 190*1*, at 11-3¼ M., and recorded 18th day of *December* 190*1* *Jno B Mayes* CLERK.

The 1901 deed. *State of Mississippi, Copiah County Chancery Clerk, Hazlehurst, Mississippi*

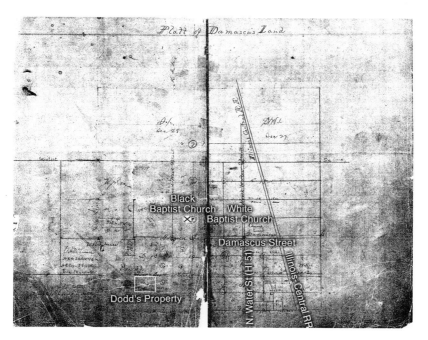

A platt map from 1901 shows the exact location of the white
Damascus church and the specific land that Charles bought.
State of Mississippi, Copiah County Chancery Clerk, Hazlehurst, Mississippi

a better lifestyle than most black families who lived in the Delta.
They had more legal and cultural opportunities. Julia and Charles
settled in Beat One in the west part of the Hazlehurst and Martinsville precincts of Copiah County and had six children in their
first eleven years of marriage. The 1900 United States Census listed
Charles Dodds, head of household (35), wife Julia Majors (25),
children Louise (12), Harriet (9), Bessie (8), Willie M. (5), Lula B.
(4), and Melvin Leroy (1).[5]

On December 4, 1901, Charles purchased "eight acres, more
or less" from a white family, the Mangolds, for the sum of $181—
more than $5,000 today. The Mangolds had owned the large plan-
tation that bore their name and were now dividing it up into sharecropper lots.

The family's new land was located on the northern side of Hazlehurst, just outside the existing city limits. The area was known for its ramshackle black homesteads near what is still called Damascus Road. The deed referred to the property as part of "Damascus Land." Two Baptist churches are now located in the area. The original white Baptist church lay to the east between North Water Street (now Highway 51) and the Illinois Central railroad. The congregation had allowed both slaves and free blacks to sit in the back or the balcony during services until its members finally raised enough money to help the black members build their own Damascus church, located on the west side of North Water Street on Damascus Road.

No record of a deed of purchase or permit for a building under the name Charles or Charley Dodds exists in any Copiah County record books. The Dodds family lived, therefore, in either a rented building or in one of the shacks that didn't require registration with the township. The town's chamber of commerce reports today that Charles built a house in 1905, although there is no recorded confirmation of this. In 1906 Charles defaulted on indebtedness and the deed to the property was lost. For someone who had been able to purchase a plot of land for a sizeable amount of money only five years earlier, this must have been embarrassing, and perhaps even infuriating for Charles. It's unknown whether he simply ran into a streak of financial bad luck or whether his misfortune was the result of a calculated plot by another local family—the Marchettis.

Frank Marchetti came to America from Italy in 1866 and married Martha Ann Tanner in Copiah County on December 14, 1872. He became both a farmer and businessman and soon had a large family.[6] Marchetti's farm was one of the most profitable in the area, and his son John also established a thriving business as a shoemaker. When Frank died in 1908 he left his estate to his sons John and Joseph. It was rumored that Joseph and Charles Dodds shared

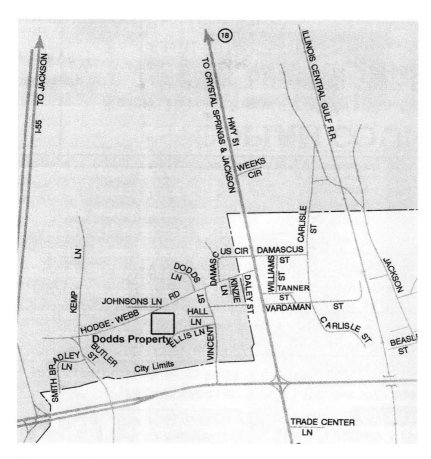

The area and property as it appears today; the land still sits just outside the Hazlehurst city limits. *Bruce Conforth*

the same mistress, a black woman known as Serena.[7] The affair is denied by surviving Marchetti family members, and a search of city directories, census, and other records do not show any reasonable candidates, black or white, named Serena in Copiah or surrounding counties, or in or around Memphis.[8] Although the story seems to be false, the rumors persisted, and were so severe, that Charles was forced to flee Hazlehurst in the dead of night disguised as a woman to avoid a lynching.

Charles settled in Memphis and changed his last name to Spencer to avoid detection. Polk's 1908 Memphis City Directory listed Charles "Spencer"—a carpenter—living in an apartment at 1 North Handwerker Place, also known as Handwerker Hill, in the center of Memphis.[9] By 1912 he moved to a larger apartment at 906 Court Avenue, and the following year to 898 Court Avenue at the corner of North Dunlap. This apartment was only a few blocks from Beale Street, the most active section of Memphis.

Joseph Marchetti.
Steve Amos, chancery clerk, Hazlehurst, `Mississippi

Back in Hazlehurst, the Marchettis succeeded in having Julia evicted from her house for nonpayment of taxes ($150) and the house and property were deeded to L. E. Matthews, a white Hazlehurst farmer. Now homeless and without an income, Julia moved from place to place doing whatever she needed to in order to try to take care of her children, and as it became increasingly difficult she sent Louise, Harriet, Willie M., Lula B., and Melvin Leroy to live with their father in Memphis. In the April 1910 census, Julia listed herself as thirty-eight years old and identified herself as "divorced." Living with her were her children Bessie (21), Caroline (Carrie, 15), John (12), and Codie (Charley) M. (10).[10] The discrepancy in the given ages of family members on the census records seems to have been a common occurrence. In 1900 Julia was listed as twenty-five while in 1910 she is thirty-eight. And by 1920 she is forty-five. Daughter Bessie was listed in 1900 as eight years old, but in 1910 she is twenty-one. Even Robert, whom the 1920 census listed as seven years

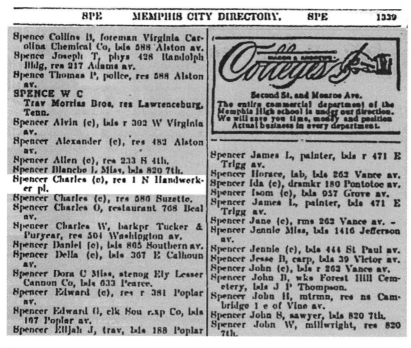

Charles (Dodds) Spencer in 1908 Memphis Directory.
R. L. Polk & Co. 1908 Memphis City Directory

old, appears as fourteen in his 1924 school record. The reason for such variation is unclear. But it was common.

In 1910 she moved into the shack on the Mangold estate occupied by Noah Johnson, a twenty-four-year-old laborer in a sawmill on that farm. Noah was also born in Copiah County to parents who came from the East Coast, or "Upper South."[11] In 1904 he had married Mary Nelson, a washerwoman with two children from her first marriage, who was fifteen years older than he was, but by 1911, just when Julia needed a home, Noah and Mary had separated, and he and his shack were available.[12] Julia and her three children joined Noah in a shed with timbers barely head high.

The house, still standing (but moved by its present owner, Hugh Jenkins, from its original location to save it from the expansion of Highway 55), is what was commonly called a saddlebag house: one room on each side of the entryway. It has cypress siding and a tin roof. The interior walls were covered with newspaper and cardboard. Julia was glad to have something resembling a real home, and on or about May 8, 1911, Robert Johnson was born there, the illegitimate son of two unmarried parents. However, an extra child was apparently too much for Noah to bear, and he and Julia would get into furious arguments about food and adequate care for her children. The incidents became so frequent that Julia and her children left Noah, and Hazlehurst, to seek a better lifestyle. She had no real plan nor any idea what she would do with her newly born son.

Probable birthplace of Robert Johnson. *Bruce Conforth*

1910 Census Record for Julia Dodds and children.
Department of Commerce, Bureau of the Census, State: Mississippi; County: Copiah; Hazlehurst City; Enumeration District 45, Sheet 6-B, April 20, 1910

National
Portrait
Gallery

Discuss our portrait of Angela Davis and *Brown Girl Dreaming*. Presented in partnership with the DC Public Library.

Tuesday, Feb. 18
5:30–7:00 p.m.
Brown Girl Dreaming
by Jacqueline Woodson

Jacqueline Woodson tells the moving story of her childhood. In vivid poems, she shares what it was like to grow up as an African American in the 1960s and 1970s, and describes the influence that civil rights activist Angela Davis had on her life.

npg.eventbrite.com

🌼 Smithsonian

Angela Davis (detail) by Stephen Shames, 1969. National Portrait Gallery, Smithsonian Institution. © 1969 Stephen Shames

❦ 3 ❦

MEMPHIS DAYS

Julia, homeless and without means of support, hired on with a Delta labor company after leaving Noah Johnson and drifted from place to place and man to man. She had difficulty taking care of her infant son and three other children: food, clothing, even a roof over their heads were no longer reliable expectations. For Robert, a lack of adequate nutrition as a newborn could have contributed to one of his most distinguishing features: he had either a lazy eye or a cataract that seemed to come and go. This latter diagnosis seems particularly appropriate, for transient cataracts were not uncommon in children with very low birth weight. Due to Julia's desperate financial conditions, the infant Robert was almost certainly undernourished at birth.[1]

Seeking opportunities in Arkansas, Julia found herself in trouble with a plantation owner there and fled, hotly pursued by one of the overseer's boss men. It must have been terrifying for the single mother and her young children to constantly feel under pursuit. Not only were the basic necessities of life now uncertain, so was their safety. After a brief period of hiding, Julia, two-year-old Robert, and his half sister Carrie relocated to Helena, an Arkansas town well known for its black community and blues music. Unskilled female laborers were in abundance there, however, and having no luck in finding work Julia was left with only one option: to seek refuge with the renamed "Charles Spencer" in Memphis.[2] She had already sent some of his other children to stay with him, and now she had no other options for a safe place for the remainder of her family.

The three-story wooden walk-up that Charles and his new wife, Mollie, lived in was already crowded when Julia arrived, but he welcomed them anyway. The new living arrangements were awkward for everyone. Charles and Julia had each moved on with other relationships, and Julia now had another son. She also had found no way of supporting herself yet and so, only shortly after arriving in Memphis, she left again to find whatever future she could create. In doing so, however, she left her two-year-old son Robert with strangers, one of a child's worst fears. This was only the first in a series of traumatic experiences that would scar Robert as a child, and it left a mark on his young life. Although he would come to consider the Spencers as his "real" family, that first year must have been a nightmare for him.

Although census records are only done every ten years and hence we have no true record of what the household looked like in 1913 when Robert became a part of it, the 1920 US Census record provides an insight into the Spencer household.[3] In the four-room wooden tenement were Mollie (erroneously identified as "Mandy"), Charles's new wife; who was forty years younger than him; Hattie Curry, Julia and Charles's daughter Harriet, now widowed with a son, George; Robert's half sister Carrie and her husband, Louis Harris; his older stepbrother, Charlie; and two more stepbrothers, Alex and Ted.

Robert adapted to his new family and environs, eventually enjoying all it had to offer, for the Spencer house was only a short walk from Beale Street, a center of attractions for all ages, genders, and races.

For family entertainment, R. R. Church's twenty-two-hundred-seat auditorium and park was located on the south side of the street near Fourth and Turley Streets. There, audiences could see the most famous black acts of the time: the Black Patti Troubadours with John Rucker (known as "The Alabama Blossom") and Madame

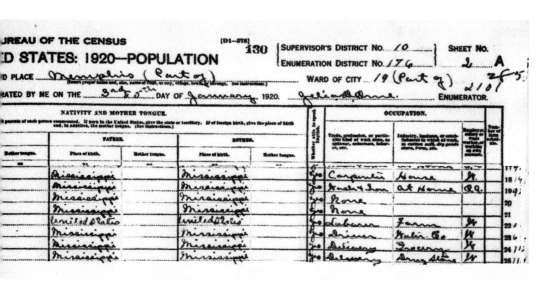

1920 Memphis census for Charles Dodds and family.
Department of Commerce, Bureau of the Census, State: Tennessee; County: Shelby; Memphis, (Part of); Enumeration District 176, Sheet 2-A, January 3, 1920

Church's Auditorium and Park.
Memphis Public Libraries, Memphis and Shelby County Rooms

Sissieretta Jones (the famous "Black Patti"), the Smart Set with S. H. Dudley (advertised as "The Greatest Colored Show on Earth"), and the Fisk Jubilee Singers.[4]

The nearby Palace Theater, originally the largest black theater in the South, was described as "hot and heavy." Couples danced and hugged tightly to the blues of black musicians. The dancers would drift almost in slow motion through the smoke-filled room, until Black Carrie, the club's tall and shapely hostess, would throw herself onto the ballroom floor. She'd lift her skintight dress to expose her knees, toss her long hair back and forth, and gyrate her body in slow erotic circles, driving the crowd almost to pandemonium. As her display grew more intense they'd yell out, "Go on, Carrie, shake it! Ah shucks, you ain't gwine tuh heben [heaven] nohow!"[5]

Farther down Beale Street, P. Wee's Saloon, owned by Italian immigrant Viglio Maffi ("Peewee"), was "a winter home for hoboes who came there to spend cold winter nights beside his red hot

Beale Street and P. Wee's Saloon ca. 1900.
Memphis Public Libraries, Memphis and Shelby County Rooms

stove."[6] Some of those "hoboes" were itinerant blues musicians, for in Peewee's club "piano and guitar players liked to gather" and they played the blues while gamblers played card games like seven-up. P. Wee's was one of the first places W. C. Handy heard the blues.[7] So many musicians gathered at P. Wee's that Handy later recalled, "You couldn't step [in the instrument storeroom] for the bull fiddles. The room was *always* that full with instruments."[8] Guitar players strolled up and down the street, and blind musicians took their posts on their favorite street corners to entertain passersby with spirituals, blues, and pop tunes.

Among the many Beale Street musicians that Robert would have almost certainly seen or heard were Frank Stokes of the Beale Street Sheiks, for jug bands like the Sheiks were prominent attractions in Memphis.[9]

Will Shade and Furry Lewis were also among the musicians who played there, and the guitarist Jim Jackson was so popular on Beale

Street that by 1919 he was performing inside the famed, and exclusively white, Peabody Hotel. Gus Cannon, along with Noah Lewis and Ashley Thompson, formed Cannon's Jug Stompers and played both at Memphis parties and on the streets. Anyone living near Beale Street was treated to a daily dose of these performers' music. The sounds of music were all around Robert—even in his Court

Charles M. L. D. Spencer and wife (date unknown).
© *Delta Haze Corporation*

Street home. Robert's own stepbrother Charles Melvin Leroy taught him a few elements of guitar and piano.

The practice of hoodoo and rootwork also thrived in the black community in Memphis. Practitioners, conjurers, and the stores that catered to them were plentiful. Hoodoo had its roots in traditional practices from Africa, Brazil, the Caribbean, and other locations that sent slaves to North America, and those practices had been syncretized. For some, hoodoo was seen as cultural resistance: a way for poor Blacks to create an agency that white culture, society, and politics denied them.[10] For Robert, hoodoo was an enticing part of Memphis culture that he would use in his song lyrics as an adult.

As early as the 1860s, reports from Memphis concerned obi or obeah men, a reference to the practitioners of folk magic, sorcery, and religion among West African slaves. The *Memphis Daily Appeal* described them as "always native Africans" who used all manner of

A. Schwab's Drug Store on Beale Street, est. 1876.
Memphis Public Libraries, Memphis and Shelby County Rooms

materials—"feathers of various colors, blood, dog's and cat's teeth, clay from graves, egg-shells, beads, and broken bits of glass"—to achieve their results.[11] There was no lack of access to hoodoo supplies in Memphis while Robert was growing up. The Pantaze Drug Store chain (several were located on Beale Street) carried a number of hoodoo-related supplies. At the famous A. Schwab dry goods store on Beale Street, a short walk from the Spencer house, one could, and still can, buy all the hoodoo and conjuring supplies one needed.

Also nearby was East Beale Street—an eerie, gloomy, swampish location—the home of Memphis's hoodoo practitioners, conjurers who sat before boiling pots mixing strange concoctions. They could make you anything you needed to cure a disease or drive away evil spirits. They specialized, however, in making red flannel mojo bags that could either protect their wearer against his or her enemy or bring good luck. These packets contained snakeroot, devil's shoestring, High John the Conqueror root, and other traditional fixings. Foot-traffic magic and other forms of hoodoo were also widely known throughout Memphis's black community well into the 1930s and beyond.

That riverport city, a fast-paced, urban society that still held onto its folk traditions, provided Robert with experiences a child previously living on a plantation could hardly have imagined. A southern urban center, Memphis was also regularly visited by the Ringling Brothers Circus, Buffalo Bill's Wild West Show, and entertainers like the Marx Brothers, George M. Cohan, magician Harry Houdini, and other exemplars of mainstream popular culture. Robert could not avoid being exposed to their presence and the excitement these entertainers created. Even without the money to attend the circus, he must have surely stood on the streets with hundreds of other children and watched the grand parade of animals and clowns as the shows entered the town.

Entertainment advertisements from the *Memphis Commercial Appeal*, 1918. *Memphis Public Libraries, Memphis and Shelby County Rooms*

Throughout Robert's time in Memphis the Spencers—Robert was now using Spencer as his last name, having fully adopted the family as his own—continued to live at 898 Court Avenue, well within walking distance of not just Beale Street, but Court Square (one of Memphis's main parks). Robert's stimuli, however, were not limited to folk culture, music, and entertainment, for he had to enter school around 1916. His boyhood friend from the Robinsonville, Mississippi, area, R. L. Windum, said that Robert told him he attended school in Memphis.[12] Actually, there was no way Robert could *not* go to school while living in Memphis, for in those years the city was the battleground of the grand champion of black education: Julia Hooks.

Hooks was a black musician, educator, and social worker who had received her degree from Berea College in Kentucky, the first southern college to be integrated. She moved to Memphis before the turn of the century and became active in various musical enterprises and churches, playing organ and directing choirs and choral groups. She also taught music, and her students appeared annually

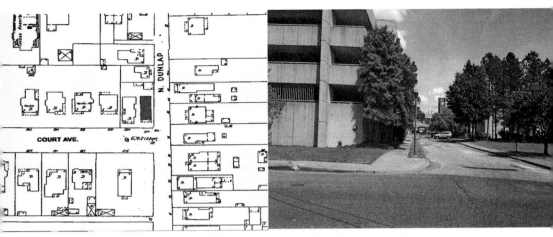

Map of original location of Spencer household and current view. *Bruce Conforth*

at Zion Hall in the Beale Street Baptist Church. Hooks also served as a teacher and principal in the city schools. Later, she became an officer of the juvenile court while her husband, Charles, took on chores as the city's truant officer. After Charles was killed in 1917, however, she began patrolling the streets of Memphis herself, seeking out errant black children who were not in school. Her two sons, Henry and Robert, became photographers and opened the famed Hooks Brothers Photographers studio on Beale Street. Years later Robert had his now-famous portrait taken by them.

The Shelby County school board archives verified that, living where he did, Robert would have almost certainly been enrolled in the Carnes Avenue Colored School, originally a two-room wooden building for black students at 942 Peach Avenue in Memphis. It was only five blocks away from his home.[13]

Robert's older half sister Carrie remembered walking with him to school, holding his hand as they traveled the few blocks to get their education. Attending any school at all, but especially an urban one, distinguished Robert from other blues musicians of his era. Robert Johnson's ability to read and write was atypical.[14] Most of

Robert's musical contemporaries were largely functionally illiterate simply because they were black plantation children.

A 1919 report, *The Public School System of Memphis, Tennessee* (based on a study done in 1917), noted that even in schools for black children (Carnes School was specifically mentioned) the subjects taught included reading, language, industrial arts (although in the poorer schools this may have been limited to scissors and construction paper), arithmetic, music, geography, and physical exercise. The report also revealed that "the Negro schools excel the standards for each grade and exceed the white schools in the third, fourth, and fifth grades."[15] It seems clear that Robert's new family intended him to be more than just a field laborer. Charles Spencer was, after all, a skilled carpenter, and therefore Robert should at least learn a good trade. For this reason, when his eye problem became apparent, Carrie, some ten years his senior, helped him secure a pair of glasses.

From 1913 until 1919, Robert lived with the Spencer household—a household that held many advantages for the young boy.[16] Memphis was full of exciting attractions that his Delta contemporaries would never see or experience. The urbanity and sophistication of the city became young Robert's norm. But Robert's foundational stay in Memphis came to an end when Julia reentered his life. In October 1916, she had married a sharecropper, Will "Dusty" Willis, and, after spending two years roaming from farm to farm, they eventually settled on a plantation in Arkansas. In 1919 Robert and Carrie were walking on Front Street when they saw Julia. As Robert looked on in surprise, Carrie cried out "That's Mama!" Julia had come to Memphis to take the young Robert back to Arkansas to help on the farm. Robert was uprooted once again.

After being abandoned by his mother with a group of strangers in a strange though exciting town, he was now, against his will, being taken from the only family he knew and forced to go with an unfamiliar woman to a place far different from what he had grown used to. Away from the city, circuses, music, and school, he was expected to acclimate to the new environment of plantations with endless cotton fields.

But the new region Julia was taking him to *did* have something unique to offer: a different type of music from that found in urban Memphis. The guitar-focused music known as cotton-field blues was played on every plantation at weekend jukes. This new sound appealed to Robert in ways he couldn't have expected. It was raw and full of feeling, probably like the emotions he might have been experiencing. He embraced it like a boll weevil did a growing cotton ball. Perhaps everything about his move away from Memphis wasn't that bad. The new friends he would make in the deep Delta would help him find his way through this period in his life and into the new music that surrounded him.

⚜ 4 ⚜

BACK TO THE DELTA

Robert Johnson stared at the endless plantation fields that lay opposite the levees shielding them from the Mississippi River. Cotton was everywhere. Gone was the life that he had known. Now there was nothing but dirt—dirt roads, dirt farms, and earthworks—as far as his eyes could see. There were no schools for Negro children. This place, Lucas Township, was vast and empty. An intelligent, citified nine-year-old had been uprooted and placed in an alien environment: the Arkansas-Mississippi Delta.

The farm where Robert was taken was on Horseshoe Lake in Crittenden County, Arkansas. It is some thirty miles southwest of Memphis, directly across the Mississippi River from Penton, Lake Cormorant, Clack, Commerce, and Robinsonville—Mississippi locations that later served as major landmarks in Robert's life. Horseshoe Lake boasted a number of plantations, and it was on one of those that Julia's new husband had decided to try his luck. Several of these plantations became legendary, among them the plantation owned by J.O.E Beck. Beck cleared the land of trees and drained the swampland, creating a huge plantation system that stretched from Hughes in St. Francis County to Lee County in the west.[1] It

47

would later become better known as Sadie Beck's Plantation when folklorist Alan Lomax recorded there in 1942.

The Snowden plantation on the northwestern side of the lake contained one thousand acres with a commissary, Baugh Store, which had the first frozen food lockers in the area.[2] Rodgers plantation occupied the islands in and the land below Horseshoe Lake. Since the January 23, 1920, US Census indicates that Willis (22), Julia (45), and Robert (erroneously listed as 7 years old) were living in the middle of the region, Rodgers plantation is the most likely candidate for their residence.[3]

Willis was known to the community as a slow-witted man, and they nicknamed him "Dusty" for his habit of walking rapidly down the dirty country roads, kicking up a cloud of dust wherever he

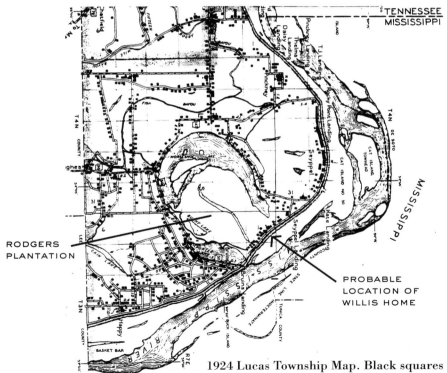

1924 Lucas Township Map. Black squares are sharecroppers' homes; thick lines between those homes and the river are levees. *Bruce Conforth*

went. Dusty could neither read nor write, but Robert, on the other hand, could do both, which created a cultural gap between the young boy and his stepfather.

Robert's new home was typical of a sharecropper's building: rough and bare, nothing like the apartment living he'd experienced in Memphis. A sharecropper's shack was usually only a two- or three-room unpainted house of unplaned lumber with either roll or tin roofing. When the insides were actually papered, newspapers or magazine pages were used for wallpaper, exactly like the house in which he was born in Hazlehurt. The only exception to the spartan decoration of plantation buildings was the house that held Saturday jukes. These were usually painted green for easy identification.

Whether he wanted to or not, Robert was forced to learn about living on a plantation. He traded his schoolbooks for a hoe and gunnysack and discovered that his days were determined by what plantation owners called a "furnish day" system instead of a school

Crittenden County sharecropper's shack, 1920s.
Margaret Elizabeth Woolfolk collection

year. March 1 of each year was furnish day: each sharecropper was furnished with one dollar per month for every acre they farmed. But it was not cash money; it was in the form of plantation scrip that could only be traded at the plantation commissary. In this system, sharecroppers resembled indentured servants more than independent farmers. Plantation owners saw to it that a sharecropper rarely, if ever, ended the year on the positive side of the financial ledger.

Robert hated farming. He told his friends that he missed the streets of the city and all it had to offer. While the rest of his new friends were content to follow a sharecropper's life, Robert told everyone he didn't want that life, and instead wanted to attend school and learn about the world around him. Sharecropping cotton was hard labor. After his new stepfather would prepare the fields by mule-drawn plow, Robert then had to help him plant the cotton seeds. As the plants grew, chopping cotton—removing the weeds that grew between the plants with handheld hoes, picks, shovels, and rakes—made his hands blister and ache. But the worst job, the picking of cotton, began in late August or early September.

Each picker carried a long white sack: twelve-foot sacks were standard for an adult male. As a child, Robert was only expected to haul a six- or eight-foot sack, but it was still backbreaking labor, and the sharp leaves of the cotton boll would hurt his hands as he pulled the white prize from its shell. After he filled his bag he'd haul it to a waiting cotton wagon, have it weighed and dumped, and then start all over again. A good adult picker could fill four or five large sacks a day—roughly 350 pounds of cotton. Robert was lucky to pick around one hundred pounds, and even on the hottest days he had to wear a long-sleeve shirt and hat for protection from the sun. In Memphis he had gone to school from morning until afternoon. On his stepfather's farm he worked "from can to can't": from daybreak, when he can see, to nightfall, when he can't. All of this to help his new family earn no more than $200 of "plantation money."[4]

Existing Abbay and Leatherman commissary/office. *Bruce Conforth*

Robert, Julia, and Dusty did not stay long on the Arkansas plantation, however. Shortly after the 1920 census they moved across the Mississippi River to the Abbay and Leatherman plantation in Commerce. There they settled in a shack along the levee near a section named Polk Place.[5] Their move was probably precipitated by the drastic dip in cotton prices from 38.5 cents per pound to 9.5 cents per pound.[6] Like other sharecroppers who only stayed one season on a farm, Willis hoped that a move to a larger, more affluent plantation in Mississippi would offer him a better living. Once again Robert's life changed.

In 1832 Richard and Anthony Abbay purchased land on both sides of the Mississippi River from the Chickasaw Indian tribe. Their land on the Mississippi side of the river would be used to create the Abbay and Leatherman plantation, one of the most prosperous in the Delta. There seems little doubt that Dusty Willis would have known about the better conditions it offered and it was onto this new farm that he moved Julia and young Robert. And, because of its proximity to the town of Robinsonville, the new plantation afforded Robert some familiar experiences. The first was that he was once again exposed to musicians: songsters, singers of older folk songs, and the new breed of Delta blues players. Robinsonville was a stronghold for the latter, and Robert could not help but hear them and become entranced with their music and lifestyle.

Famous for its extremely fertile soil, and infamous for its desolation and frequent flooding by the Mississippi River (in spite of attempts to build protective levees), the Delta in which young Robert found himself was divided into two different areas—the south and north regions. The south Delta began at Yazoo City and Vicksburg and extended above Greenwood and Greenville to Clarksdale. The area above that, Coahoma County toward Memphis, was termed the north Delta by those who lived there. Railroads helped further divide this region. The Columbus and Greenville Railroad (C&G, or the "Southern") ran from Columbus in the eastern part of the state to Greenville on the Mississippi River. Another historical railroad, the Yazoo & Mississippi Valley (YMV), commonly called the "Dog," used two routes to run from Yazoo City, where the Delta began, to Clarksdale. One route came through Moorhead and the other branch went through Indianola, past Parchman Penitentiary, to Tutwiler, where the two branches once again met. W. C. Handy, the "Father of the Blues," wrote that he had first heard a bottleneck guitarist playing at a depot there in the early 1900s, which inspired him to begin writing blues for sheet music and recordings. It has been conjectured by scholars writing about Handy that the guitarist he heard might have been Henry Sloan, mentor to Charley Patton and a resident of the Dockery plantation.

The long layover from early December until spring planting began again allowed for musicians to drift in and out of the area making easy money by playing for dances and parties. David "Honeyboy" Edwards said that the "off-time" gave musicians an opportunity to "sit around and play. Mississippi and Arkansas had the largest group of musicians. They didn't have nothin' to do but sit around and play and drink that old moonshine whiskey. They didn't work in no cotton fields."[7] The music and lifestyles of these musicians suited Robert just fine. The proximity to Robinsonville also permitted Robert to renew another routine he had begun in Memphis: attending school. The 1924 Tunica County school records document Robert Spencer attending classes at the Indian Creek school in Commerce.[8]

That school record also noted he was still using the last name Spencer—his first stepfather's adopted name. Julia had not yet told him about his biological father, Noah Johnson, and Robert signed the school attendance record as his own guardian—Robt. Spencer. His classmates all had parents or guardians sign on their behalf. Compared to people like Son House or Charley Patton, Robert received a considerable amount of schooling, and continued a unique habit he established in Memphis: keeping a notebook of his ideas and lyrics.

Memories of Robert's education varied widely. Johnny Shines, who didn't meet Robert until he was an adult in 1937, believed that Robert had little schooling. "Robert didn't have no education at all as far as I could tell. I never saw him read or write, not even his name. He was a natural genius, but he was definitely 'anti-education.'"[9] Shines was surprised when he saw Johnson's signature many years later and confessed, "Robert had beautiful handwriting. His writing looked like a woman's writing."[10] People like R. L. Windum, with whom Robert attended school in Commerce, had a much different understanding of Robert's education. "I become acquainted with Robert Johnson when we were boys. And we were going to school at that St. Peter's school. We were about fourteen years old or something like that, and going to school."[11]

As credible as Windum's recollection was, however, previous researchers have been confused about what, or where, St. Peter's school was. No actual school in Commerce was ever identified by that name. To make matters more confusing, there was a St. Peter's school in Memphis, and some researchers maintained that this was the one Robert attended. But St. Peter's in Memphis didn't accept black students, and it is now known that he attended the Carnes Avenue School in the city. The location of the school Windum mentioned has previously been a mystery, but further recollections from his boyhood friends helped solve it. According to Windum, Robert's family lived in a shack on Polk Place, near a fishing lake.[12] Israel "Wink" Clark added credence to Windum's account by asserting that he and Robert first met via school, church, and fishing. "His mother and my mother would fish together. That started us and we would—had to go up to the lake for them because they would skin our heads about staying with them fishing."[13] Archival maps show Polk Place at the eastern end of the Abbay and Leatherman plantation, and a small one-room church, St. Peters Church, also sat on Polk Road. Next to the church was a small tributary, Indian Creek. Both locations are less than a mile away from Fish Lake. Indian Creek School was obviously named because of its location next to that stream. Wink Clark provided the first real clue in identifying the one-room school by noting it was actually the "small wood-frame church."[14] The location and identity of St. Peter's school was ultimately verified by Dr. Richard Taylor, director of the Tunica County Historical Museum.[15]

Robert was used to getting a very complete education in Memphis, and Indian Creek School was nothing like the Carnes School he had attended. Its main function was to teach its students the most basic reading and writing skills that would be needed by sharecroppers or other laborers—Robert had already acquired more education than most of his classmates would ever get. Regardless, Robert took advantage of whatever opportunities were provided to further develop his educational and intellectual habits, in the

Polk Place today. St. Peter's Church/Indian Creek School was on the immediate right, and the Willis home was in the background on the left. Fish Lake is below the water tower. *Bruce Conforth*

Fish Lake, where Robert fished with his boyhood friends. *Bruce Conforth*

process becoming a voracious reader. His later musical friend and "stepson," Robert Lockwood, spoke warmly about how much Robert loved to read. "I have to say that he done quite a bit of studying in his life. He did a lot of reading and stuff like that. Just about anything you could read, he read it."[16]

Going back to school introduced Robert to new friends like Windum and Clark, and they would spend their days like many other Delta youth: fishing and playing together. "Everything would go smooth," Clark recalled. "We'd just run around, fish, play around. My mother and his mother were great friends, and that's how come we grew up together, we got to be teenage boys. And all up and down this river here we'd fish, and his mother lived [on the plantation] back there near the levee, and that's where me and him got many a spanking, right there."[17]

Whatever Clark was spanked for, Robert's punishments were usually caused by his reluctance to work in the fields. He hated farmwork now more than ever, and his way of avoiding it was to frequently run away to his family in Memphis. He was now old enough to travel on his own—and close enough to Old Highway 61 that he began leaving Dusty Willis and fieldwork and returning to the Spencers. R. L. Windum said that Robert would often be gone from the Delta for long periods of time precisely because he was visiting the Spencer family.[18]

Robert at this time still considered Charles Dodds Spencer in Memphis his father, especially since Julia had yet to tell him about his biological father, Noah Johnson. Robert saw Charles as a much better role model than Dusty Willis. Even the latter's nickname went against Robert's better instincts. Why would he want to be a dusty field worker? Robert wanted to be something special, and Charles Spencer understood that. And so Robert continued to use Charles's last name, at least for a while longer. "I always knowed him by Spencer," Windum stated. "That's how I knowed [him]. I didn't know nothing about that Johnson till his music come up. I just knowed his mother, and his sister and his brother. And his mother, she was named Julia."[19] Willie Mason had similar memories: "We used to call him Robert Spencer and then Robert Johnson, I don't know where that Spencer come from, the name Robert Johnson Spencer or what, but folks used to call him Robert Spencer a lot."[20]

Once Julia informed Robert that his biological father was from Hazlehurst, the confused boy suddenly had two last names. "He called himself Spencer and Johnson," Clark explained. "Robert Spencer and Robert Johnson, both of them. [Robert's mother] had about three different husbands. So I wouldn't know [who his father was], but when I knowed him as Robert Johnson."[21]

Elizabeth Moore was one of their neighbors on the Leatherman plantation and recalled Robert using a variety of names during the time she knew him. "He had three names. Sometimes they used to call him 'Dusty' [after his stepfather—Robert made it known that he hated this] but most of the times looks like they enjoyed callin' him 'Sax.' I don't know why people called him that but he had three names when I first moved around Robinsonville and that's when I got acquainted with him. I learned him as Robert Johnson, see, his name, but I'd hear from somebody else, like people come in here to get you on a Saturday night, to play. 'Where Robert Sax is?' And I said, 'I don't know him. There's a guitar player here but his name is Robert Johnson.' 'Well that's him! That's him!' Or I'd hear from somebody else: 'Where Robert Johnson is?'"[22] The use of nicknames such as "Dusty," "Sax," or "Son" were prevalent in rural areas of the South in both black and white cultures. It was also considered rude, or even threatening, to challenge someone's nickname. Many times musicians didn't even know the last name of their playing partners. They never asked.

But Elizabeth's recollection reveals far more than just confusion over Robert's name, because she talks about people looking for

Robert to play guitar at their parties. This contradicts conventional wisdom based almost exclusively on Son House's recollection that when House first met Robert, the "boy" couldn't play guitar. Both Elizabeth and Willie Moore repeatedly asserted that Robert was not just playing guitar but performing publicly by 1928, when he was only seventeen. If their information is correct, Robert had taken the first steps to become a professional musician years before previously believed. Robert was not just a kid living on a plantation in Robinsonville. He was already on his way to developing his own musical style.

❦ 5 ❧

MUSICAL ROOTS AND IDENTITY

In 1926 Robert Johnson became a musician. He was fifteen years old, living on the second plantation of his young life, and dividing his time between Memphis and his Delta home. His trips to see his Memphis family made him ever more sure that he had no interest in farming; his major interest was *music*. By his early teenage years Robert had already become an accomplished harmonica and Jew's harp player, and he could play some guitar and piano (both learned from his older stepbrother Charles in Memphis). Now his half sister Carrie moved from Memphis to join his Delta family, bringing her son, Louis, to become his neighbor on Polk Place near Robinsonville. Although most of Robert's friends were still primarily interested in playing games and going fishing, he discovered that he and R. L. Windum had a musical interest in common: they both played harmonica. "We used to blow harp together," Windum recalled. "When we would be together we would blow harp just like the boys that was in those times to get around."[1] A harmonica was cheap, pocket-sized, and easy to carry. It could play both single notes and chords, imitate a train whistle or steam engine, and its percussive nature allowed it to provide a driving rhythm for juking. And Robert was good at it too. But his main musical interest was the guitar.

Young boy playing a diddley
bow on the side of a shack.
Library of Congress – Johnson

Dusty Willis, on the other hand, was only interested in Robert
working on his land. The idea of Robert playing guitar instead of
farming was out of the question. In spite of his stepfather's opposition, though, Robert, like many blues musicians before and after
him, resorted to building his own stringed instrument.

Wink Clark remembered Robert's earliest musical attempts: "He
had him one built on his wall, outta three strands of wire. And
that's the way he started, on the three strands of wire and three
bottles. He'd drive in three nails upside the wall. And he'd have one
string tied from this nail down to this nail . . . then he'd put him
a bottle under it and put him one up [at the top] and push 'em

up tight and it's just like tuning a guitar. And he could play what he was singing but I never could get no sense out of it [*laughs*]."[2] The instrument Clark described was a diddley bow: a simple string instrument sometimes constructed on a building or sometimes as a stand-alone instrument. It could have been built on a plank of wood, a rake handle, or whatever piece of lumber was available.

Music consumed Robert's life. Willie Mason said if Robert couldn't play his diddley bow, or later his guitar, he'd play his harmonica, even when he was out in the fields. Wink Clark corroborates: "We was working on the farm together and the boss man told him to leave once 'cause everybody in the field chopping cotton, and [Robert] ran inside the house and had some wire, some hay-bale wire tied around his mouth with his harp."[3] Robert had fashioned his own homemade harmonica holder that allowed him to play the instrument even when he was working. Invariably his playing would slow down his work, and his farm production would suffer, repeatedly causing Robert to get beatings from Dusty. But not everyone in Robert's Delta family was opposed to his music or his ambitions. Carrie—who had cared for Robert when they both lived in Memphis, bought him glasses when he needed them, and walked him to school every day—was once again there to help her younger half brother.

Now living with Wink Clark's brother Leamon, Carrie saw that Robert was no farmer and that his interests lay in music.[4] She knew what Memphis and its culture meant to him. She had been living at the Spencer home when he would run away to seek refuge in his childhood environs. As she was there for him then, so would she be the rest of his life, and if Robert wanted to play guitar she would help him do so. Although neither she nor Robert could afford to buy even a cheaply manufactured instrument, Carrie helped him move up from the diddley bow on the side of his shack to the next best thing: a homemade cigar-box guitar. They pieced one together using bailing wire from the farm, a scrap of wood for a neck, and a cigar box from Wink Clark's father. While Robert was practicing on that instrument, both he and Carrie began saving whatever change they could accumulate to reach their goal: a store-bought guitar. In early 1927 they were able to walk into a general store and purchase their prize: an old wooden guitar that was missing two strings.[5]

Robert played those four strings constantly, driving everyone within earshot crazy from his practicing, until he was finally able to acquire a dime to buy the two missing strings. Having a real guitar not only began to improve Robert's playing, it also helped him grow up and leave behind the things his other friends still found interesting. Wink Clark spoke about how that change manifested itself. "We'd go out on the levee, side of the road somewhere, and we'd shoot marbles, [but] he'd play guitar."[6] For the rest of his life Robert and a guitar would be inseparable.

Wink Clark's father, who had been helpful in assembling the cigar-box guitar, next assisted in making Memphis more accessible to Robert when he purchased a Model T Ford. Robert, now sixteen, and Carrie began getting rides from Clark to make regular visits to Charles Spencer, his wife Mollie, and their two new daughters. Instead of hitching a ride as best he could, now Robert was driven the short thirty-two mile trip every few weeks. And as they always had, these trips to the city only served to intensify the differences between him and his country friends as he changed from a boy into a man.

For Robert, one of the most life-changing lessons was learning how to drink. "Did he [drink]?" Clark queried. "You ought to ask, how much did he try to drink? He tried to drink up all that corn whiskey was made, but he never would get too drunk to play his guitar, but he sure drank it. He drank a lots. He drank all night. Just about like you see these women sipping on these Coca-Colas. That's just the way he would do a bottle of whiskey."[7]

Carrie Dodds Spencer Harris. *© Delta Haze Corporation*

As he matured, Robert grew as a musician too. His musical growth
had been given a huge boost only a year earlier when one of his first
mentors, a guitarist who had been playing for ten years, moved to
Robinsonville. His name was Willie Brown.

Brown was known as a highly talented guitarist and even mentored Memphis Minnie while living near Lake Cormorant, Mississippi. As gifted as he was, however, he was best known for playing second guitar accompaniment behind Charley Patton and Son
House. Brown was probably born near Perthshire, Mississippi,
around 1897, and had played music from Dockery's plantation
near Cleveland all the way up to Tunica. Prior to arriving in Robinsonville he lived on Arthur Peerman's plantation, just northeast
of Cleveland. Willie Moore, who met Brown in 1916, explained
Brown's friendship with Patton. "He [Brown] told me that he had
some fella he used to play with down the road; he told me, 'twas a
fella stayed down here in Hollendale. And he said, 'Man, you oughta
hear him play!' Said, 'Me and him plays together!' He's talkin' about
Charley Patton!"[8] Brown learned well, for he easily matched Patton
in both musicianship and histrionics, something that was called
"clowning" on the guitar. "He stomp his foot, barefooted. He say,
'Give me that *Pony!*'" Moore explained. "Slap that guitar, boy, back
there, say, 'Set it over yonder!' He just played his own style all the
time."[9] Brown's own style included playing the guitar behind his
head. And his repertoire was diverse enough that he could play for
either a black or white audience, including pop tunes like "You
Great Big Beautiful Doll" or "What Makes You Do Me Like You
Do Do Do?" His jobs with Son House or Patton usually consisted
of one-night stands throughout the area's jukes and house parties.
Robert Johnson began to sneak out to see Brown play at these jobs,
and the two became fast friends. Brown gave the younger player
at least some guitar tips, as Elizabeth Moore confirmed. "[Robert]
didn't have to talk about [Willie Brown], he knowed him. He could

Photo alleged to be of Willie Moore, Willie Brown, and either Fiddlin'
Joe Martin or Billy Dickson. Found near Pritchard, MS, and identi-
fied by local connections and comparisons with other photos.
Randy Meadows collection

talk about him because he played with him. He [Robert] could play
pretty good. I imagine there's some things he learned from Willie
Brown, but he could play pretty good. [He went around with] both
of them [Willie Brown and Son House]."[10]

Robert quickly realized that he could avoid field work, attract
more attention from young women, and pick up some spending

money by playing his guitar. But to do that successfully he had to get better, and so he became a musical sponge: soaking up playing tips from everyone who would give him some of their time, no matter how talented they were. "He'd come out here to me and my husband's home near Robinsonville," Elizabeth Moore said. "We lived out on the same plantation, out from Robinsonville. So my husband could pick one old tune, you know, and he'd come there to get that tune all the time. Lord, I'd get sick of them playing that old song, 'I'm Gonna Sit Down and Tell My Mama.'" Eventually, she protested her husband's commitment to the young journeyman. "I'd say, 'Fella, why don't you put that old guitar [he had his own] down?' 'Miss Harvey [her married name at that time],' he'd say, 'don't say that.' He wanted to learn how to make them notes. I'd say, 'Well, you all worrying me.' I'd go to bed and leave 'em sittin' up there on the porch and he'd be plunkin' on his old guitar. Plunka, plunka, plunka. My husband couldn't play but that one old tune

Willie and Elizabeth Moore. *Gayle Dean Wardlow*

he done learned up in the hills [before he moved to the Delta]. He was primarily a piano player."[11]

After learning basic skills, Robert did what young musicians have always done: he sought approval. In his case, it would come from older sharecroppers who basically had only live music for entertainment. Robert traveled from house to house, and whenever he could find someone willing to listen, he would give them an impromptu concert. Almost always he was met with a kind reponse: "You just go right on, child. You just keep on, child." By now, Robert had completely turned his back on anything but music. Dusty Willis still expected him to help on the farm, but Robert would have no part of it. "He quit farmin.' His mama and them was farmin' out there on the place where we all was, all of us makin' crops, you know," Elizabeth Moore recollected. "Well, he got to the place where he didn't wanna chop no cotton."[12]

Robert's insolence made his relationship with Dusty more unbearable, increasing the frequency of beatings he would receive. Each argument between the two men always ended the same: Dusty would insist that Robert get into the fields and work, and Robert would grab his guitar and leave. Their fights were intense enough that Elizabeth Moore could hear Dusty's rantings: "I told you to work! How come you didn't do that like I told you? You got to help me work!" She could also hear Robert's response: "I don't wanna work. I'm tryin' to learn how to make my livin' without pickin' cotton. I got this here old guitar music on my mind and that's what I wanna learn more."[13] And indeed, at some point around this time, according to Mack McCormick and Steve LaVere, Robert did learn more from Ernest "Whiskey Red" Brown, a friend of Willie Brown and Charley Patton.

By 1928, only two years after he had built a diddley bow on the side of his shack and only one year after acquiring his first guitar, Robert was playing professionally at local small parties and dances.

Before long he was going to Tunica, a few miles below Robinson-ville and the county seat, to play at the local roadhouses and then on to another location, and finally back to Robinsonville.[14] Nat Richardson, whose father owned a juke where Robert would per-form, recalled that "people from all around" would come to the juke to hear Robert play, "people even outta Memphis."[15]

According to Delta musician Hayes McMullan, who lived on a plantation near Sumner, at first people held house parties, or "frol-ics," where no alcohol was served. The homeowner often sold food. When alcohol was added and the parties became a place to drink and dance, the term "juke" became widely used. Playing in a juke was quite profitable by Delta standards. The musician got paid as much as five dollars, plus free food and whiskey. That was more money than Dusty made on his farm, and that fact only alien-ated him from Robert even more. During the off winter months the pay was less, but as long as people liked to frolic after long workweeks in the fields, they always sought relief. Guitarists such as Robert provided the perfect entertainment. In addition to the money was a benefit that Robert found especially interesting: the attention he received from young women. Robert was becoming quite a womanizer.

Wink Clark affirmed that by the late 1920s, a teenaged Robert was already traveling to Lake Cormorant, Pritchard, Banks, and occasionally into Arkansas to play music.[16] By this time Robert offered his audience a variety of musical talents: harmonica, Jew's harp, piano, pump organ, and guitar. As he got better and better on the guitar, Clark saw him less and less. "He began to get profes-sion and he would go out and stay out. He used to try to get me to go—come and go, stay all night long with his lady. . . . Take him anywhere around Robinsonville, Tunica, Banks, Prichard—they wanna have a big picnic or a big party Saturday night, Sunday, they would get Robert."[17]

Hayes McMullen. *Gayle Dean Wardlow*

Willie Moore, a musician turned "juke house gambler" who had toured with Handy's Orchestra from Memphis, teamed with Robert in the late 1920s as a "complimenting guitar." Moore's memories are important: they attest not only to Robert's musical abilities but to how early they developed. Moore swore that Robert was already a somewhat accomplished musician when the two met. "It was before high water [the 1927 Mississippi flood] that I met Robert. He wasn't twenty years old."[18]

They first performed together on a Saturday afternoon, when sharecroppers came to buy groceries for the week and socialize in Robinsonville, a typical plantation town. Robert was playing guitar on the town's only paved street. Moore saw him for the first time "at the Chinaman's store—little Chinaman used to follow us all the time. He [Robert] was there and he seen me with a guitar. I was goin' to play for a dance, and he asked me, he said, 'Can you, what, you play lead or just play that?' I said, 'Well, I tell you one thing, I hardly play lead, I play by myself.' He said, 'God knows I need one [an accompanist] so bad.' He said, 'I got a boy but he can't make B flat. He can't make a B flat, but he lays his fingers down, but he don't know how to put that introduction in there.' I said, 'He musta learned on his own. I learned in school; I can make a B flat so slick.' He said, 'Well, look, you got time to go around here.' We went around there and got to rehearsing there on the street, right there by the Chinaman's store and the folk couldn't get by, we hadda quit that. [We had] two guitars. I had mine and he went and got his."[19]

Robert and Willie stood for hours outside of the Chinese-owned grocery store until they made enough money to buy drinks and food. Such stores were common in the Delta. Robinsonville, where they played, had a population of only a little over three hundred but featured three such groceries.[20] Just after the Civil War, Mississippi planters began recruiting Chinese workers as a possible replacement for the freed black laborers. It was quickly obvious to the new arrivals, however, that plantation work was not a way to obtain economic success, so many opened grocery stores. Their small stores carried meat, cornmeal, molasses, and other simple basics—exactly the items poor black farmers working on plantations needed.[21]

Robert was performing a combination of folk songs and standards that had filtered into black communities: songs that he had heard other local musicians playing. He had yet to begin composing his own songs. According to Moore, his earliest pieces included "Captain George," "Make Me a Pallet," and "President McKinley." "'Captain George, did your money come? Captain George, did your money come?' And he would say, 'Reason I ask you, I wanna borrow me some.' That's the first song I ever heard Robert sing. Next thing he played about was 'Make Me Down,' but he never would say, 'Make me down a pallet.' He'd say, 'Flung me down [a pallet] on your floor, and make it so your man would never know.'"[22]

Robert used a bottleneck slide while singing about McKinley's assassination in Buffalo, New York, in 1901. The song included a standard verse employed by such earlier musicians as Blind Lemon Jefferson: "Rubber-tire buggy and a decorated hat. They carried McKinley to the cemetery, but they didn't bring him back." Many of Robert's earliest pieces were peppered with verses drawn from earlier blues or oral tradition, because that's what he learned. But one of Robert's songs struck Moore as particularly special. It seemed to address the whole idea of rambling, a concept that Robert would personally embrace. "I played with him lots of times but you know, he had a song he sang all the time, 'Black Gal Why Don't Ya Comb Your Hair,' but the most he played was, 'He walked all the way from East Saint Louis with a lousy dime.'"[23]

Robert's other pieces included "You Can Mistreat Me Here but You Can't When I Go Home" (perhaps an early version that later became "Dust My Broom"), "East St. Louis Blues," and a bottleneck version of "Casey Jones" that he renamed "A Thousand and Five on the Road Again." He began to develop a small reputation as a guitarist of modest but entertaining skills. His notoriety and playing, while usually drawing the kind of attention he did want—money, drink, and women (and not necessarily in that order)—would sometimes draw attention he didn't want: trouble with people even beyond his stepfather. On one occasion Willie Moore and Robert were both jailed because they named the sheriff of Robinsonville in a song.

"Mr. Woolfolk was the high sheriff. [We were singing,] 'Mr. Crump don't like it, Mr. Smith ain't gonna have us here.' We was in Robinsonville [and] come out with a song, you see. I didn't know it; Robert, I don't reckon he heard it neither. They had a whole racket about Mr. Smith don't like it and Mr. Woolfolk ain't gonna have it here. He put us right in that jail, I'm tellin' you. We didn't stay in there long, stayed in there about two hours, man got us out, you know."[24]

In or out of trouble, Robert was focused on pushing his music forward. He wanted to be known and make an impression, and he wanted to be wanted. To appear more modern and flashy, he bought a wooden-bodied guitar with an imitation resonator to provide more volume. True resonator guitars had just started being manufactured, and many companies, such as Regal, began releasing imitation resonators: plain wooden guitars with a fake metal resonator plate on the top of the body. Robert swore to all who would listen that the metal plate (which actually did nothing) increased the volume of the instrument, and that with this new guitar he was leaving the old folks behind. "We asked him many times, 'Why do you have it on there?'" Willie Moore related. "He say, 'Well, that makes my guitar sound louder, see. This here's put on there to make it sound louder. He didn't have no electric to it."[25] Robert wasn't the only guitarist to try to impress people with such a piece of musical chicanery. Years later, a very young B. B. King fashioned a fake resonator plate out of an old piece of tin and attached it to the top of his guitar. Like Robert's, the plate did nothing, but it looked special and unique.[26]

Robert and Willie Moore became regular musical partners for a brief period. Whenever he needed to find Moore to go juking,

Robert used the country form of "gettin' up together" to find him. "Like, if he need me to meet him, he'd get in a buggy, or get on a mule or a horse, or something or another, or get a car and come get me and we'd play."[27] Moore lived on the nearby Black plantation, just south of where Robert's stepfather sharecropped. But Moore never went to Robert's house; he knew Dusty disapproved of Robert playing music instead of working on the farm.

As his talents grew, Robert wanted to appear more professional, and on one of his trips to Memphis he made a five dollar vanity record to impress his friends. "He told us about it then—where he say he got the first one of his records demonstrated," Elizabeth Moore recalled fondly. "He say a little opera house. He just had that little stuff [song] demonstrated for hisself, and he just go to carryin' it 'round among the colored people where he'd be."[28] The record got the exact response Robert wanted. "He would show it to the people, sit down and play it for the folks. You know, people say, 'Oh, child, that do sound nice.' 'Boy, you did that? That do sound nice.'" Robert had the encouragement he needed. "They say, 'Boy, you keep on.' You know, makin' 'em. And he just kept on."[29]

The life and music Robert sought could be found in the Robinsonville area, which was quickly becoming a main center for the blues in the northern Delta. The liquor flowed as freely as the music, and Wink Clark believed this was a good reason why Robert began to spend more and more time playing in that town. "I think most of what it was, it was a lot of corn whiskey was cooked around Robinsonville. And most of the people, you know, just like they is now, followed whiskey."[30] Robert didn't just follow whiskey, however, and his drinking habit continued to grow.

But he was still looking for something that seemed to elude him. He still split his life between Memphis and the Delta. He had used several different names. Although he had two stepfathers, he still had never met his biological father. Robert Johnson had already been through many life changes. So he began searching for his own identity: who was he and what would he do with his life?

Folklorist Mack McCormick called him a phantom. In reality he was more of a chameleon, finding ways to become whoever he needed to be, whenever it fit, as long as he could play his music. But he faced more heartbreak and disappointment in the months to follow. The changes ahead would alter his life forever.

6

MARRIAGE, DEATH, AND THE BLUES

Let's imagine a summer scene in the black community of New Africa.

A short young man struggles behind his horse and plow. He is trying to tend a small field but is clearly not used to the tools he is using. His neighbors watch his struggles with some amusement, but he also looks oddly familiar. They have seen him before, but not behind a plow. He was playing guitar in a local juke only a few weeks ago. He's that young musician they like so much: Robert Johnson. Robert is working on a farm! And while Robert toils in the field, his young wife works in their shack: mending, cooking, and taking care of other domestic chores. Robert's surprised neighbors thought he was from Robinsonville and was a sworn musician. What is he doing here with a plow in his musician's hands? Robert is, after all, a local favorite, playing guitar in the local jukes and parties, giving any crowd a good time with his music. And he enjoys that life: the music, the drinking, the women. But something has changed.

Robert had been, in fact, having the time of his life playing guitar and reaping the attention it brought him. He played all over the upper Delta region, anywhere he could easily get to from Robinsonville. Two of the places within walking distance of that town were the small cotton-farming communities of Clack and Penton, in Desoto County, Mississippi. Those two hamlets, near the Mississippi River on old Highway 61, were near several cotton plantations, and included house after house of sharecroppers. Their one grocery store served a dual purpose: to provide food and be a major meeting place for Saturday night jukers. By late 1928 this was a regular place for Robert to perform.

Robert's presence at that Clack grocery store would change his life in ways that his music never could, for it was there that Robert was attracted to a fourteen-year-old named Virginia Travis. She was living nearby with her kin, and Robert was almost immediately smitten by the girl's beauty and sweetness. He used his best songs to court her, and before long the two were a couple. Only a few months later—on Sunday, February 17, 1929—they were married in Penton. Like on his mother's February wedding to Charles Dodds some forty years earlier, the weather that day was clear but cool, with highs in the upper fifties and the promise of

Clack Grocery Store. *Gayle Dean Wardlow*

spring soon to come. The wedding was held at the Penton home of Virginia's sharecropping grandmother Lula Thomas. In that small, tight-knit community, their wedding was a noteworthy affair, and Robert even provided some of the music for the party that followed the ceremony.

Because Virginia was so young, both bride and groom lied on their marriage license. Robert claimed to be twenty-one years old, living in "Leathers," the Abbay and Leatherman plantation, a future address as Robinsonville, and his occupation as a farmer. Virginia listed her age as eighteen. Born in Lamont, Mississippi, she was one of several children of Jessie Travis and Lula Samuel.[1] Signing as a witness for Robert was Dave Phillips, and for Virginia, Johnson Smith. The Reverand W. H. Hurley officiated their ceremony. Hurley was a local preacher with a congregation in a small nearby church that had an accompanying cemetery.[2]

Something profound had indeed happened in Robert's life: he was in love, and although it went against his natural inclinations, he uncharacteristically agreed to put his musical ambitions aside to become a sharecropper to support his young wife. It took love for Robert to accept, at least temporarily, the field work that Dusty Willis had so long wanted him to do.

The couple probably started married life living with Robert's half sister Bessie and her husband, Granville Hines, on the Klein/Kline plantation just east of Robinsonville in Penton. Unfortunately, in October the Great Depression began, and farm prices would plummet as much as 60 percent.[3] This economic disaster came just as the Delta region was beginning to recover from the devastation of the Great Mississippi flood of 1927 that covered more than twenty-seven thousand square miles, displaced more than two hundred thousand black residents, and killed more than five hundred.

If Robert and Virginia ever did live on the Klein/Kline plantation, however, they soon moved elsewhere. The April 12, 1930, US

Robert and Virginia's marriage license and certificate of marriage.
Tunica County Clerk's Office, Tunica, Mississippi

Census records for Bolivar County, Mississippi, lists eighteen-year-old Robert Johnson and his fifteen-year-old wife, Virginia, living in Beat 3, District 24, some seventy miles from Penton. The same record also lists Granville and Bessie Hines as their neighbors.[4] A year after Robert and Virginia married, therefore, they were living with kin in or near the all-black New Africa community in Bolivar County.[5]

New Africa was an all-black community. By 1900, two-thirds of the owners there were black farmers. It made a hospitable environment for a young black couple whose male partner had hated farmwork and preferred playing music.

According to research conducted by Steve LaVere, their life together was one of happiness and love, and sometime in the late summer of 1929 Virginia became pregnant with their first child. Robert became a proud and protective husband. Once, while the two couples were out riding in Granville's car, they hit a rough patch in the dirt road causing the car to bounce wildly and Robert to shout out, "Man, be careful! My wife's percolatin'!"[6]

The following year, with the birth of their child growing near, Virginia sought the comfort and protection of her family's home. Her decision to go to the safety of a family home, traveling the many miles north to Clack and Penton, left Robert behind to work on their farm while she gave birth. But with Virginia gone, the lure of his guitar and playing in jukes was too strong for Robert to hold out against any longer.

Attempts to find any evidence of where Jessie or Mattie Travis, Virginia's father and mother lived, have been fruitless—no records for either name have been discovered. Virginia, however, didn't go to her parents' home but rather back to the home of her grandmother. Another census record, this one from Monday, April 7, 1930, lists Virginia as staying on a cotton plantation in Clack with her grandmother Lula Thomas and five of Thomas's other grandchildren.[7]

As she lay in labor, Virginia began to experience a difficult birth, and Doctor G. M. Shaw of Robinsonville visited her on Wednesday, April 9, to try to help her deliver. But her condition grew worse, and Virginia died in childbirth at 2:00 AM the following morning at her grandmother's house. Shaw listed her cause of death as "Acute Nephritis (Child birth)" and "Eclamsia [*sic*]." Less than seventy-two hours after she was enumerated in the April 7 census record, she and her unborn child were dead. Robert was nowhere to found.

Virginia's April 10 date of death, however, conflicts with the April 11 census record, which still listed her as living with Robert.[8] Whoever provided the latter information did not know that Virginia had died two days earlier. Although technically correct—Virginia and Robert had been living in that location—at the time the Census was taken it seems that neither of them were in residence. If the information was wrong about Virginia's presence, could it also have been wrong about Robert? Almost certainly the answer is yes, for informants told researcher Mack McCormick that Robert had taken advantage of the time that Virginia was away to play his guitar at various jukes up Highway 1. In fact, several weeks passed

Virginia Johnson death certificate. *Mississippi State Board of Health*

April 7, 1930, census record of Virginia Johnson.
Department of Commerce, Bureau of the Census, State, Mississippi; County, DeSoto;
Beat 3 (part); Enumeration District 17-10, Sheet 3-A, April 7, 1930

before Robert, still unaware of the deaths of his wife and baby, appeared at the family doorstep, guitar in hand. This seems to point to him spending the intervening time playing in whatever juke or party he could find.

There may be evidence of his absence in another census record, providing an answer as to where he had been, and why he was so late arriving for his child's birth. The April 12, 1930, US Census record lists a Negro man named Robert Johnson, age nineteen, rooming in Mrs. Ophelia Morgan's Rosedale boarding house.[9] Obviously Robert Johnson is a very common name, and if the coincidence stopped there it would not be a lead worth following. But there are other curious happenstances that make it worth a second look.

The Rosedale Robert Johnson gave his occupation as a farmer, just as the musician Robert Johnson had stated on his marriage license and as he was described in the April 12 record with Virginia. This designation of a nineteen-year-old Robert Johnson as a "Laborer—Farm" is of particular interest because, of the three-hundred-plus people enumerated on the Rosedale census pages that day, this Robert Johnson is one of only three individuals identifying himself in that way, and the two other Johnsons lived with their families. Why would someone who identified himself as a farm laborer be a temporary roomer in a boarding house when all his neighbors identified themselves as factory workers, lumber hands, fishermen, or merchants? Could Robert Johnson the musician have been only traveling through Rosedale as he played his way across the Delta? Did this census record capture his temporary appearance in Rosedale much like the April 7 census record had captured Virginia while she was temporarily in Clack? If Virginia had been enumerated in two different places, couldn't the same be true for Robert? Rosedale, after all, played an important enough part of Robert's life that he sang about it in his song "Traveling Riverside Blues": "Lord, I'm goin' to Rosedale, gon' take my rider by my side / We can still barrelhouse baby, 'cause it's on the river side." It must be seen as a possibility that Robert Johnson, Virginia's husband, was in Rosedale when she died. His probable intention was to play his way up Highway 1 while Virginia gave birth and recovered with family, stopping anywhere there was a juke or a party to make some money.

When Robert arrived at the Thomas home in Penton he was horrified at the news of Virginia's death, but his sorrow and guilt did not end there. According to Mack McCormack's research, her family and friends, still reeling from the tragedy, condemned Robert for being absent when she died. And, seeing his guitar, they believed his pursuit of a godless lifestyle as an "evil musician" contributed to her death. Their anger focused on that instrument, and

April 11, 1930, census record for Robert and Virginia Johnson, Bolivar County.
Department of Commerce, Bureau of the Census, State, Mississippi; County, Bolivar; Beat 3 (part); Enumeration District 6-24, Sheet 4-B, April 11, 1930

Memphis Slim.
Blues Archive at the University of
Mississippi Libraries

they harassed him about why he would have brought his guitar and taken so long to arrive if he had not been playing jukes and parties on his journey. They claimed that Virginia's death, and that of her child, were due to Robert being out "playing the devil's music."[10]

Robert's friends said he began to believe that he *was* to blame for her death, and he turned his back on the church and God. He began to blaspheme so badly when he was drinking that those around him would leave in fear of being struck down by the Almighty.[11] Piano player Memphis Slim (John Len Chatman) observed of Johnson's

PLACE OF ABODE				NAME	RELATION	HOME DATA				PERSONAL DESCRIPTION					EDUCATION		PLACE OF	
	House number or dwelling in order of visitation	Number of family in order of visitation	of each person whose *place of abode* on April 1, 1930, was in this family	Relationship of this person to the head of the family					Sex	Color or race	Age at last birthday	Marital condition	Age at first marriage	Attended school or college any time since Sept. 1, 1929	Whether able to read and write	Place of birth of each person enumerated and of their parents. If born in the United States, give State or Territory. If of foreign birth, give country in which birthplace is now situated. French from Canada—English, and Irish	
																	PERSON	FATHER
1	2	3	4	5	6	7	8	9	10	11	12	13	14	15	16	17	18	19
32				Johnson Robert	Roomer			✓	M	Neg	19	S		No	Yes	Mississippi	Missis
33				Carter Anaelina	Roomer			✓	F	Neg	23	S		No	Yes	Mississippi	Missis

Dark Corner Cemetery. *Bruce Conforth*

behavior: "And he was about one of the most evil men. Robert Johnson, every time he'd get drunk he'd cuss God. He'd go to cursin' God out and he could empty a house quick. 'Cause nobody wanted to be around him. They were afraid. He'd done called God some of the worst names you ever heard of. Then he'd look around and it wouldn't be nobody in there but him. Everybody said, 'Get away from that fool, 'cause God gon' strike him—and he might kill me, too.'"[12] Such behavior branded Robert a marked man, in league with otherwordly forces.

April 12, 1930, Rosedale census record for a Robert Johnson.
Department of Commerce, Bureau of the Census, State, Mississippi; County,
Rosedale City; Enumeration District 6-8, Sheet 21-A, April 12, 1930

Previous research only noted that Virginia was enumerated by the census on April 12 at home with Robert in Boliver County. But through our research, and some luck, Virginia's count at her grandmother's home in Tunica County was found as well. That information led to the discovery of her death certificate and the information that she was buried in Dark Corner Cemetery. But that raised another mystery: where was that cemetery? No graveyard exists by that name today, nor is it mentioned as such in any specific records.

Dr. Richard Taylor, director of the Tunica Museum, located an elderly undertaker in Tunica who was able to provide an answer. He remembered that Dark Corner Cemetery sat just behind the current Rising Sun Missionary Baptist Church on Green River Road. That was the same church Rev. Hurley used as his home congregation. It lies off Old Highway 61 in Penton, just over the Tunica-DeSoto County line, less than two miles away from Clack. No grave marker for Virginia exists today.

❧ 7 ❧

THE MUSIC BEGINS

Robert Johnson, now a nineteen-year-old who had just lost his wife and baby, fell back on his old habits. He visited his Memphis family to share his grief, and then in May 1930, still devastated, he moved back with his mother, Julia, and stepfather Dusty Willis. He was a totally different person than when he had left them, and life in the Willis home had changed. Dusty and Julia had moved into Tunica, some twelve miles south of the Abbay and Leatherman plantation, and they had taken in a boarder, a woman named Dove Jones. Yet Willis still expected the now adult Robert to work with him, and when he did not, his stepfather would beat him yet again. Robert found every opportunity to leave and spend nights, or even days or weeks, at the homes of sympathetic neighbors or at the Spencer house in Memphis.[1] The more Willis beat him, the more Robert rambled. Willie Moore reiterated his perception of Robert's life at this time: "He was young. He couldn't whup the old man nohow. He'd just come by here. [He'd stay] with anybody. Anybody let him stay two or three weeks he'd stay with that person and leave there and stay [with] somebody [else] two, three weeks. [Playing music]—that's what he'd be doin'."[2]

It seems odd that Robert would continue living with his mother and stepfather under such conditions. He could have easily gone to stay with his family in Memphis, with whom he had a better relationship. But it was the proximity to musicians like Patton, Brown, and Moore that kept him in the Delta. A few months earlier, Charley Patton had moved to the Joe Kirby Plantation near Lula, and after seeing Patton perform locally, Robert recognized Patton's enormous talent, even if he was critical of Patton's clowning. In addition to the two Willies—Brown and Moore—Robert now had a real recording star to watch and learn from, for Patton had already recorded more than three dozen songs. As often as possible, Robert would go to watch Patton play and even began to emulate a few of those clowning techniques, beating on his guitar and stomping his feet. And, for the time being at least, Robert continued to follow Patton's lead of having Willie Brown play backup for him by using Willie Moore as his own second guitar. "When Robert be playing, he wanna play lead all the time. I tell you we played, [but] sometimes it'd be a year before I'd see him. I'd go out, and he'd be there. I'd get off and be back and he'd be there."[3]

Already considered a professional musician by Delta standards, Robert now honed his musical skills and once again began to attract young women by the score. Moore remembered that the girls would get so excited by the blues he'd need protection from them. "I tell you one thing. He wasn't wild, but I tell ya them gals pulled at him all the time. We'd be playing, have to put up a protection around. Them gals you see would jump up."

At the same time that Robert was gaining more local fame, Eddie "Son" House Jr. was being released from Parchman Penitentiary. After serving some two years for killing a man named Leroy Lee, allegedly in self-defense, House relocated to Robinsonville in June 1930 to work on the Tate, Cox, and Harbert plantations where Willie Brown was already living.

Son House, 1964. *Photo by John Rudoff*

Robert was excited when he heard that House and Brown would be playing in a nearby location. He was anxious to learn whatever he could, from anyone he could, and this in part accounts for the stories about him that House would later tell. But House played a very different style than Robert was used to. Robert was playing mostly standard folk tunes, and House was playing rough, in-your-face, original bottleneck dance tunes. People didn't want to hear the old songs Robert was playing. They wanted to get down and dirty, and that's what Son's bottleneck playing offered them: harsh, sweaty music that gave them the cathartic release they needed after a week of hard labor.

House was a conflicted man. He was also drawn to preaching, and the battle between that calling and the blues would be one he would face all his life. Originally, House wanted nothing to do with music, especially such secular music as the blues. When he was only fifteen, House began a career as a preacher. However, in 1928, he was attracted to bottleneck-style guitar and began playing the blues. In Commerce and Robinsonville he tried to straddle both worlds and started his own congregation. Elizabeth Moore considered him a great preacher. "He *really* could sing and he *really* could preach. He got baptized four times in four different churches." But his reputation as a drinker, womanizer, and blues singer ended his religious career. As Moore remembered, "Them members up there put him outta business."[4]

After being tossed out of the preaching business—though he would continue to pepper his performances with impromptu sermons—House, along with Brown, became regular performers at the Oil Mill Quarters, a juke joint in Robinsonville run by bootlegger Nathaniel Richardson. Robert would sneak away from the watchful eye of Dusty Willis and go to hear both men playing together. He already knew Brown and wanted to use that familiarity to become part of their musical scene.

Charley Patton.
*From the collection
of John Tefteller and
Blues Images. Used
with permission,
www.bluesimages.com*

Many years later, House related his first memories of Robert: "We'd play for Saturday night balls and there'd be this little boy standing around. That was Robert Johnson. He was just a little boy then. He blew a harmonica and he was pretty good with that, but he wanted to play a guitar. His mother and stepfather didn't like for him to go out to those Saturday night balls because the guys were so rough. But he'd slip away anyway. Sometimes he'd even wait until his mother went to bed and then he'd get out the window and make it to where we were. He'd get where Willie and I were and sit right down on the floor and watch from one to the other. And when we'd get a break and want to rest some, we'd set the guitars up in the corner and go out in the cool."[5]

Aside from Robert not being a "little boy," this first part of House's recollection is fairly accurate, and most blues writers have accepted it as truth. But when describing what would happen when Robert appeared at their jobs, House's story begins to lose credibility. He claimed that when they would take their break, Robert would *try* to play their guitars, but he could only make noise. "Robert would watch and see which way we'd gone and he would pick one of them up. And such a racket you never heard. It'd make people mad, you know. They'd come out and say, 'Why don't y'all go in there and get that guitar away from that boy! He's running people crazy with it.' I'd come back in and I'd scold him about it. 'Don't do that, Robert. You drive the people nuts. You can't play nothing. Why don't you blow the harmonica for 'em?' But he didn't want to blow that. Still, he didn't care how I'd get after him about it. He'd do it anyway." In spite of House's alleged annoyance with Robert he relented and showed him some guitar riffs. "I learned him stuff from me. Started out when we was living, oh, not two miles apart. He was at home with his mother and father."[6]

But House was wrong about several of his facts. Robert was not a little boy; he was a nineteen-year-old widower. Robert was also not a noisemaker on the guitar or even a novice. He had been playing with other musicians at jukes for at least two years.

House's later claims downplaying the skills of the younger musician are understandable, because a year after House's story ends Robert returned and amazed them with his skills. He would literally take House's seat. The archetype of a younger musician replacing his older master is both iconic and mythic, and House must have resented Robert displacing him. It was Son House's show, not Robert's. The jobs at which House accused Robert of just making noise *were* House and Brown's gigs after all, and this could account for

House's interpretation of Robert's skills. The people who had come to those jukes came to hear the two men, not Robert. After frolicking to the house-rocking music provided by the two older players, the standard folk and pop songs that Robert played, no matter how well he played them, were *not* what people had come to hear. They could very easily have been annoyed by anything that was different.

But in spite of what might or might not have happened there, Robert was honing his guitar skills with every chance he had. When he wasn't practicing he never passed up an opportunity to play with other people. He played with a woman from West Helena and House's cousin Frank in a juke in Bowdre, Mississippi. He also experimented playing with a pianist, Punk Taylor, from nearby Lost Lake.[7]

Along with music, however, there was one other constant in Robert's life: his family in Memphis. No matter how focused he was on playing guitar, Robert always found the time to assist his family in any way he could. That summer, Charles Spencer decided to move his family from Memphis to Eudora, Mississippi, east of Robinsonville. He had been a success at carpentry in Memphis, and perhaps he was just looking for some time to raise crops for the winter. He called upon Robert to help them, and he was quick to respond. His "Baby Sis," Annye (no blood relation but the daughter of Charles and his wife Mollie), said that even after Robert helped them move he would return again and again to help Charles with the plowing. Robert wouldn't help Dusty Willis with *his* field work, but he had no problem helping his first and lifelong father figure. The Spencers didn't stay long on that plantation, however, for by that fall Charles and his family returned to Memphis to move into a Hernando Street apartment with Robert's half sister Carrie and her husband, Louis Harris. Once again, anxious to help, Robert hitched a ride from Clarksdale with a friend of Carrie's who had a truck, and helped that move.[8]

As much as things seemed to be settling down for Robert, he was facing another crossroad in his life. If he continued his musical path he had to face certain realities. "The bluesman was low class. He couldn't intermix with people," Jackson music storeowner and record scout H. C. Speir observed. "[He] smelled a little and had to have a drink before he could play. He was what we call the meat barrel type. Bessie Smith come along and they [companies] dolled it up. They put a little perfume on her type singing. Pulled it out of the meat barrel. . . . He wasn't going to work; hold no steady job. He just wanted to play on the streets and pick up nickels and dimes."[9] Robert Johnson wanted that lifestyle. He wanted to be a "meat barreler" and just play music. He would never go back to being a sharecropper.

Unhappy living with Dusty and Julia, Robert needed a respite from going back and forth to Memphis. Ever since Julia told him that his father was Noah Johnson, Robert had wondered who he was, and who that made him. So as soon as the Spencers were safely back in Memphis, Robert headed south to seek out his biological father and possibly establish a relationship with him. (He didn't leave, as Son House maintained, because he grew tired of House and Brown chasing him away from their gigs.)

And so he headed south to Hazlehurst in Copiah County. What Robert actually found was his most important guitar mentor, living near the small communities of Martinsville and Beauregard, a musician who had no reputation outside of that area. Soon everything in Robert's life would change once again.

8

HERE COMES THAT
GUITAR MAN

Robert Johnson was back in Hazlehurst for the first time since he and his mother, Julia, had left it when he was an infant. He had come to look for his biological father, Noah Johnson, and had no idea where to begin. As he stood on its streets and looked at the strangely familiar surroundings he began doing the only thing he could think of: to go into every store and ask if anyone knew of someone named Noah Johnson. The name sounded famailiar to many, but no one had seen or heard of him for years. Robert went from store to store and plantation to plantation, but he was left with no information. It's not known how long he kept up his inquiry, but eventually Robert decided his attempts were in vain and gave up his search.

What happened to Noah Johnson remains a mystery. Even today, although records exist for individuals with the same name in other locations, he is not listed in any Copiah County records after 1910. Quite possibly, not long after he and Julia separated, he left the area to begin another family in a place where he had no history, where he could make a fresh start. Whether Robert's birth father is one of the other Noah Johnsons that appear in later census records from Bolivar, Madison, or Pike counties in Mississippi, or whether he died without leaving a trace, will probably remain unanswered. Whatever the truth may be, Robert had traveled almost 250 miles from Robinsonville to Hazlehurst in search of a father he couldn't find. He wasn't just searching for his father, however, he was searching for his own identity. He was nineteen years old, a widower, and a good musician. Or so he thought.

Unable to find his father, Robert resorted to what he knew best—playing guitar to earn nickels and dimes. He played at whatever opportunity he could find, and even played for one of the road gangs on the highway. During the early months of 1930 a road crew began constructing the road bed for Highway 51 to be paved. The construction work brought many new people to Martinsville, Hazlehurst, and the surrounding towns. As one local resident, Eula Mae Williams, said, "You know, strange people would be coming in and up."[1] Robert Johnson was one of them.

To almost everyone in that little town he seemed to be just another moderately talented guitarist who happened to be passing through. In "passing through," he chanced upon the small community of Its, just south of Hazlehurst, another of the many small Mississippi towns that no longer exists: the only remnant is an abandoned general store. A small, circular dirt drive enters and exits in front of the building and back onto the main road. Local residents said this building was also known as a juke. Hearing the music and seeing the crowd, Robert couldn't help but go in to see who was playing and what was going on.

The man who was playing guitar was better than anyone Robert had ever heard. He had to know this man—Ike Zimmerman, one of the road crew members. Loretha Zimmerman, one of Ike's three daughters, recalled Ike and Robert's first meeting. "My understanding [is] that Robert came back [to Hazlehurst] to find his daddy. He found my daddy instead."[2]

Loretha Zimmerman. *Bruce Conforth*

But who *was* Ike Zimmerman?

Henry Townsend said, "I'm not sure . . . I wouldn't want to declare on that because the name sounds but that don't mean anything. Zimmerman might mean somebody else's name."[3]

Willie Mason never heard of him: "No. I never did hear tell of him." Wink Clark claimed Johnson never mentioned him: "No, he never did tell me about him." And Johnny Shines was even more puzzled: "Who?"[4]

Isaiah "Ike" Zimmerman was born April 27, 1898, in the small Alabama village of Grady. Once full of sharecroppers, Grady, like so many other Delta towns, is now virtually nonexistent. Ike's great-grandparents moved to Alabama from Virginia before the Civil War. The 1870 census records showed they were farmers in the post–Civil War era. Ruth Sellers Zimmerman, Ike's wife, came from

Montgomery, Alabama, just north of Grady. They were married in the late teens or early 1920s.

Ike and Ruth had seven children, one boy and six girls, and they raised them in a shotgun house in the small town of Beauregard, Mississippi. A shotgun house is a narrow, rectangular building, no more than about twelve feet wide, with rooms arranged one behind the other. The allignment of the rooms and doors at each end of the house was responsible for the saying that "you could shoot a shotgun in the front door and have it come out the back without hitting anything." In shape it was not that different than the saddle-bag house in which Robert was born. The main difference was that the shotgun house had more rooms.

Physically, Ike was short like Robert, but "a strong man, a good man, who wanted everything to go smoothly." His daughter said Ike was a good-natured, generous man and always provided well for his family. "He was really kind and I can't ever remember him raising his voice at me, 'cept for one time when I got married. He didn't want me to do that. But when I was a kid growing up I had long hair and he combed it, would plait it, and all that stuff. 'Cause my mother would tell him he put too many pigtails, they be just flopping on my face. She told him, she'd have a hard time taking it back down. But they [my parents] got along good. I never, never did hear him misuse us any way. We didn't never lack for nothing!"

Ike played guitar for as long as his daughter could remember, but his own musical origins are uncertain. Neither Loretha nor grandson James had any idea how or where he learned his guitar skills. His brother Harmon owned a guitar and could play a few simple songs, but clearly he was not Ike's mentor: "[Harmon] could not play but he could hit a chord or two. He played something, saying, 'Chicken, chicken, you can't fly too high for me.' But that's all he could do, do that. And Ike just started on those two chords and he just went on. Just learned hisself. When I came into this world he was carrying a guitar with him. I tried to find somebody who could beat my daddy. B. B. King, he couldn't touch my daddy. I don't know, my daddy he acted like he had electric fingers."

Because Ike earned more money on his highway job than a sharecropper's average pay, he was able to buy a good guitar. Most sharecroppers could only afford cheaper mail-order instruments: Stellas, Regals, etc. Loretha remembered that Ike bought a more expensive Gibson guitar. Musically his repertoire ranged from blues to pop tunes, but at home he only played the blues.

"He was playing blues," Loretha remembered, "'cause I remember him playing a song about 'going.' He was going on the road, you know, it concerned, it had the road in it. . . . There was one traveling, going away somewhere, he was going, and that was one of the songs . . . Since I been grown he was a spiritual [person], but when I was growing up it was the same music like he taught Robert. That's what he was playing [the blues]. [He made up a] lot of them. I think that Daddy made that one up: 'Going, going away and baby

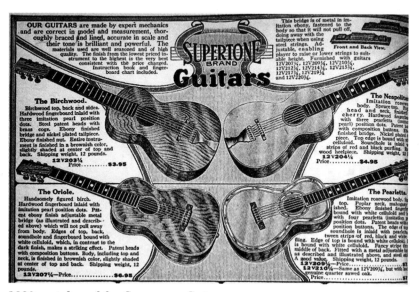

1920s catalog ad for Supertone Guitars. *Bruce Conforth*

Ishman Bracey

Ishmon Bracey.
Promo photo used in
Victor Record Catalog

don't you wanna go. But going, going away and baby don't you want to go.' Daddy made that up."

In his later years, Ike abandoned the blues and devoted himself to the church and gospel songs, like many other bluesmen did. Perhaps it was their way to atone for having played the devil's music. Son House, both a preacher and bluesman, in later life was not allowed to play the blues in his house.[5] Ishmon Bracey, Rube Lacey, and Robert Wilkins were blues musicians who also shifted from the devil's music to religious spirituals in their older age. "[Ike] played blues then," his daughter remembered, "but he ended up playing church songs later. When I heard him play church songs it was after Robert."

Zimmerman alternated between fingerpicking and playing bottleneck slide—his slide was homemade from a bone. He was also a skilled harp player like the young Robert Johnson. And Ike understood how to work an audience. He was a showman like

Last known photo of Ike Zimmerman playing guitar.
Loretha Zimmerman

Charley Patton, playing behind his head and performing other guitar gymnastics.[6]

Also like Patton, Ike used his musical and showmanship skills for more than making money. "Well he did [play guitar to chase women]! He did! My daddy was a womanizer," Loretha admitted. "He really was." Robert didn't need any encouragement to seek out women in his life, but watching Ike use his musical talents to impress women could have only given the young apprentice more encouragement to use his guitar as a tool of seduction.

Ike's generosity was apparent when he invited Robert to live with his family. "He [Robert], far as I know, like I told you, he fitted in our family, and he had to be nice, because my daddy was a strong man and he would've had . . . he'd make everything go smoothly, and so he wouldn't have taken up no time with someone who wasn't a good person." Robert and Ike were such a good team that to Ike's daughter he seemed to be part of the family. "He was just like a family member. I was thinking he was! I really was! Robert lived with Mama and Daddy there. For a long time I thought he was related. I really did! For a long time, look like one of the family just be there with us, and he just fitted in."

To have found a mentor and family after fruitlessly searching for his father must have been very reassuring to Robert. Although he was in their home like kinfolks, Loretha didn't remember how many months Robert actually stayed: "I couldn't even think about how long it was because like I said he lived there." In actuality Robert lived there for less than a year, but in that time he left happy memories for the little girl. "I can remember my daddy when, oh well, I had to be five, and I can remember him wrapping me up in a sheet, and he would put the guitar over [me] and he would be in that chair, and see I remember Robert because he was in that other chair. See when he was holding me on his lap there was Daddy, and there was Robert. And my feets was down there on the floor. I don't know, why *did* he hold me? And they was going at that guitar like some . . . it sounded just so good, just like they was competing. He was teaching him then." When she'd wake up in the morning Ike and Robert would be right there as her mother cooked breakfast and served the family until Ike had to leave for work. As soon as Ike returned the two men would start playing guitar again, but until that time Robert had the day to explore his new surroundings and make himself known to the community, especially the women.

Eula Mae Williams, another local Martinsville resident, remembered meeting Robert shortly after he came to the area. His first appearance was striking to her. "He came in here from somewhere. Didn't say where he come from. [The first time I saw him,] he come walkin' slowly across that field towards the house. He come up to the porch, stopped and asked to come on up, and he introduced hisself as 'R. L.' He wudn't no big man. He wudn't no more than five-eight. He didn't weigh more than a 140 pounds. Seems like he

Eula Mae Williams. *Gayle Dean Wardlow*

had one big eye and one smaller eye."[7] But Robert impressed her for another reason. "I never saw him, not once, without that guitar. He had this here [leather strap] across his chest on his guitar. He always had that old guitar with him." Later, she and her sister would always say when they saw him: "Here comes that guitar man."[8]

Robert also carried several smaller instruments with him and he was quite adept at entertaining with them all. He'd play a piano if he had access to one. "He had this little funny thing in his mouth [Jew's harp] that he played with this here finger. He made himself acquainted with me and my folks and after he sat a while, he went on off. R. L., that's what we called him. He never said he was named no Robert. He always called himself R. L." But it was his guitar playing that Robert took seriously, and he knew the ways he could use it to impress the ladies. "He had a guitar swinging on his neck. . . . He put his hands on it and it would sing just like—[he] could make it sing songs and such."[9]

Eula Mae soon discovered that Robert was playing house parties near Martinsville, close to where the Zimmermans lived. "There was a little quarter like. Eight or ten houses around in a circle. It just would be one special house that on Friday, Saturday, and Sunday that they would move all the furniture out of this room. And they would sell fish and hot dogs and different things, and he and Ike would play the music. That would pull the crowd from all the other houses, and from different places they would come." Eula Mae walked to those parties with her girlfriend Virgie Jane Smith and Virgie's uncle Clark Williams. As a friend of the family, she also heard Robert play at the Zimmerman house and confirmed that Ike was "the one who taught him a lot about music," and that Robert "mostly stayed with" the Zimmerman family.[10]

Whether Robert was just being shy about his family background, embarrassed that he could not find his father, or was just trying to create a new identity, he would spend the next few years introducing himself as R. L. to everyone he met. Back in the Delta he had been Robert Spencer, Robert Johnson, Robert Sax, and was even referred to, to his displeasure, as "Little Dusty." Now he just wanted to be R. L. "[He] had a nickname because I'm thinking he was, his name was Robert Lee," Loretha Zimmerman remembered, "[but] we never called him Robert."

Ike and Robert may have played at home to entertain his family, but the place the older guitarist loved to play, the only place he said you could really learn to play the blues, was in a cemetery at night. Southern black belief in hoodoo, especially in rural regions so close to New Orleans, was particularly accepted since "two-headed doctors" or "conjure" men or women were often the only medical and psychological resources available. Ike subscribed to those beliefs, and he often claimed that he learned to play the blues while sitting on gravestones at midnight.[11] Such an idea certainly fed into the stories connecting blues musicians to the devil or the supernatural.

Ike's daughter did, in fact, verify that her father practiced guitar in a graveyard. Ike even used the local cemetery to instruct R. L. But at the same time that she validated the cemetery story, she also disparaged the crossroads myth. "They would leave and go to that cemetery. It's got them old tombstones, you know some of them new, it was some of them old ones. He'd sit back there with him. He wasn't at no crossroads. [It] was just a path. There wasn't no crossroads. They went 'cross the road [*laughs*]. 'Cause you gotta go across [the] road and go to that cemetery. They went over there and sat on the tombstones. Exactly. And that's where they was. Sitting there playing."

Some current Copiah County residents believed that Ike played in Hazlehurst graveyard, but that was incorrect. The cemetery in which Ike and R. L. practiced was, as Loretha indicated, in Beauregard. "Now I just got through reading the [newspaper] my granddaughter brought me and told me this man had been in Hazlehurst looking around saying that Robert Johnson was his idol and they was taking, snapping pictures. They put that in the paper. And he went to the cemetery in Hazlehurst and I saw that, I read that, and I got tickled, I laughed. He went to the wrong cemetery. He said he done been to the cemetery in Hazlehurst where Robert learned to play. And they mentioned my daddy but I knew that wasn't the [right] cemetery."

Although Loretha initially scoffed at any notion of the supernatural, within the Zimmerman home and family the idea was not out of the question. "My daddy ain't no devil," Loretha said laughingly. But her son James, Ike's grandson, was less willing to disparage the idea of darker forces being at work in the blues: "I don't know, that crossroad thing, [a newsman] said that, uh, Robert sold his soul to the devil at the crossroads. And Aunt Kimberly [Loretha's sister] said, 'Well, you know Daddy walked around here talking that stuff.'"[12] Protective of her father, Loretha quickly shushed her son, but she still allowed for the possibility that there was something more to the story than *just* practice: "I don't care what Kimberly say. Daddy, he would, Daddy would always scare people and say he'd go pickin' the guitar and the haints would come out at the graveyard." Did Ike just want to scare people away "talking that stuff" or was he a believer? According to Loretha, Ike liked playing in the cemetery because it was quiet, and he knew no one would disturb his playing. But in explaining his rationale her recollections hinted at deeper reasons. "He'd come back and tell [us] he played for the, he said the haints. He said I been up there playing for the haints." And according to grandson James, it was always at midnight: "The thing I could never figure out, I mean I knew he went to the graveyard, ever since I was a little kid; that was the story he used to tell us, that we grew up with. That was what our granddaddy did. It was always at twelve o'clock."[13] Loretha once again agreed but held on to her belief that it was more natural than supernatural: "When everybody was asleep. I think because it was quiet and nobody around to walk and interfere. He wasn't never scared, but he wasn't meeting the devil neither."

Soon R. L. progressed enough in his lessons that Ike began taking him on his regular playing route, locations where people had money to spend: lumber camps with sawmills (probably the Piney Woods section of Copiah County), fish frys, and jukes. The two guitarists walked all over the rural roads that took them to their next job. "They used to go everywhere in those little towns. And they did a lot of walking. They did *lots* of walking. They really did," Loretha remembered with a laugh. "Back then you know they didn't make a whole bunch of money. It was cheap, but they made money." R. L. also ventured out without Ike by his side. "He would go away and come back," Loretha noted.

R. L. made at least one trip from Hazelhurst to see his Memphis family, who were still living together on Hernando Street. It was

Gravestones where Ike Zimmerman and Robert Johnson played guitar.
Bruce Conforth

always a good time when Robert was back in town. Carrie might
hold a house party for him to play at, or he'd spend time entertain-
ing Charley and Mollie's little children and their friends. His Baby
Sis, Annye Spencer, remembered how he used to entertain them:
"He would sit at the window. [There would be] too many children
to come into the house. But he would sit at the window and play.
And the steps would be lined with children. Because when he came
I would gather all the children and he would play his songs for us."[14]

True in his devotion to his Memphis family, Robert journeyed
back in early March 1931 to help them move from their Hernando
Street apartment to 285 East Georgia, where they lived until Charles
Spencer died on November 28, 1940, at age seventy-three and his
wife, Mollie, passed on March 12, 1942, at age forty-seven. He

would use this as his contact address for the rest of his life. If someone needed to reach him they could do it by sending either a note or a telegram to this address, or by physically inquiring at the home. Carrie lived only a mile away at 1219 Texas Street. By mid-March, after helping with their move, Robert returned to Hazlehurst to play every Saturday on the steps of the Copiah County courthouse, where Eula Mae Williams would see him when she went to town with her relatives. "He never had nobody else play with him on the streets. He had this little old hat he laid there on the ground so people could drop a penny in it. But he didn't carry no crowd with him. People just walk up and listen and stop, but they didn't come here when he played up there."[15]

Robert initially tried to court Eula Mae's younger sister, Johnnie Pearl, but a musician's reputation as low class got him run off from the Williams household. "He come up here to court my sister and Granny ran him off. He wudn't no church person 'cause he played the blues. She knew that so she wouldn't let him see her. She knew what he wanted."[16] Unsuccessful with Johnnie Pearl, Robert set his sights on Eula Mae's friend, sixteen-year-old Virgie Jane Smith. "Me and my girlfriend Virgie Smith used to sneak off and hear them all playing together on Saturday nights. We didn't go in, we were still girls and our parents wouldn't allow us to go inside. So we'd listen outside to the music."[17] But, just as Eula Mae's parents had turned him away for playing the devil's music, he also ran into resistance with Virgie's parents and grandparents. "We were Christian folks and they didn't allow us to be where the blues was played."[18]

But it wasn't just the devil's music that made some people wary of Robert; it was also personality traits that the local people thought were rather odd. Eula Mae always saw him alone and thought of him as being "moody." "He'd sit a while then just get up and leave. Wouldn't tell you bye. Just get up and go."[19] That Robert exhibited such traits is not hard to understand. He had been through a series of traumatic life changes, and when he came to Hazlehurst in hopes of finding his father, and at least a clue to who he was, he failed. Even for a young black man in 1930s Mississippi, life had been unkind. In addition to his odd social behavior, Robert didn't try to change in order to impress the God-fearing families of the young women who interested him. He had no interest in religion or the church. Eula Mae recalled, "I ain't never heard anyone say R. L. went to church. He never sung no church song at all. I never heard him sing nothing but the blues."[20]

In spite of any opposition to him as a person, Robert's music still served as a siren call for the young women in the area, and both Eula Mae and Virgie would stand outside the parties at the house of Callie Craft, who ran a Martinsville juke. Virgie wanted to meet him and convinced Eula Mae's uncle Clark to introduce them. Robert, looking for someone to replace his lost Virginia, took advantage of Virgie's attention, and the two quickly became romantically and ultimately physically involved. They would go walking around the country roads at night as Robert would use all his talents to woo the young schoolgirl.

In late March or early April, Robert and Virgie met Eula Mae and her boyfriend walking down the Martinsville Road. Virgie confessed: "We gone play around tonight." Eula Mae later testified that the two couples stood in the woods kissing and then watched each other have sex. "R. L. and Virgie were laying on the ground over there. R. L. was on top of her."[21] The couple continued to have sex for several weeks. Sometimes Robert even met Virgie to have sex "on [her] way to school" near her aunt's house.

In either April or May Virgie confided a secret to Eula Mae: "I done missed a month. It's R. L.'s and I don't know what I'm gone do now. Because it's gone tell on us." Eula Mae remembered that "she just told us that 'I'm pregnant.' I said, 'Yeah, it's sure gone tell on us.' And so Clark [Vergie's uncle] asked R. L., said, 'Well, what you gone do?' He said, 'Well, whatever she want to do.' And she said, 'Well I don't know, because I'm afraid.' Clark told her, 'Well, you have to go on home to Little Sis.' That's what we called her mother. And she was afraid, said, 'But I guess I have to go.' And it wasn't long before her mother came and got her. R. L. didn't say anything, but just said, 'Well, what you gone do?' She says, 'I don't know.' He said, 'Well, I'll do whatever you want to do.'"[22]

Robert wanted Virgie and her unborn baby to leave with him and go to Memphis. This time he wasn't going to lose another potential wife and child. But in what must have been heartbreaking news to him, Virgie decided to neither marry nor leave with him. Once again Robert was facing a profound loss because he was playing the devil's music. Virgie's decision weighed heavily on him, and perhaps in an attempt to make her jealous, or to try to get over her, Robert turned his attention to the much more available Callie Craft. An older, stocky woman who had three children, Callie ran the house juke that he played at in Martinsville. It was the home of a bootlegger named O'Malley. Flattered by the attention the young guitarist was giving her, Callie tried to please Robert any way she could: dancing with him, sitting on his lap, bringing him breakfast in bed.

Perhaps as a reaction to being rebuffed by Virgie, on Monday, May 4, 1931, Robert and Callie were married in a civil ceremony in the Hazlehurst courthouse. Robert gave his age as twenty-three (although he was barely twenty) and Callie listed hers as twenty-eight (although she was actually older).

Shortly after they married they left for Vicksburg for a brief honeymoon, but Robert could not stop thinking about Virgie and his unborn baby and made every effort to see them.

Robert and Callie would eventually head north to the Delta, but before their departure, Robert went behind Callie's back and made one last attempt to carry Virgie with him to Memphis. The

Caletta "Callie" Craft.
© *Delta Haze Corporation*

May 4, 1931, marriage license for Robert Johnson and Callie Craft.
Copiah County Clerk's Office, Copiah County Courthouse, Hazlehurst, Mississippi

result of his efforts to win her hand were met with a response he'd heard too many times before: he played the blues, "the work of the devil," and Virgie's religious parents refused to let her go with him. And besides, Virgie had heard that R. L. was married to Callie, and she wasn't going to run away with a married man, no matter who he was.[23]

Robert never appeared to show any true affection for Callie. To him she was primarily a meal ticket and someone to pamper him. When Virgie refused to go with Robert, this time claiming it was because he was married, Robert resented his new wife even more.

Claud, Robert and Virgie's son, was born on December 12, 1931.

After Virgie turned Robert down he took Callie in tow and, with Ike Zimmerman along for the trip, went back to the Delta. Ike had gone with his student to bolster Robert's musical confidence. "They stayed [in Vicksburg] awhile. Then they went on up in the Delta," Eula Mae remembered.[24] Robert, Callie, her children, and Ike settled in Clarksdale for a while.

"Daddy always, I think, he wanted to push him," Loretha claimed. "I don't think Daddy really wanted, or cared about—I don't think he really wanted to record. I think he just pushed Robert. I think he did push him. I think that's the reason he went all up through there [the Delta region]. I guess he just stayed in the background is what I figured. They tell me he went back to play that guitar, he just tore it up, but . . . but like I said, my daddy taught him well. Because my daddy was a real blues player. He was really, really, a guitar player."

But Loretha also recalled that Ike soon returned to Hazlehurst rather than staying in the Delta. She thought his return is what ruined any opportunity he might have had to record. "If he stayed out there, like knowing what he did, you know, he'd have been in the right place" to have been discovered and recorded.

Virgie Jane Smith and son, Claud Johnson. *Robert Johnson Estate and Robert Johnson Blues Foundation*

Back in Copiah County, Eula Mae heard that in December 1931 or early 1932 Callie took desperately ill. Robert, uninterested in anything or anyone other than his music and his Memphis family, abandoned Callie, first for short periods of time, and then forever. Callie's illness soon caused her death. She died in early 1933 without ever returning to Copiah County. Eula Mae said, "We heard she died up there. They never sent her body back. You know, she was my cousin."[25] She died without her husband by her side.

This was the second time Robert lost a legally married wife while he was off playing the blues. But unlike when Virginia died, Robert seemed not to care about what happened to Callie and neither tended to her illness nor paid attention to her death. He had a more important task at hand: finding Son House and Willie Brown and showing them how his guitar skills had improved.

❦ 9 ❧

RAMBLIN' AT THE CROSSROADS

When Robert returned to Robinsonville, he heard that Son House and Willie Brown would be playing at a nearby juke on a Saturday night, so he and Ike made plans to go show them his new skills. When they arrived the two older, more established musicians were playing to a rowdy, drinking, carousing crowd. The shack was lit up like a holiday, with candles in all the windows and a drum full of flaming kerosene-soaked wood providing heat for the men standing outside smoking, drinking, and swearing up a storm. Robert could hear women shrieking and other men laughing. And through all the extra noise he could hear House's slide guitar and Brown's second guitar accompaniment working the crowd to a frenzy.

Robert had been to many such jukes before, but he never had so much to prove. This was to be *his* time, not House's or Brown's. With his guitar strapped to his back he made his way through the outside crowd and stood for a second in the doorway, wanting to get a good view of his competition. Both musicians were every bit as good as he remembered, and when House sang, his head rocked back, his eyes rolled, and he became totally possessed by the song he was singing. They were still, at least for the next few minutes, the best any of the crowd had seen or heard, and Robert knew he had his work cut out for him. He had returned to display the superior skills he learned since he left the Delta almost a year earlier, and he paused for a moment wondering if he was really that good. But Ike Zimmerman, still with him, pushed him through the door and spoke only three words: "I taught you."[1]

Robert walked through the room and stood before the two musicians. It was the first time he ever thought he could "cut somebody's head"—he was there to outperform the competition. Son House recalled the night well when asked about it in 1964.

He remembered Robert had been away for some time. Then, "Willie and I were playing again out at a little place east of Robinsonville called Banks, Mississippi. We were playing there one Saturday night and, all of a sudden, somebody came in through the door. Who but him! He had a guitar swinging on his back.

"I said, 'Bill!'

"He said, 'Huh?'

"I said, 'Look who's coming in the door.'

"He looked and said, 'Yeah. Little Robert.'

"I said, 'And he's got a guitar.' And Willie and I laughed about it. Robert finally wiggled through the crowd and got to where we were."

House asked him, "'Well, boy, you still got a guitar, huh? What do you do with that thing? You can't do nothing with it.'

"He said, 'Well, I'll tell you what.'

"I said, 'What?'

"He said, 'Let me have your seat a minute.'

"So I said, 'All right, and you better do something with it, too.' And I winked my eye at Willie.

"So he sat down there and finally got started. And man! He was so good! When he finished, all our mouths were standing open. I said, 'Well, ain't that fast! He's gone now!'"[2]

After impressing House, Brown, and everyone else in the juke, Robert sat and smiled in satisfaction. He had cut their heads and had literally taken the seat of the master. Robert played a few more songs before letting House take his place alongside Brown and finish the evening, but the attention was still on Robert.

House, the more experienced bluesman, took Robert aside over the next few days and tried to give him some advice. He tried to warn Robert of the dangers he faced. "He hung around about a week or more, and I gave him a little instruction. 'Now, Robert,'" House told him, "'you going around playing for these Saturday night balls. You have to be careful 'cause you mighty crazy about the girls. When you playing for these balls and these girls get full of that corn whiskey and snuff mixed together, and you be playing a good piece and they like it and come up and call you "Daddy, play it again, Daddy"—well, don't let it run you crazy. You liable to get killed.'" But Robert, still reeling from successfully cutting heads, seemed to disregard these warnings. "He laughed it off, you know. I said, 'You gotta be careful about that 'cause a lot of times, they do that; and they got a husband or a boyfriend standing right over in the corner. You getting all excited over 'em and you don't know what you doing. You get hurt.' I gave him the best instruction. So he said, 'Okay.' Finally he left and went somewhere else again with his guitar."[3]

Although House's often-quoted story would later attain mythical proportions, resulting in many untruths about Robert, his basic facts remain accurate. Unfortunately, some blues writers, inserting their own personal beliefs, implied that House's alleged comments indicated that he believed Robert had used supernatural forces to gain his remarkable guitar skills. Their conclusions, not House's comments (for he never actually made such an assertion), were the first steps in building the long-enduring crossroads legend: the most famous story in all of blues history. What makes this mythical reliance on what House supposedly said about Robert even more absurd is the usually unnoted fact that House had also under-gone a similar transition: he was playing professionally within a year of acquiring his first guitar. His biographer, Daniel Beaumont, described his rapid development: "Once House took up the guitar what happened next is . . . surprising—the rapidity with which his new career progressed. Within a matter of weeks he was performing at house parties on his own."[4] Such rapid musical development was certainly no less remarkable in House's case, yet no one has ever associated his accomplishment with a deal at the crossroads as they have with Robert. To the community who knew him, Robert was a musician who went from being a "good player of old time songs" to "an excellent player with his own songs." Somehow, his progress allowed southern superstition to be intertwined with reality. How this happened is a case study in folkloric creation.

Both African and European folklore include stories of pacts being made at a crossroad. In both traditions the crossroad is a supernatural place with unique powers. Similarly, the Faustian bar-gain was a very familiar theme in the African American tradition, predating the development of popular blues. Blues scholar Julio Finn contends that "the tradition of making a pact at the crossroads in order to attain supernatural prowess is neither a creation of the Afro-American nor an invention of blues lore, but originated in Africa and is a ritual of Voodoo worship," and indeed, the African roots of the African American version of this belief seem beyond dispute.[5] As it was adopted by many members of the American black community and syncretized with Western religious beliefs in a devil, the idea of selling one's soul or making a deal with a "Big Black Man" or the devil became a common theme in folk narratives and music. The key to understanding the prevalence of such a belief is to understand the time and place in which this narrative existed and the mainly rural, African American people for whom it held meaning. The culture was full of such folklore.[6]

As early as 1926 Niles Newbell Puckett collected beliefs about making a deal at the crossroads in *Folk Beliefs of the Southern Negro*.[7] The Federal Writer's Project (1935–1939) actively collected tales of conjure in the black community. In 1931 Zora Neale Hurston published "Hoodoo in America" in the *Journal of American Folklore*.[8] And in 1935 she published *Mules and Men*, describing her personal initiation into voodoo/hoodoo.[9] Between 1935 and 1939 folklorist Harry Middleton Hyatt collected several dozen folk versions of that belief, all similar in content: a person may go to a crossroads at midnight and make a deal with either the devil or a "big black man."[10] In her 1939 book, *After Freedom: A Cultural Study in the Deep South*, Hortense Powdermaker asserted that a connection between Christianity and voodoo/hoodoo wasn't contradictory: "Often, however, those who are devoutly religious are also devout believers in current folk superstitions and do not look upon Christianity and voodoo as conflicting in any way. . . . For a large number in the middle and lower classes they [the superstitions] still have significance. The older generation is the one that adheres most strongly to superstitions, but there are also younger believers."[11]

When questioned about the legend decades after Robert's death, Willie Mae Powell, one of his girlfriends and cousin of Honeyboy Edwards, believed what Edwards allegedly told her about Robert: "He [Robert Johnson] told Honeybear [Honeyboy Edwards] that he sold hisself, at the fork in the road, twelve o'clock one night. Honeybear says it's the truth! He told me so. He did! He wanted to be a sworn musician, and that's the kind that can play anything."[12] Another of Robert's girlfriends, "Queen" Elizabeth, also from Quito, Mississippi, was even more adamant that Robert made a crossroads deal. "He done went to the crossroads and learnt, went to the cross, and he started playing. I done heard. I asked him. If I want to know anything, I ask 'em. Well that's where you have to play! You sold your soul to the devil."[13]

It's important to remember that these declarations were made in the 1980s, almost fifty years after Robert's death and twenty years after the rerelease of his music made him a cultural icon. It is uncertain, therefore, whether these "recollections" can really be attributed to Robert making the claim himself or whether they are the result of folk-iconic creation: people saying what they believe others want to hear. One thing *is* certain: hoodoo belief survived in the black community at the time Robert was performing and recording. But as Queen Elizabeth indicated, however, it wasn't just the crossroads myth that was culturally important, it was also the belief in a personalized devil.

Reverend Booker Miller, a former Greenwood-based bluesman, explained: "Them old folks did believe the devil would get you for playin' the blues and livin' like that."[14] Deacon Richard Johnson, pastor of the Payne Baptist Church in Quito, Mississippi, echoed Miller's insights: "My father used to tell me about singers who made pacts with the devil by selling their souls. That's what they used to say about Robert Johnson. I think he wrote a song about that. It kind of reminds me of that old story about the Devil's Son-in-Law [Peetie Wheatstraw]. That crazy old boy thought the devil had a nice daughter."[15] Henry Townsend, the Saint Louis blues musician who knew and traveled with Robert, reflected on the power of belief in the devil in southern folklore: "That word, devil, you'd be surprised how effective it is."[16] The blues and its association with the devil's music created great division in black families in the South. One blues writer points out that "grandparents and parents warned that singing reels and blues guaranteed a quick road to hell."[17]

Robert had run face-to-face with these beliefs. To assume that he was not aware that he had been implicated by those around him in the deaths of two wives as a part of his association with the devil's music would be to ignore common sense. Blues guitarist Jimmy Rogers confirmed that he too had been given such a warning: "My grandmother, she raised me, and she was a Christian-type, church-type woman, and man, they's really against music, blues, period."[18] A very similar story was related by guitarist John Cephas: "They used to say [the blues] was the devil's music, and even today my mother's still living now and she always asks me that I should give some time to the church and stop singing blues. She still says that, you know."[19]

The early history of the blues is replete with people either using an association with the devil as a marketing tool or mentioning him in their lyrics. As early as 1924 blues singer Clara Smith sang "Done Sold My Soul to the Devil":

> *I done sold my soul, sold it to the devil, and my heart done*
> *   turned to stone,*
> *I've got a lot of gold, got it from the devil, but he won't let*
> *   me alone.*
> *He trails me like a bloodhound, he's slicker than a snake,*
> *He follows right behind me, every crook and turn I make.*
> *I done sold my soul, sold it to the devil, and my heart done*
> *   turned to stone.*[20]

In Smith's song her deal was rewarded with gold riches, but in exchange the devil turned her heart to stone. The bloodhound that trails her is unquestionably similar to Robert Johnson's wail, "I got hellhounds on my trail."

Peg Leg Howell, an Atlanta bluesman, sang, "I cannot shun the devil, he stay right by my side" in his 1928 recording "Low Down Rounder Blues."[21] Bessie Smith's 1929 "Blue Spirit Blues" declared, "Evil spirits, all around my bed / The devil came and grabbed my hand / Took me way down to that red hot land."[22] In 1931 Texas/Oklahoma bluesman J. T. "Funny Paper" Smith sang: "You know this must be the devil I'm serving, I know it can't be Jesus Christ."[23]

African American conjure doctor wearing nutmeg and red flannel.
*Newbell Niles Puckett Memorial Gift, Cleveland Public Library, Fine Arts and
Special Collections Department*

Also in the 1930s, pianist and guitarist Peetie Wheatstraw billed
himself both as "the High Sheriff from Hell" and "the Devil's
Son-in-Law."

Without a doubt, the folk belief in a personalized devil, hoodoo,
and the power of the crossroads existed well before Robert Johnson.
But also, without a doubt, the Robert Johnson who returned to the
Delta was a changed man. Musically, he was a better guitarist and
lyricist, who now played original songs. Personally, he had become
a heavy drinking, womanizing, blaspheming individual who preferred being a loner. Regardless of which side of Robert's transfor-
mation people saw, he was now a man ready to make his living by
playing the devil's music. And regardless of House's words of warning, Robert was embarking on a new phase of his career that would
ultimately lead to a degree of fame—and then death.

৯⅄

After returning to Clarksdale, Robert started to make plans for using his new talents. Ike Zimmerman, seeing the success of his young mentor, returned to his family and job in Beauregard. Robert began to use all his new skills to perform at as many jukes and parties, and to attract as many women, as he could.

One of the small jukes he frequented was Elizabeth Moore's place in Friars Point. "He come in and played for me," she recalled, not remembering how much she paid him. "It was just a few dollars," she said. And whenever Robert told her that he would someday make records and become famous she would just laugh him off. She had no idea she was hosting a legend-to-be. He was just another juke house friend that she loved to party with and to listen to play "them thair old mud line blues." She preferred Robert's music over that of his mentors House and Brown, whom she also had heard numerous times at jukes. "Now this here Robert Johnson was over Son," she believed.[24]

Running a juke was not an easy task, and it was dangerous. Hernando bluesman Joe Callicott, who recorded in 1930, recalled an incident in which "one man was shot dead and the other was cut up so bad, and left for dead, he shoulda been dead" at a house party in a nearby town. "You had to watch where you went and whom you played for," Callicott warned. He and his friend Garfield Akers (aka Garfield Partee), who had recorded together in 1929, always sat facing each other when they played. "I could watch his back and he could watch mine. That way nobody could slip up on you from behind and try to kill you."[25] Booker Miller always carried a .38 pistol in his belt and said he would "have killed anyone" who tried to harm Charley Patton while he was playing at jukes with him from 1930 to 1934. Elizabeth's common-law husband, Willie, said the doormen in jukes in cities like Memphis always collected weapons at the door ("knives and guns") to hold down violence. But a country juke was different. It was up to the host to provide protection, liquor, and food for the musician.

Pete Franklin, a former juker who grew up in the Alabama Black Belt, recalled a typical Saturday night in the late 1930s at a juke in Marengo County, Alabama. "It'd start about five o'clock and you'd go there and stay all night. You paid twenty-five cents to get in, twenty-five cents for a half pint of moonshine, and twenty-five cents for a fish sandwich. As long as you had some money you could stay all night, 'til the sun come up on Sunday morning. They'd have one or two guys who played so you could dance."[26] As dangerous as these jukes could be, Robert relished performing in such places. They represented the life he loved: music, drinking, and women. The only things Robert wanted more than that lifestyle were Virgie and his son, Claud.

In May 1932 Robert returned to Copiah County to attempt a reconciliation with the mother of his child, but once again he was turned away. Virgie's parents and grandparents were very religious and opposed Robert's very presence on their property: first because he had impregnated their daughter, and second because his music was "the work of the devil."[27] Finally, in August, Robert tried, for the last time, to take Virgie and their son, Claud, to Memphis, but Virgie again refused to go. Robert gave her twenty or thirty dollars to help with Claud. That was the last time he would see them: "When Claud was five months old," Virgie later related, Robert "came by my mother's and again when he was eight months, he came by my mother's. Then he asked me to go with him to Tennessee. The last time he came he asked me to go to Tennessee with him. But I refused. So he left and I never saw him again."[28]

Although deeply disappointed that he had yet again been denied because of his music, Robert had other relatives living near Virgie in whose homes he could find solace. Both the Majors and Dodds families were large, and Robert had relatives on both sides of the family spread throughout Mississippi, some of whom he had never even met. One of these was his aunt Clara Majors Rice, Julia's youngest sister, who lived in Hazlehurst. Robert probably didn't know her when he had first visited Hazlehurst to look for his father, but his mother might have told him about her when he returned to Robinsonville. Neither the Zimmermans nor Eula Williams remembered her, so it's unlikely that Robert had met her before this point. When they finally did meet, Robert told his aunt Clara that he had become a musician because he "didn't want to work for fifty cents a day" sharecropping.[29]

From that point on, every time Robert was near Hazlehurst he would stop at Clara's house. Her son Howard remembered Robert displaying a variety of musical abilities. He would arrive with his guitar "strapped across his back in an old bed ticking—striped bed ticking. I don't think they make them anymore. Blue and white striped bed ticking. He carried it in a bag. And when he left, he just had it strapped across his shoulders."[30] But the guitar was not all Robert would bring. His blue ticking bag was full of clothes that needed washing. "He would come and visit. And if he had clothes he would need washing [Clara] would wash them. And she would cook and feed him. And he would stay a day or two, and probably move on."[31] The music he played during his visits made him a hero to his younger relatives. Just as he entertained his Baby Sis and her friends in Memphis, Robert was happy to entertain the children here as well. Perhaps it was his way of making up for the two children of his own he had lost. "Well, we would go out to the woods and things and he played guitar," his cousin would remember, "and we'd have one more, air organ, which you had to pump on. He could play that. He could also play the piano. So he played music and sang. And he was just, you know, our idol. A kid's idol."[32]

Even though he could get his clothes washed in Hazlehurst and entertain his relatives there, Robert chose to make the much larger town of Hattiesburg his new home. Hattiesburg had more piano players than guitarists who worked its streets and jukes, and with his superior guitar skills Robert would have no real competition. Ninety miles southeast of Jackson and Hazlehurst on Highway 49, Hattiesburg had a population of more than ten thousand. Robert could make a better living playing music in a town that size than in the small community of Hazlehurst. Two railroads—the Norfolk and Southern, and the Gulfport Ship Island—ran through the town. If Robert wanted, he could use either to get to Gulfport to the south or Jackson to the north. It was a perfect place for a budding blues musician.

Soon Robert was railroading from Hattiesburg to Jackson, where he met another young bluesman, Johnnie Temple, who lived on South Jefferson Street and who grew up listening to musicians at his stepfather's house. Bluesman Tommy Johnson, who lived in Crystal Springs (between Jackson and Hazlehurst), and Temple's stepfather, Lucien "Slim" Duckett, had been playing together many years. It may have been through this association that Robert learned of Tommy Johnson's alleged deal at the crossroads and decided that this myth fit his own life. "He came in here one Friday afternoon on a freight train and I run into him. He said his name was R. L. That's what's he told me. Said he was from Hattiesburg." Temple had no reason to doubt the young musician, and right after their meeting Robert began a weekly routine: on Friday afternoons he would ride a freight train from Hattiesburg to Jackson. Then the two of them would "go out in West Jackson and play on Friday nights and he'd catch a freight train out of here on Saturday mornings. He was going up there to Sunflower County [another hundred miles north of Jackson]. He'd come back through here on Monday afternoons and go on back to Hattiesburg. He did that for a couple of months. I never saw him after I left for Chicago."[33]

Hattiesburg, Mississippi, ca. 1926. *Bruce Conforth*

Robert stayed in Hattiesburg until at least the end of 1933 or early 1934, according to Temple. Some blues historians have posited that it was Temple who taught Johnson the stomping bass that Temple first recorded on *Lead Pencil Blues* in May 1935. But Temple freely admitted that R. L. taught *him* the pattern. "Now I tell you, as far as that beat there [the boogie bass pattern], R. L., the boy that I was telling you about, [was] the first one I ever heard use it, and I was the one carried it to Chicago. And I'm the one that made that beat popular. It was similar to a piano boogie bass. But R. L., the boy that learned me, yes sir, I learned that from R. L. in '32 or '33. I was the first person to carry that stompin' bass to Chicago," he boasted. "I learned it from that boy R. L."[34] That particular boogie shuffle became one of the most important riffs in blues music. While Temple did beat Robert to the studio by a year, he honestly admitted that he learned the bass pattern from him at least two years earlier. In return, Temple showed Robert the open E minor tuning that he had learned from Skip James. Robert appropriated the tuning only one time on record, for "Hellhound on My Trail."

Johnnie Temple.
Gayle Dean Wardlow

Temple's recording of "Lead Pencil Blues" must have bothered Robert when he heard it, for with it he lost his chance to be the first to record his new dynamic guitar sound. This could help explain why he later became so secretive about his playing.

By now Robert had settled into a regular traveling itinerary. On Saturdays he would take the train from Jackson up to Sunflower County. The Yazoo and Mississippi Valley line took him straight into Moorehead—where the Southern cross the Dog—which was also near Indianola, Holly Ridge, Itta Bena, and other small towns with jukes. Robert would return to Hattiesburg and repeat the same route week after week.

But the curious behavior that Eula Mae Williams had noted in Robert while he was still in Hazlehurst soon returned: he would once again show up someplace, stay there for a short time, and, without saying goodbye, just disappear. After playing with Temple for several months, Robert once again vanished. This time he went back to the Delta. His ramblin' days were just beginning.

10

TRAVELING RIVERSIDE BLUES

Robert was now constantly on the move. No one place could hold him after he had finished his playing and loving whatever woman he could seduce. His ramblings took him up and down the length of Mississippi, and on one such ramble he again ran into Eula Mae Williams. She was working in a small café that her sister owned in the Delta town of Shelby. Unbeknownst to Williams, Robert had been been hired to play a brief engagement there. "He come in the café my sister had. He knowed who I was and he was kinda surprised to see me. He said, 'Hello, girl,' and I said hi back to him."[1]

Eula Mae inquired if he was planning to go back to Hazlehurst to see Virgie and Claud and he pointedly told her no. Robert knew that Virgie had married a man named Smith and went on to tell Eula Mae that he was "too busy" with his music.[2] As much as he wanted to carry Virgie and Claud away with him, Robert couldn't stand to be let down one more time. He stayed in Shelby only long enough to play that job, not even looking for a woman to spend the night with, and left as quickly as he had come.

Soon after, he left for Arkansas, particularly Helena, where blues music was all the rage. Either late in 1933 or early in 1934, Robert landed regular gigs playing at the Hole in the Wall juke. The Helena of the 1930s was a good-sized town with all the amenities of a more urban environment: its own hospital, a thriving downtown, and a bus service. In the main blues center of Arkansas, Robert met and played with Sonny Boy Williamson II, Robert Nighthawk, Elmore James, Hacksaw Harney, Calvin Frazier, and many others who came through the riverfront town.

Helena was a perfect home base for Robert, because from there he could also easily travel to jobs at the Blue Goose juke off Eighth Street in West Memphis and another juke in Marianna, Arkansas, twenty miles northeast. In Helena he teamed up with a guitarist, Wash Hamp, who backed him up as Willie Brown had done for Son House. Willie Moore heard about their music together: "[Robert] and another boy called . . . that Hamp boy from Helena. Wash Hamp. He was from Helena, you know. He just second on him. Him and Robert played together."[3]

In addition to the Hole in the Wall there were enough jukes and clubs to keep the blues going seven nights a week. Helena's downtown streets—Elm, Phillips, Walnut, and part of Cherry—were filled with venues where bluesmen played all night long to packed houses. Even the sidewalks were a popular performance site for many musicians.

Most of the jukes paid the local white police for protection through shares of their revenue. People went to the jukes to play cards, gamble, drink, and carouse: they were rough and dangerous places. Johnny Shines, who would soon meet Robert, recalled that the clientele could get so out of control that certain restraints were required: "Beer was served in cups; whiskey you had to drink out of a bottle. You didn't have no glasses to drink the whiskey out of, so you drank it from the bottle or you used your beer cup, and they were tin cans usually. See, they couldn't use mugs in there because people would commit mayhem, tear people's head up with those mugs. Rough places they were."[4] The bluesmen knew that there was good money to be made in Helena's jukes, and they competed heavily for it. To get a job in one of these jukes a musician had to be both talented *and* lucky, and Robert was both.

If a juke owner had heard of a musician, he'd generally seek him out and make him an offer, perhaps a dollar and a half a night plus tips. It was the tips that could make or break a gig because if the crowd didn't like you, or if you couldn't play their requests, you ended up only with the dollar and a half the owner had offered. If, on the other hand, you could play the latest tunes from the radio and records and fill the crowd's requests then you could literally be showered in money. Johnny Shines recalled that "sometimes people just throw you money anyway, just come up and chuck it into your guitar, anything."[5] Robert had a great ear for the latest tunes. He was now performing popular blues, a few originals (many based on previous recordings by other artists), and pop standards like "My Blue Heaven" and "Yes Sir, That's My Baby." He knew all too well that without being able to play the most recent hits of the day, no matter how good his other songs were, he wasn't going to make decent money. People didn't yet want to hear Robert Johnson, they wanted to hear what they heard on the radio, and Robert was particulary adept at reproducing these songs.

Robert was making decent money for a black blues and pop musician, but for him the most intriguing aspect of Helena was a local woman named Estella Coleman, the mother of Robert Lockwood, the only person with whom Robert would share his guitar-playing techniques. Robert was used to seducing women with his music, but according to Lockwood, he basically invited himself to move in with Estella and her family. "Robert followed [my mother] home, and she couldn't get rid of him. I don't know if that's the first time he met her, but I never knew anything about no Robert Johnson till he followed her home. I don't think she knew anything about him till that day. She couldn't get rid of him."[6] A very light skinned, thin woman, Estella was treated like a queen. She wasn't just another juke-joint pickup for Robert but someone for whom he had real feelings. When he wasn't playing his guitar he doted on her, spending his money on the family and buying her little gifts. Robert fused himself to her family, which must have been a whirlwind courtship for Estella, for she had been through a series of failed relationships.

The 1920 US Census showed that Robert Lockwood and Estella Lockwood originally lived in Big Creek, Arkansas, and along with their four-year-old son, Robert Jr., were two boarders: Milton Staines and Lonzo Williams.[7] Robert Sr. and Estella divorced shortly after that census was taken, however, and Estella married Staines.

The April 1930 US census contains several surprises about Estella, who was by then living in a building on Hospital Alley in Helena. It mentions her son, Robert, but also includes a daughter, Omega Washington, age seventeen, who had been absent from previous census records, and Milton is conspicuously missing. There are also two different lodgers: Joe Coleman, and Cinderella Mattley, who was accompanied by a cousin and daughter.[8] It is unknown what happened to Milton, but on July 1, Estella and Joe Coleman married. Apparently the two had known each other from Big Creek, and when Coleman moved to Helena, the two reunited. Coleman was a private chauffeur and made a decent living without having to do manual labor. Estella and Joe remained together for at least three years, and only then did Robert Johnson become intimate with the family.

All records indicate that Robert Lockwood was born in 1915 or 1916, yet at various times he claimed to have met Robert Johnson as a boy, as early as when he was only eleven years old. At other times Lockwood asserted that he was thirteen when he met Robert.[9] But these ages correspond to dates that don't fit with what is known about Johnson. Lockwood was eleven years old in 1926 or 1927, and at that time the sixteen- or seventeen-year-old Johnson was still living with his mother, Julia, on the Abbay and Leatherman plantation. When Lockwood was thirteen years old, in 1928 or 1929, Robert Johnson was courting and marrying his first wife, Virginia. Further, Lockwood claimed that the first song he learned from Robert was "Sweet Home Chicago," but that song was based on Kokomo Arnold's "Old Original Kokomo Blues," which was recorded in Chicago in September 1934. Arnold was firmly a part of the Chicago scene and had no reason to travel to the Delta, and

1920 Big Creek Arkansas census record for Lockwood family.
Department of Commerce, Bureau of the Census

Robert had not yet traveled to Chicago, so it is unlikely that Johnson heard a live performance of "Old Original Kokomo Blues" but rather adapted "Sweet Home Chicago" after Arnold's record was released. We also know that Robert had been in Hattiesburg and Jackson with Johnnie Temple until at least 1933 and that he did not move to Helena until after Callie Craft's death. Although Robert may have been in Helena for several months before meeting Estella, he did not become a part of that family or meet and begin to teach Lockwood guitar until very late 1934.

Before Lockwood even met Robert, however, he had already started playing music on the piano and organ. "I was eight years old when I was introduced to play the piano, and I played the piano until I got twelve years old. My grandfather was a preacher, and we had an old organ in the house, you know. So when he used to leave, my grandma would let me play the blues. I had a couple of cousins who could play a few tunes on the piano and that was my beginning."[10]

Lockwood was also very familiar with the blues before Robert entered his life. His family had a whole supply of blues records: Blind Blake, Ma Rainey, Ida Cox, Texas Alexander, and Blind Lemon Jefferson. But one particular artist was his favorite. "I was crazy about Leroy Carr. He had such laid-back stuff. Scrapper [Blackwell] and Leroy was workin' together."[11] Although he liked the blues, the guitar didn't particularly interest the young man. He was annoyed by what he deemed the musical limitations of the instrument. Robert Johnson's playing, however, changed not only his opinion of the guitar but also ultimately his life. "I really never did have a desire to play the guitar until Robert Johnson came along. All the guitar players at that time—it was always two of 'em, one playin' chords and the other playin' melody and I just didn't like that. Robert showed up playin' it all by himself. That was really a thrill to me. I always wanted to play something that I wouldn't really have to have no help, you know. I didn't think that could be done. And then when I seen him doin' it, I decided that's what I wanted to do, you know, so I kept worryin' him until he finally started teachin' me."[12]

Robert was a surprisingly patient teacher. He even helped Lockwood make his first guitar, remembering what it was like when his half sister Carrie helped him make one back in 1926. "He mentioned makin' me a guitar one time, and I said okay. And I helped him. We took the little thin vinyl part—the finishin' part of the wood that they puts on furniture—we took that off the Victrola,

1930 Helena Arkansas census record for Estella Staines, Robert Lockwood Jr., and boarders. *Department of Commerce, Bureau of the Census*

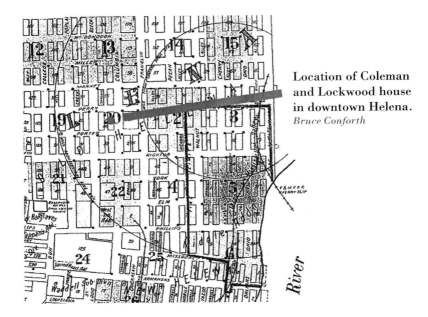

Location of Coleman
and Lockwood house
in downtown Helena.
Bruce Conforth

and that's what we used to make the guitar. We also used an old cheese box—what cheese used to come in a long time ago. Robert carved the neck out of some wood, and planed it out with a planer and put frets in it. I helped him do that. It stayed together about six, seven months. We didn't have the kinda glue that you have to put things together, you know? It stayed together pretty good."[13]

Lockwood practiced on that homemade guitar with an enthusiasm that must have reminded Robert of his own youthful infatuation with the instrument, and when Lockwood's aunt gave him a real guitar, Robert's memories must have flooded back about his own first store-bought guitar. "When it [the homemade guitar] tore up my auntie bought me one," Lockwood remembered. "Then *everybody* was in trouble."[14]

Robert appears to have felt more of a kinship with the younger musician who was just starting out than he did with any of the contemporaries with whom he was in competition. Everything that Lockwood recalled about those times were almost mirror images of the experiences that Robert had gone through in learning to play.

The only difference was that no one was beating Lockwood for favoring guitar over field work.

With that store-bought guitar, Lockwood admitted that he was "learning fast." "At first he would tell me where to put my fingers, but he didn't have to after the first three months. If I asked him something, he'd sit down and show me. He'd set the guitar down, and I'd ease in and pick it up. I'd go get it. He wouldn't hear me when I pick it up. . . . Well it wasn't hard to learn—I learned real fast. I learned so fast I excited both him and my mother. He showed me something one time and when he look around I be playin' the shit out of it."[15] Lockwood also remembered, "I played all night and I played it all day and my mother had to take a stick of stove wood and chase me outta the house. I played it all night and all day. When I wasn't asleep I was playing the guitar. That's how come I learned so fast. 'Cause I slept with the guitar."[16]

In time, Lockwood became so associated with Robert's music that many people believed he was called Robert Junior solely because of their relationship. But being called Junior for that reason annoyed him: he had been known as Junior from birth, named for his father.

For the first time since his wife Virginia died, Robert made at least a temporary commitment to someone. But ultimately not even Estella and her son could stop Robert's rambling and carousing. Lockwood soon grew competent enough to accompany Robert and second him wherever he performed. In very late 1935 those ramblings took them to one of his traditional playing locations, Tutwiler, Mississippi, where, in a rather bizarre bit of bad luck, Robert got run over by a truck. After less than a year together, that accident caused their musical and personal relationship to come to an end. "I went to Mississippi with Robert that time he got hurt by a truck," Lockwood recalled, "and we stayed in Tutwiler. I was part of the cause of Robert getting hit, because I was not fixing to go in that direction. I was fixing to go back home. And he turned around, and backing up, turning around, he slipped off the fender of the

DEPOT.   TUTWILER. MISS.

Tutwiler train depot. *Mississippi Department of Archives and History*

truck and fell under it. I stayed around for three or four days until he got well, but I just decided I wouldn't be with him no more."[17] Robert wasn't badly hurt, but the incident was enough to help him decide that he preferred to stay on the road by himself: to ramble where and how he wanted to.

When they returned to Helena, Lockwood found a new playing partner, Sonny Boy Williamson II (Aleck "Rice" Miller). "The first time I met Sonny Boy Williamson, Robert brought him to my mother's house. They would run across each other and stuff like this. So he come home with Robert one night. He and Sonny Boy come back and begged Mama to let me go to Mississippi with [Sonny Boy]. And she sure didn't want me to go. Sonny Boy had heard me play at home. He made it sound so good, so she finally said okay. I left with Sonny Boy in 1936."[18]

With Lockwood off playing with Williamson, and Robert's urge to ramble growing every day, he left Estella and started preparing himself to reach his ultimate goal. He wanted to make records, but he had to find someone to make that happen.

A white man in Jackson, Mississippi, would provide that opportunity.

⚜ 11 ⚜

I'M BOOKED AND BOUND TO GO

In the fall of 1935 music store owner H. C. Speir was contacted by Art Satherly, recording director for Vocalion/ARC, to search for talent for a session to be held that October in Jackson. Satherly planned to record in Dallas with Don Law, his Texas sales manager for the Brunswick owned companies, and then stop in Jackson on his return trip. Speir had been a valuable asset in finding excellent talent for previous companies. Satherly had begun working for Paramount in the early 1920s, rose to direct the QRS piano roll company's short-lived record label, and joined ARC in 1930 and then Brunswick. In the ARC mergers of the early 1930s, Brunswick was combined with the Vocalion labels and all race and old-time music recordings were placed under Satherly's control. This meant that if Robert was to have a chance to record, Speir and Satherly would be his main contacts.

The two men scoured both New Orleans and Handy Park in Memphis searching for talent and made a quick stop in Helena on the return trip, where they found a piano playing bluesman. They recorded him and some others at the weeklong session on Farish Street at the Crystal Palace, a second floor dance hall. In Memphis they located two previously recorded singers and arranged for them to be part of a session. Both were veterans of recording sessions and one, country bluesman Robert (Tim) Wilkins, had at least five records issued from 1928 to 1932. The other, Minnie Wallace, was a cabaret band singer who had been featured with some of the Memphis Jug Band personnel on her Victor recordings.[1] The most dynamic recordings from the session, however, were by guitarist Isaiah Nettles from neaby Utica in Hinds County. Speir remembered finding him near a depot in the small community of Rockport near Taylorsville in south Mississippi. "I found him takin' up nickels and dimes at the depot there in Rockport," Speir recalled. "When I went into a town looking for talent, I always checked out the train station first." Nettles's rendition of a Blind Lemon Jefferson song that he titled "It's Cold in China" had an up-tempo Mississippi dance rhythm and his high-pitched moaning prompted Satherly to issue his lone record as by the "Mississippi Moaner" with his real name listed below that pseudonym.

Although Robert Johnson was doing all he knew to become a recording artist, both Speir and Satherly somehow missed him on this talent search. Undoubtedly, Robert knew of Speir's importance in getting bluesmen on records. His association with Johnnie Temple in 1934 would have provided that information, as would a number of Temple's mentors, including his stepfather, Slim Duckett, whom Speir had helped record in 1930. Speir did not remember Robert auditioning for him before 1936—if he had, the only way Speir would have rejected him would have been for a lack of four original songs. An original repertoire was extremely important to Speir. Four original songs enabled companies to release a first record and have a backup for a second issue if a hit occurred. If that happened they could then arrange for a follow-up session. Companies did not record songs they already had in their catalogs or want a new artist covering a previous hit. Robert's version of "My Blue Heaven" might have been terrific, but it wouldn't have gotten him

H. C. Speir, 1920s. *Gayle Dean Wardlow*

a contract: the white crooner Gene
Austin had already had a multi-
million-selling hit with the song in
1928. From a young black guitarist from Mississippi, record companies would only be interested in
what they considered Robert's blues
songs, which would fit into the race
record catalogs. Record companies
considered ten thousand copies sold
to be a hit, and they worked on a
one-in-ten recording ratio: "They
always told me it took one hit to
pay for the other nine, they put it,"
Speir noted. "They were always looking for something different. He [the
bluesman] had to have something
different from the others that didn't
sell for them." Speir did believe that
the lyrics were important, but also
that a song had to have some drive or
rhythm to complement the words.

After the 1935 session Speir
arranged a follow-up deal with ARC
for a July 1936 session in the Hotel
Hattiesburg. Satherly sent his national
sales director, W. R. "Bill" Calaway,
who had used Speir in 1934 to locate
Charley Patton and bring him to
New York to record for Vocalion. In
addition to Patton, Speir had also
been responsible for the recordings

WANTED

**Blues Singers and Old
Time Tuners to Make Re-
cords AT AN EARLY
DATE.**

For many years Mr. Speir
has been associated with
all the leading record companies of America.

Arrangements are under-
way to record here in
Jackson real soon. If you
can sing or play any in-
strument, see

for further details.

SPEIR'S

**111 N. Farish Street
Tel. 985
Jackson, Miss.**

H. C. Speir 1935 newspa-
per ad for musical talent.
Gayle Dean Wardlow

Hotel Hattiesburg. *McCain Library and Archives, University of Southern Mississippi*

of legendary Mississippi icons such as Son House, Willie Brown, Skip James, Ishmon Bracey, Tommy Johnson, Bo (Chatmon) Carter, and the Louisiana Delta bluesman Blind Joe Reynolds. He even advertised in newspapers in an attempt to find talent.

In the end, Calaway never paid Speir for that July session, which had produced more than seventy race titles by the talent Speir provided. Speir was disgusted: "I really lost my shirt on that deal. Calaway never paid me a dime. I made up my mind to never work with him again." He also vowed never to work for Satherly either.

Robert, hearing about the Hattiesburg sessions after the fact, appeared at Speir's Music Store in the early fall of 1936 to audition for him. He must have presented quite a stereotypical image, for Speir remembered him as just another one out of countless musicians who came from as far away as Georgia and Texas to audition for a record deal. If earlier descriptions of Robert remained accurate, he arrived at Speir's store with guitar slung over his shoulder, perhaps even carrying his striped bed-ticking bag of belongings. But whatever he looked like, his playing and singing were enough to impress Speir, who liked the way he "threw his voice up like Ishmon [Bracey] and Tommy [Johnson] did." After his audition, during which Speir made a test recording of "Kind Hearted Woman Blues," Robert made use of Speir's equipment to make another personal record like the one he had made at a Memphis opera house that he played for his friends in Robinsonville. Robert paid Speir five dollars for a metal-based one-sided aluminum disc that would eventually wear out from numerous plays on a windup Victrola that used a steel-tipped needle.

Speir's store at 111 North Farish Street was unique for the area, for he had purchased a recording machine in 1925, thereby providing the only private recording opportunity between Memphis and New Orleans. Speir was the only person in his area who could make demos of his talent and private recordings at a reasonable price. "Seems like I remember that boy makin' a record for himself," he recalled. But in dealing with so many itinerant musicians, Speir developed a way of protecting his interests through an informal, self-written contract that stated:

> For and in consideration of $1.00 receipt of which is hereby acknowledged and other good and valued consideration, I hereby assign and convey to H.C. Speir, manager of the Speir Phonograph Company, Jackson, Mississippi, Hinds County, what ever commercial value and musical talents I might possess, for a period of one year, with an option of renewal and additional year. In other words, I appoint H.C. Speir sole manager in securing the best value for my musical talents, and leaving this entirely up to him.

Speir's Music Store, 111 Farish Street, Jackson, Mississippi. H. C.
Speir is on the right. *Gayle Dean Wardlow*

I, or we, have read the above agreement, and state that in
the presence of these witnesses, that I, or we, are sound men-
tally, and do understand the above agreement.[2]

Thirty years after Robert's audition, Speir could not remember
whether he signed that contract or not, but he *did* remember that
Robert had at least four original songs.

Normally, Speir would have telegrammed Satherly in New York
or Law in Dallas. Law had begun recording Texas talent in 1934 in
both San Antonio and in a makeshift studio at the Burrus Flower
Mill between Dallas and Fort Worth. But because of his bitterness
over his treatment by Calaway, he didn't. Instead he told an excited
Robert that he would contact Vocalion salesman Ernie Oertle from
New Orleans, and that Oertle would find him if the company
was interested. Speir did have some reserverations about Robert's

possible success. Recent trends in race recordings were beginning to feature more city-oriented bluesmen such as Big Bill Broonzy, Bumble Bee Slim, Washboard Sam, Memphis Minnie, and Peetie Wheatstraw. These were not just solo artists, but musicians who used sidemen playing piano, drums, bass, and sometimes even horns on their Chicago recordings. "When they got in the mid-thirties, they started recording the piano blues with other instruments, and they didn't have no real interest in them old guitar blues," Speir said. "It just wasn't selling like it had." If Speir had paid attention only to the change in musical styles, Robert might never have been recorded. But Speir also realized that the emerging jukebox market might be the perfect vehicle for Robert's songs.

By the time Vocalion got Speir's test pressing of Robert they were using both a hotel in San Antonio and the company's Dallas headquarters to make recordings and would continue to do so until World War II. Ernie Oertle, the Vocalion salesman Speir contacted, worked the Louisiana-Mississippi area from New Orleans, placing records in other outlets such as hardware, furniture, and drug stores in small towns. His territory included New Orleans to Columbus, Mississippi on Highway 82, then over to Greenville, and finally to Shreveport in northern Louisiana.

Speir gave Oertle Robert's name and his Memphis family's address when Oertle made his monthly sales call, and before long news arrived at the Memphis home that Robert had been offered a chance to record in San Antonio.

Ernie and Marie Oertle.
Jane Templin

1936 Hooks Brothers studio photograph of Robert Johnson.
© *Delta Haze Corporation*

Robert could barely contain his pride and told all his friends he was going to San Antonio to record. He even bragged to Elizabeth Moore about it. "I'm leavin'. I don't know when I'll be back, 'cause I'm goin' over there for a good while. But I'm goin' over in Texas." Elizabeth asked, "'Yeah, boy you gonna get way over there?' He say, 'Yeah, but I'm gonna be makin' music whilst I'se over there.'"[3]

At the 285 Georgia Street home of the Spencer family that also housed Carrie and her husband, Louis, there was great excitement. Their son Louis Jr., who had recently joined the navy, was home on leave dressed in his military apparel. Robert wanted to have a formal photo of him taken as a professional musician, just like the ones he had seen of Charley Patton, Blind Lemon Jefferson, or Blind Blake. Borrowing Louis Jr.'s slightly undersized hat and pinstripe suit he proudly walked into the Hooks Brothers studio on Beale Street to have his photo made.

Normally, photographers like the Hooks Brothers took several poses from different angles as backup pictures, but only one pose from that day has survived. That photo, originally in Carrie's possession, shows Robert as a cheerful, optimistic young man, believing he was soon to achieve national success. His long fingers are prominently displayed holding a 1928 Gibson L-1 guitar while making a complex chord on the fretboard.

His family's Georgia Street location also provided the background for his one true hit recording, "Terraplane Blues." Little Sis Annye testified that Robert admired a 1936 green Hudson Terraplane that was frequently parked down the street from the Spencer home. "We had a neighbor that had a minister that visited the address at 277 Georgia Avenue. And he visited this family often. He had a 19—I don't know whether it was a 1936—and he had a green Terraplane. The children that lived at 277 were around our ages, and my sister and the other two girls played together and we knew the family. And brother Robert would walk through on his way to

Highway 61 and often I would walk with him. And he would walk by and admire this car. He would always take a good look at it. And of course we all looked at it because during that time cars were few. But most of them out there were the old T Model Fords and old cars. And this car was new."[4]

While Robert was reveling in his new status as a recording artist, Oertle started to drive to Memphis with his wife, Marie, to find Speir's new discovery. This was the first trip Marie had accompanied him on, but it would soon be Thanksgiving and she wanted to spend the holiday with her husband. By Saturday morning November 21, Ernie Oertle, Marie, and Robert Johnson were on the road to San Antonio. It was a trip Oertle had made many times before, but this time he had two passengers with him. The trip, more than seven hundred miles, took them three days, Marie recalled. It must have been a strange—and potentially dangerous—sight for 1936 Mississippi, Louisiana, and Texas: a white couple driving with a young black man in their car. According to Marie's recollections, the

1936 Hudson Terraplane advertisement. *Bruce Conforth*

Oertles took a cue from the trick that John Lomax had developed while driving through the South with Lead Belly. Not wanting to be seen as a "nigger lover," Lomax would sit in the backseat and have Lead Belly drive, pretending to be the white man's chauffeur. The Oertles did the same. [5] Driving was not their only concern, however, for Robert would certainly not have been able to stay in the same accommodations as the Oertles. The two nights they needed lodging meant locating a colored hotel or boarding house for Robert and a whites-only room for the Oertles. But San Antonio was a hot recording location, so the three settled in for the long drive.

Speir explained why San Antonio was so important to the recording business: "They had two hundred thousand Mexicans living there, and they could record and sell their music in Mexico and South America. It was the best place in the country to find Mexican talent." This Mexican context would feature prominently in Robert's music, recordings, and myth.

The Okeh label had recorded in San Antonio as early as 1928, when Speir worked a session with Polk Brockman, the Atlanta-based director for their southern recordings. Satherly, who since 1934 had been working closely with Law, said they recorded in San Antonio for the emerging jukebox business, just as Speir had predicted. "We saw a real opportunity to sell more records to the jukebox market in the South and Southwest, so we started recording in Texas."[6] Recording in southern locations also saved the companies the added expense of bringing talent to either New York or Chicago. These savings could be used to pass on reduced costs to jukebox companies and increase total sales numbers. Satherly said Vocalion gave such companies new releases for nineteen cents each, instead of the normal thirty-five-cent retail price. Such savings were a natural inducement to buy more product. Vocalion had other methods of disseminating its artists' music, however, in the form of releases in dime and department store markets. These records were not issued under the Vocalion name but rather were transferred to labels such as Perfect, Oriole, and Romeo, each selling for only twenty-five cents. While we have no actual numbers detailing how many records Vocalion pressed (save for the notion that Robert's only hit, "Terraplane Blues," sold in the thousands), we have exact numbers for the dime store pressings.[7]

Perfect Records (whose motto was "Better Records Can't Be Made") sold quite well, while Oriole Records (associated with the Sears & Roebuck stores) and Romeo Records (associated with S. H. Kress & Co) were far less successful, and for that reason accounted for fewer pressings. "Kind Hearted Woman Blues"/ "Terraplane Blues," Robert's first Vocalion release and his only hit, was, not surprisingly, the first release for the dime store market. The cheap versions came out on January 4, 1937. Perfect Records pressed nine hundred copies of the recordings, and Oriole ordered seventy-five. On February 10, 1937, Perfect Records led again with a pressing of nine hundred copies of Robert's "32-20 Blues"/ "Last Fair Deal Gone Down." Oriole again ordered a pressing of seventy-five copies. The companies must have seen promise in "Dead Shrimp Blues"/ "I Believe I'll Dust My Broom" for on March 10, 1937, Perfect pressed eight hundred copies of the songs, with Romeo pressing one hundred. "Cross Road Blues"/ "Ramblin' on My Mind" was released on April 20, 1937, with eight hundred Perfect Records and seventy-five Romeo Records. "They're Red Hot"/ "Come on in My Kitchen," released on June 1, 1937, only interested Perfect Records enough to have them press five hundred copies, with Romeo pressing one hundred. After a brief hiatus Perfect was back on August 1, 1937, with a more modest four hundred, and Romeo with again seventy-five copies of "From Four Until Late"/ "Hell Hound on My Trail." "Milkcow's Calf Blues"/ "Malted Milk," songs that the companies must have thought would have only minor appeal, was released by Perfect and Romeo on September 15, 1937, with Perfect pressing four hundred copies of the record and Romeo only fifty. Apparently, only Perfect Records had any interest in "Stones in My Passway"/ "I'm a Steady Rollin' Man," for on November 15, 1937, they became the only budget record company to release it, and then only in a short run of three hundred copies.

Whether these declining numbers are indicative of a deepening economic depression or a shift away from Robert's style of blues to the more urban Chicago sound is unknown, but in this secondary market Robert's sixteen songs (eight records) accounted for five thousand total pressings by Perfect Records, four hundred pressings by Romeo Records, and only one hundred fifty by Oriole Records. But Robert was not getting paid by the number of records pressed or sold; he received a flat rate for each song he recorded. He probably had little knowledge of the number of sales his records would generate. His main interest was the personal pride he felt in becoming a recording artist and with his records issued and heard. With that in mind he prepared to fulfill his dreams.

By the time of the 1936 recording session, Satherly, who had to travel from New York to record in Texas, began shifting responsibilities to Don Law so that he could remain in the Big Apple to work primarily with other groups. After Law solved some technical problems for Vocalion in 1934, Satherly turned over most Texas sessions to him. Since Oertle had wired Law that he was bringing Robert to record, they met as soon as the three travelers arrived in town.

On Sunday, November 22, Robert and Ernie met Law at the Gunter Hotel in San Antonio, but since the hotel was whites only, Law found Robert a room in a boarding house on East Commerce Street in the city's black section. Law paid for the room (about two dollars per week) and told him to be ready to record on Monday morning (November 23, 1936) in room 414 of the Gunter Hotel.

Previously, Johnson researchers have claimed the recording sessions were made in radio station KTSA, which had its offices on

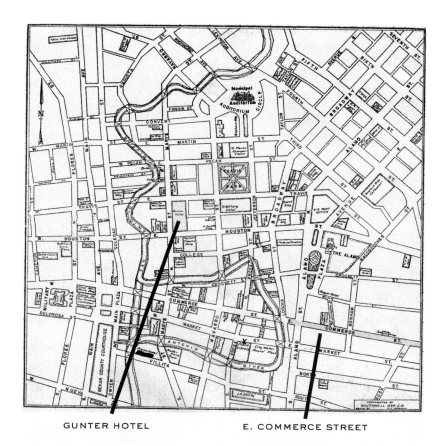

GUNTER HOTEL   E. COMMERCE STREET

Downtown San Antonio. *Bruce Conforth*

the mezzanine of the Gunter and its studios on the third floor. But Don Law was adamant that he rented and recorded in two rooms on the fourth floor: the company's recording equipment was placed in one room and the musicians performed before a microphone in the second.

San Antonio was particularly active that week celebrating the upcoming Thanksgiving holiday and the end of the Texas Centennial Year celebration. It was a jumping town, just as Robert liked it. Newspapers were filled with articles about celebrations in both the black and white communities. Aware of the city's upbeat party mentality, the performer in Robert drove him to look for a place to play and sing. He wasn't aware that only a week earlier the city's mayor, C. K. Quin, had declared "war" on street crime, especially vagrancy, because of the influx of people for the holidays.

Robert, buoyed by his imminent recording session and used to playing before crowds of strangers, tried to take advantage of the holiday throngs by playing his music on the street as he had in dozens of other towns. He tried performing by the Southern Pacific railroad depot and the Harlem Grille, but police chief Owen Kilday had his officers out in force and Robert was quickly accosted and roughed up. The beating was severe enough to be noticeable several days later.

Robert protested that he wasn't a vagrant but was in San Antonio to record for Vocalion, but to the police he was just another

Gunter Hotel ca. 1930s.
University of Texas at San Antonio Libraries Digital Collections

intinerant musician with no visible means of support. On his very first night in San Antonio, therefore, Robert was arrested, had his guitar broken beyond repair, and was thrown into jail on false vagrancy charges. False, of course, because Robert was right: he *wasn't* a vagrant, was legitimately in San Antonio on business, and had a room in which to stay. After being booked into the San Antonio jail, Robert was given his one phone call, and he made it to Don Law at the Gunter Hotel.

Years later, Law's son provided a detailed story of that Sunday night: "[My father] told the famous story of how once Robert came to San Antonio he took responsibility for putting him up in a boarding house and he cautioned Robert, he said that he'd be recording that next morning at ten o'clock and to get a good night's sleep, maybe suspecting that that wasn't likely. My father then went with my mother to the Gunter Hotel to have dinner with some friends, and as they just started dinner there was a phone at the hotel for my father and it was the local police. My father went to the phone. 'Mr. Law, we have a young man here says his name is Robert Johnson and that he's here to work for you. Is this correct?' And my father says yes. 'Well, we've arrested him and he's in jail.' [My father] went down to the police station and found that Robert had been roughed up, he'd been arrested for vagrancy. And my father, with some effort, extracted Robert from the police and brought him back to the boarding house. He said, 'Robert, please, we're going to try to record early, here's breakfast money'—which in those days was forty-five cents—'we'll see you in the morning.'"[8]

Law made arrangements for Robert to play a borrowed guitar on Monday morning and returned to complete his dinner.[9] Robert, without a guitar, at least wanted some company. Law's son explained what happened next: "My father then went back to the hotel, sat back down with my mother, and hadn't gotten very far into the meal when he was again summoned to the phone, and on

the other end of the phone was Robert. 'Mr. Law, I'm lonesome.'
And my father said 'Bob, what do you mean you're lonesome?' And
he said, 'Well it seems that there's this young lady here and she
wants fifty cents and I lacks a nickel.'"[10]

The next morning Robert reported to the Gunter to begin his
first recording session, but as a black man he was not allowed to
enter through the front doors, and this irked him greatly. When he
came to record he was forced to enter from the rear of the building,
the colored only entrance. This was not the way he expected to start
a career as a recording star. Rising above the racist slight, Robert
began his first sessions around 10:00 AM. He was the *only* artist in
the studio for his entire session. Other artists that day recorded as
late as 10:00 PM. Vocalion demanded a lot from its artists for the
little money they paid them, and recording fifteen to eighteen different songs—with at least two takes of each—was considered an
excellent day of work. It's extremely important to remember that on
that first Monday Robert Johnson was the *only* musician to record:
he was alone in the studio. The only other people present were Don
Law and Vincent Liebler, the recording engineer. This helps destroy
a long-held myth about his recording technique.

Law and Liebler had the two rooms set up exactly as they wanted
to ensure the best recording quality. H. C. Speir noted the physical
setup of such a recording session: "We always put a person twelve
to fifteen inches back from the mike. That way, you got the best
recording of the voice." Robert walked into room 414 and, receiving instructions from Law and Liebler, sat down in front of a microphone that had been placed in the middle of the room. In front of
Robert, to the right of the mike, were two lights. One indicated the
start time, and when the second light flashed on it signaled that the
artist should end the song. Blind musicians would be accompanied
by the recording director, who would stand next to them and used
a friendly tap on the shoulder for the signal. Speir recalled: "We'd

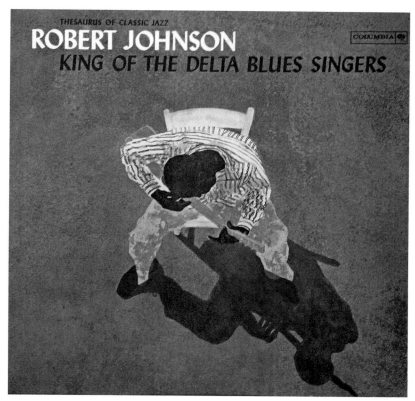

Cover design for the 1961 Columbia release *Robert Johnson: King of the Delta Blues Singers*. *Courtesy of Sony Music Entertainment*

tap him on the shoulder when to start, and we'd tap him again at the end of the three minutes." Most recordings ran from two and a half to three minutes, although some did exceed that time slightly. Songs were always timed before the actual recording began.

Robert took his position in a chair in front of the mike, as depicted in the cover artwork on the 1961 Columbia reissue. Looking at the first Columbia album cover artwork, Elizabeth Moore said that was the way he always played. "He'd sit in a straight back chair and sway from side to side as he sung, pattin' his feet to keep time with that old guitar of his."[11]

The 1970 release of *Robert Johnson: King of the Delta Blues Singers Vol. 2*, however, showed Robert sitting before a microphone now located in a corner. That image of him represented both the speculation and myth that developed about how Robert recorded. It was simply wrong. This new artwork, based on an erroneous interpretation of actual events and how they were described, caused a number of blues historians to believe that Robert recorded facing the wall. He did not.

Lawrence Cohn, producer and record executive who was involved in the 1961 release and who won a Grammy for the production of the 1991 boxed set, said that he spoke to Don Law, Don Law Jr., and Frank Driggs, a jazz historian, about that session. Driggs was also Columbia Records' producer for both Robert Johnson albums and wrote the original liner notes for the 1961 release. In contrast to the idea that Robert recorded his songs facing the corner, Cohn recalled Law saying that Robert only turned his back several days later when asked to play for some Mexican musicians.[12] Driggs confirmed this in his 1961 liner notes: "He [Law] asked [Johnson] to play guitar for a group of Mexican musicians gathered in a hotel room where the recording equipment had been set up. Embarrassed and suffering from a bad case of stage fright, Johnson turned his face to the wall, his back to the Mexican musicians."[13]

In a letter from Law to Driggs in 1961, Law reiterated that the only time Robert turned his back was when he was asked to perform in front of Andres Berlanga and Francisco Montalvo (who also recorded on Thanksgiving). "He reluctantly complied [to play for them] but sat on a chair in a corner facing the wall."[14] Law, like Driggs, believed this was because Robert was shy. Others, however, such as guitarist Ry Cooder, believed the myth that Robert recorded into a corner to purposely "corner-load": playing into the corner so the sound of his guitar would be enhanced by bouncing off the plaster walls.[15] This is wishful thinking: Robert's guitar sounds the same

Cover design for the 1970 Columbia release *Robert Johnson: King of the Delta Blues Singers*, **Vol. 2.** *Courtesy of Sony Music Entertainment*

on all his takes, even on the Dallas recordings where there were no corners into which he could turn. Attempts to attribute his sound to some unique circumstances are simply wrong. They are as mythic as the notion that he sold his soul to attain his guitar-playing skills.

And Robert Johnson was certainly not shy: he was a seasoned street performer who played before any crowd he could gather, as well as at jukes, parties, and picnics. The very concept of corner-loading is improbable since the places Robert played wouldn't have been conducive to him finding any corners to develop such an odd technique: listeners surrounded him, and plantation jukes were flimsy structures. Moreover, he wouldn't have been a very entertaining performer if he faced the wall. Further, Law never actually mentioned Robert facing the corner during a recording. It was *only* when Robert was asked to demonstrate his music for a group of other musicians that he turned his back on them. He wasn't turning into the corner because he was shy or to produce a loaded sound, he was protecting his techniques. He had learned his lesson when Johnnie Temple had used his boogie bass pattern in "Lead Pencil Blues" a year earlier, beating Johnson to the studio. He did not want that to happen again. Johnny Shines addressed that very fact: "It wasn't that he was shy. He just didn't want you watching what he was doing. See Robert was very particular about nobody learning his style of music. If you watched him he'd turn his back."[16] Robert Lockwood stated that Robert "wouldn't sit and face another guitar player and let him see what he was doin'."[17]

Robert's dream had been realized. But he hadn't had to go to New York City to make records as he often proclaimed he would. He only had to go to Texas.

❦ 12 ❦

KIND HEARTED WOMEN

Recording sessions in 1936 were laborious affairs for both the artists and engineers. Magnetic tape was still years away, and if you
made a mistake during a recording there was no way to fix it: you
had to start all over again. There was no way to cut or splice in a
new section on a disc. In addition, several complete takes of each
song needed to be recorded. The first take timed the song before
an actual master was recorded. An alternate take, or an insurance
take, was made to protect against the possibility of breakage. And
perhaps even another take was required if the producer decided
that the song should be slower or faster. All together this meant
that a single song could take a long time to complete, and when the
musician finished he or she could be exhausted. This was especially
true if you recorded more than four different songs at one sitting.

Robert was already used to playing for hours at a juke or party,
so playing to a microphone, although a new experience, was certainly no more difficult than playing for several dozen drunken and
carousing men and women. Showing his adaptability to recording rules, and his stamina, the twenty-five-year-old Delta musician
completed eight songs his first day.

Most country bluesmen, as opposed to the more polished city bluesmen like Big Bill Broonzy, varied their songs greatly between takes, holding true to their performance practices. Each performance of a song by Patton or House, for instance, could be wildly different from the previous rendition: they played it as they felt it, and that could mean taking great liberties with their lyrics or musicianship. Robert had a different perspective on his songs, however, and his second or alternate versions are almost identical to his first ones. The only differences in the takes occurred when the speed at which he performed a song was changed, necessitating either the addition or deletion of a verse to meet the three-minute time limit. Importantly, both such changes were initiated by the producer or engineer and not by Robert. Other than that, his takes are very similar to each other. His codifying of his material made an indelible impression on Saint Louis bluesman Henry Townsend. Townsend had already recorded numerous times for three different labels—Columbia, Paramount, and Bluebird—but Robert's standardization of his songs was something new to him. "In my opinion, what made Robert's music different was this—the older music was more or less various tunes but it didn't have no specific body to it. What I mean when I say body; they didn't play in any certain direction. They would play it this way this time, and the next time it was altogether different—the same tune but it was altogether different. But Robert, he was not like that. Each time, whatever he played, was uniform, and this could make you notice."[1]

Robert was beginning to develop a lyrical and musical consistency that would bring a new self-consciousness to the blues as art. While most of his contemporaries accepted that their verses could vary both in number and content, Robert believed a song should not be changed but should be played the same way every time: it was a finished and fixed product. That Robert saw his songs as finished compositions is evident in the fact that he wrote them down in the little notebook he kept. He was, after all, a product of the technology of his time. The songs he heard on the radio or a record were identical each time he heard them, so why should his songs be any different?

This new type of self-consciousness as a musician was relatively innovative in the country blues. It placed Robert into a more modern category than Son House or Charlie Patton. This approach is evident right from the first song he recorded: "Kind Hearted Woman Blues." "They always did their best four songs first," Speir explained. "They did the ones they thought were their best."[2] Robert wanted to make hit records, and he borrowed "Kind Hearted Woman Blues" from a number of sources that were already hits for other bluesmen. It was both musically and lyrically aligned with Leroy Carr's "Mean Mistreater Mama" and Bumble Bee Slim's "Cruel Hearted Woman Blues." But Robert's genius was beyond just knowing good songs to copy: he rewrote them, changed the tempo, synced his guitar more closely with his vocal than those who preceeded him, added a guitar riff, and literally remade the piece. Although inspired by the original, the new song was really all his. Several aspects of his playing accentuated his ownership. First, Robert saw "Kind Hearted Woman Blues" as a complete composition. The song's lyrics are thematically cohesive and the overall effect is of a musical whole, and not the type of whole that one would normally hear in a juke joint. This wasn't a rollicking good-time piece designed to keep jukers dancing. On the contrary, "Kind Hearted Woman Blues" was a well-thought-out composition with a beginning, middle, and end.

This was the song that Speir remembered Robert playing at his audition. Played in the key of A in natural tuning, Robert recorded two takes. The first included a guitar break that added a unique dimension to his performance. Most guitar blues recordings did not feature guitar breaks but rather consisted of a continuous

stream of lyrics. "Kind Hearted
Woman Blues," for whatever reason, was the only recorded song
he performed with such a guitar
break. The second take of the song
was more up-tempo and included
one different, additional final lyric
verse. Musically, with the exception
of having to add an extra verse, the
two takes are virtually identical.

Leroy Carr. *Promo photo for*
Vocalion Race Record Ad #1432

Robert tuned his guitar one-half
step (one guitar fret) lower than most bluesmen when he used an
open tuning such as D, G, A, or E. That was apparently a technique
he had learned from Willie Brown, whose influence on Robert was
undeniable. Brown had used the A flat tuning on his legendary
1930 Paramount recording of "Future Blues." Robert also either
tuned or capoed his guitar (usually on the second fret) to match his
singing voice, as had Patton and House.[3]

Shifting to what was probably open E tuning, Robert next
recorded "I Believe I'll Dust My Broom," a song made even more
famous by Elmore James in 1951 as "Dust My Broom" for the
Jackson Trumpet label. Ironically, Robert did not use the bottleneck on the tune as James would. Instead, Robert slid his fingers
up the neck to play a triplet riff against his driving boogie bass
pattern. Possibly also displaying Robert's awareness of current
events obtained from newspapers, he mentioned Ethiopia—where
Emperor Hallie Salassie was fighting Italian invaders—as well as
China and the Philippine Islands in the song. For local color, he
used an old Patton trick and also sang about his home area. "If
I don't find her in West Helena, she must be in East Monroe, I
know," referring to the county adjacent to Helena. Robert was,
perhaps because of his education and urban upbringing, turning

his songs into more cosmopolitan pieces than the usual good old down-home blues.

Melodically the song borrowed from another Carr tune—"I Believe I'll Make a Change"—as well as lyrical influences from Kokomo Arnold's "Sagefield Woman Blues" and "Sissy Man Blues." Although always assumed to be about leaving, being unhappy with your cheating girlfriend and packing up (dusting one's broom), Robert may have included his first reference to hoodoo practice in the song. The first verse ran, "I'm gon' get up in the mornin', I believe I'll dust my broom. Girlfriend, the black man you been lovin', girlfriend, can get my room."

Hoodoo references abound concerning the use of the broom as a means of ridding oneself of an unwanted visitor. Harry Middleton Hyatt collected black folklore in the 1930s, and among the beliefs he found were that to rid one's home of an unwanted person "one needed [to] sweep salt and pepper out the door when they leave and they'll never be able to come back."[4] Other references stated that dusting one's broom with magic powder and then using it to sweep your house would free it of unwanted houseguests.[5] There are literally dozens of documented hoodoo folk beliefs involving the use of a broom and "dust"—some form of magic powder—to rid oneself of someone or something. When Robert sang, "You can mistreat me here, but you can't when I get home" it was almost certainly because he knew about the hoodoo practice he had described.

Musically, "Dust My Broom" is a hard-driving, forceful song in which Robert's signature high-note triplet riff increased the tension of his boogie-driven bass. He was the first blues guitarist to make such a boogie pattern a standard part of his repertoire, and thereafter the song became a standard among many Chicago blues stylists.

Robert then shifted back to natural tuning for more of the walkin' boogie that he had earlier taught Johnnie Temple. "Sweet Home Chicago," with its even heavier and more intentional bass boogie pattern and rhythm, became another classic that surpassed "Dust My Broom" in its musical influence on postwar musicians. It was his adaptation of Kokomo Arnold's "Old Original Kokomo Blues." Arnold's version employed a virtuosic slide guitar performance that bordered on the manic. At times there seems little relationship between Arnold's playing and his vocal. Robert's adaptation, on the other hand, synced the music and lyrics into a thick and driven whole.

Robert's fourth song, "Ramblin' on My Mind," stands out as a unique piece because of its unusual open tuning. Somehow Robert developed a tuning that was apparently never used by any other guitarist. Computer analysis of his recording produced a transcription identifying an inventory of the notes he played in his opening guitar riff, revealing his tuning: to play all the notes identified, Robert could have only tuned his guitar to an open F chord (from low E to high E) C F C A C F, but not just an ordinary open F. Interestingly, prior to this research, guitarist Rory Block had for years been using this same tuning for this song after arriving at it through her own painstaking process of listening to what Robert was playing and testing the various tuning possibilities. This computer analysis confirmed that her tuning was indeed accurate.

Opening notes to "Ramblin' on My Mind."
Bruce Conforth and Michael Malis

Robert tuned his low E string down to C, his A string down to F, and his D string down to C. But he tuned his G string up to A, his B string up to C, and his E string up to F. He kept this "split open F" original tuning from being displayed to any other guitarists. It belonged to him alone. Almost certainly this could not have been the only song he used this tuning on. In live performance it would have taken too much time to tune his guitar to this unique set of notes only to have to retune it again for his next song. It would have made much more sense for him to use the tuning for several songs before changing back to another tuning. Unfortunately, we only have this one recorded example of his musical ingenuity.

Like "Kind Hearted Woman Blues," Robert's first take of "Ramblin'" was slow. He repeated one verse twice: as the second and last verse of the song. His second take was considerably faster and he never repeated a verse. Otherwise, the takes are quite similar. According to former Delta bluesman Johnny Shines in a 1966 article by *Down Beat*'s music historian Pete Welding, "Ramblin'" was autobiographical. Shines noted that by 1937, after Robert's first records were released and the two men began to travel together, rambling was their way of life. "His home was where his hat was, and even then a lot of times he didn't know where that was. We used to travel all over, meet the pay days (Saturday) in the lumber camps, the track gangs—anywhere the money was." Like other bluesmen, they traveled mostly by rail. "Used to catch freights everywhere. Played for dances, in taverns, on sidewalks. Didn't matter where, far as he was concerned."[6] The lyrics and powerfully driving guitar in "Ramblin'" seem to reflect Robert's itinerant lifestyle: rough and urgent. His friends back in Robinsonville, House and Brown, were never driven to ramble the way Robert did; they stayed largely in the Delta regions where they lived. But by the time of this recording Robert had already established himself as a rambler inside *and* outside Mississippi. And musically, neither House nor Brown used the piano boogie in their guitar arrangements that Robert showcased on these two recordings that Monday.

The bottleneck style was probably based on a combination of the African one-string instruments that so many blues players started out with such as the diddley bow, the Hawaiian sound that had become popular in the early years of the twentieth century, and various tunings used by Mexican laborers. As they helped clear Delta forests and swamps around 1900, Mexicans brought the guitar to the Delta. They used an open G tuning, and when black laborers adopted it they called it Spanish tuning. Charley Patton often tuned two frets higher to a Spanish A (E-A-E-A-C#-E), capoed at the second fret to make his bottleneck sound more effective by pitching the song in the key of B. But while Robert's elders tended to use a highly formulaic guitar pattern, almost always returning to the starting chord after their variations of the standard twelve bars, Robert was among the first Delta musicians to feature a piano turnaround at the end of the normal twelve bars of music. Robert also displayed his damping effect on the bass strings to provide more rhythm for dancing. Few, if any, Delta blues musicians had ever recorded a similar damping sound prior to Robert.

Lyrically, "Ramblin'" may have been even more autobiographical than even Shines realized, for in the third verse Robert sang a line that has usually been interpreted as "Runnin' down to the station, catch that first mail train I see." But more likely Robert was singing about the "Fast Mail" train: the precise name of a train that ran on the Southern Railway line from Memphis to New Orleans. His lyric was almost certainly a personal reference from his time traveling back and forth to his Memphis family.

"When You Got a Good Friend," Robert's fifth song, was musically structured in the same manner as "Kind Hearted Woman." It varied only slightly in both takes: the first was shorter than the alternate, which Robert added an extra verse to. A very personal song, Robert bemoaned his unaccountable mistreatment of his woman. He was puzzled by his own behavior and both opened and closed the song with the same admonition: "When you got a good friend that will stay right by your side, give her all your spare time, love and treat her right." This was a tender side of Robert he rarely made public. Perhaps due to such an open admission of his vulnerability, the song was never released by the record company.

Considered one of Robert's masterpieces, "Come on in My Kitchen" was his sixth selection that day. He used the Spanish tuning for his adaptation of the old melody that had been an enormous hit for the Mississippi Sheiks in 1930, "Sitting on Top of the World." His ability to showcase a song in two different ways included one take that produced a fast Delta dance rhythm, while the other was a slow, haunting version painting images of a chilling Delta winter wind, blowing across barren cotton fields. His first take, slower and more deliberate, mournful, sensitive, and eerie, is almost certainly the version that Johnny Shines repeatedly stated would "make grown men cry." Shines recalled that during their last trip together in 1938 he particularly noticed the effect this song could have on a crowd. "One time in Saint Louis we were playing one of the songs that Robert would like to play with someone once in a great while, 'Come on in My Kitchen.' He was playing very slow and passionately, and when we quit, I noticed no one was saying anything. Then I realized they were crying—both men and women."[7] Apparently the slower version did not impress Satherly, who chose to release the second, faster take. But Robert's first run-through is still acknowledged as the greater of the two.

Robert's seventh selection, once again with bottleneck, became his best-selling signature song among record buyers at that time. "Terraplane Blues" featured the fast-car image with highly developed sexual overtones. These "get dirty" lyrics helped sell more records in the Depression, according to Harry Charles, a Birmingham-based scout who began to use that technique before 1930. "I'm gonna' h'ist your hood, mama, I bound to check your oil," Robert sang. "I'm gonna get deep down in this connection, keep on tanglin' with your wires."

Sexual innuendoes had always been in blues but they made a career for Bo Carter of Edwards, Mississippi, who later worked from the small town of Anguilla, just below Leland. Carter was considered "the dirtiest man" on records for recordings with such titles as "Banana in Your Fruit Basket," "Ants in My Pants," and "Please Warm My Weiner." No respectable churchgoer would have dared purchase such a record (or at least admit to it). Such records sold well, though, and Robert used his fixation with the Terraplane he repeatedly saw parked near his Memphis family's home to create his hit.

But in all probablility "Terrapane Blues" was not a hit for its sexual innuendo alone but also due to the newfound public attraction to highways and speed. Road construction had grown enormously throughout the 1920s with federal highways—numbered routes—gaining designation in 1926. America was becoming a motorized nation, and the car was even more of a status symbol than it had been before. Mississsippi, with its relatively flat terrain, boasted miles of straight flat-top upon which cars could travel faster than ever before. Ike Zimmerman helped build one such highway—Highway 51. And of all the cars being manufactured at that time the Terraplane was highly prized. The eight-cylinder 1933 Terraplane was believed to be one of the fastest production cars being made and was favored by such gangsters as John Dillinger and Baby Face Nelson. This, along with its sleek design, made the Terraplane even more attractive to the general public.

Robert ended the session with "Phonograph Blues," another of the five unissued songs from his two Texas sessions. Interestingly, "Phonograph Blues" is one of only three songs Robert recorded in which he mentions a woman by name (the other two being "Honeymoon Blues" and "Love in Vain"): "Beatrice, she got a phonograph, and it won't say a lonesome word. What evil have I done? What evil has the poor girl heard?"

The lyrics to "Phonograph Blues" are somewhat confusing. Played in the style of "Terraplane Blues," a first listen seems to reveal just another double entendre song. The phonograph needle as Robert's penis; "playing it on the sofa, we played it 'side the wall" apparently describing some sexual gymnastics. However, Robert offers that her phonograph won't say anything anymore because of some evil he did or some evil that she heard. Then he bemoans that his needle has gotten rusty and won't play anymore. Instead of the typical bluesman's bragging about sexual potency, Robert seemed to be admitting, or at least addressing, the issue of impotence. And finally he begs Beatrice to gather up her clothes, come home, and "try me one more time." It must have been confusing to the record company as well because it was never released during Robert's lifetime.

With that awkward finish Robert ended the day's sessions. Masterfully, however, he had recorded eight songs, a total of at least sixteen takes, in one day's sitting. At three minutes per take, with at least several minutes set up and review time between each start, those recording efforts amount to several hours of concentrated focus. That was no easy task for someone who had never been in a studio before and who had been beaten up and spent time in jail the night before. Yet Robert had some idea what to do from the stories Willie Brown and Son House had told him about recording for Paramount, so he was probably somewhat prepared for the experience. "He always told us he was gonna go to New York some day and record like Son and Willie did," Elizabeth Moore noted. "He heard 'em talkin' 'bout how they had made them records they made."[8]

Robert Johnson left the Gunter Hotel late that afternoon with more than one hundred dollars cash in his pocket. It was late Monday, Texas was still celebrating its centennial year, and Thanksgiving was only two days away. He had Tuesday and Wednesday to do as he pleased. What did he do? Speculations abound, but the most compelling account was told by Shirley Ratisseau, a white woman who grew up around Houston in the 1930s. George Ratisseau, Shirley's father, owned two of the main blues bars in the area, and both T-Bone Walker and Sam "Lightnin'" Hopkins played at his jukes. The Ratisseau family also owned the Jolly Roger Hunting and Fishing Club on Redfish Point near Rockport, Texas, a club well known to members of the black communities of both Houston and San Antonio. That club always welcomed them, and it was a prominent place for black Texans to vacation, fish, and relax. Needing just that kind of relaxing after being beaten by the police and then completing a strenuous day of recording, Robert seems to have used Tueday to ramble out to Rockport where, just before Thanksgiving, still looking battered, he showed up at the vacation grounds. Shirley, who was only seven or eight, met him there and offered to take him fishing. They made up a song about it together. After a few hours of sitting on the pier pulling in redfish, Shirley took Robert home to dine with her family, a most unique event for a young black man from Mississippi. Not to be outdone by her daughter's kindness, Ratisseau's mother, Thelma, felt sorry for the beaten and exhausted Robert and invited the musician to spend the night in their home. Robert had found a "kind hearted woman" to take care of him that night. After a good meal and a better night's rest, Robert returned on Wednesday to San Antonio the next day to prepare for his second recording session.[9]

Robert had disappeared for two days before returning to San Antonio, and it seems likely that for that reason on Thursday, November 26, Robert recorded only one song, "32-20 Blues," his arrangement of Skip James's Paramount recording of "22-20 Blues." In his version, Robert identified Hot Springs as being in both Arkansas and Wisconsin, an obvious reference from James's

1931 recording. This recording would lead to an erroneous report by Sam Charters in his 1959 book, *The Country Blues*, that Johnson had recorded more than one master. Charters claimed the other recordings from that day were destroyed in a pool hall fight where the recordings reportedly took place. He provided no source for this information and no other researcher has substantiated his claim. The most probable reason Robert recorded only one song that day was very simple: Law had been unable to find Robert while he was in Rockport with the Ratisseaus and had booked other musicians for that day's sessions not knowing when or if Robert would return.

Among these other musicians were the Texas gospel group Chuck Wagon Gang, who recorded six masters before Robert returned. Law continued to record this highly popular sacred group well into the 1950s after he became director of all country music artists for Columbia Records. Formed in 1935 by D. P. (Dad) Carter, and featuring son Jim (Ernest) and daughters Rose (Lola) and Anna (Effie), they recorded "The Engineer's Child" (a Vernon Dalhart song of some ten years earlier) among other numbers. Following Robert's one-song session, Tex-Mex performers Andres Berlanga and Francisco Montalvo recorded "Que Piensas Tu que Mi Amore (You Think You're My Love)" and "Ay! Que Bonitos Ojitos (Oh! What Pretty Eyes)." Another Mexican duet, Hermanas Barraza and Daniel Palomo, followed with some additional Tex-Mex songs. They were released on Vocalion's Mexican series. It was at this time, and *only* this time, that when asked to demonstrate his playing for Berlanga and Montalvo, Robert, already done recording for the day, turned his back on them to protect his techniques. Although he made his skills secret, the two musicians might still have been of some interest to Robert. They had established themselves as the Mexican equivalent of southern bluesmen by singing narrative corridos such as "Corrido de los Bootleggers (The Story of the Bootleggers)." And their songs contained the exploits of outlaws and outsiders.

Also like American bluesmen, Berlanga and Montalvo rode freight trains as itinerant troubadours during the Depression. And, like their Delta juke joint partners, they had also played for dances that went from dusk to dawn. "They just keep playing and the people just keep drinking and dancing," Berlanga recalled. "Man, those were wonderful days."[10] Even their Tex-Mex lyrics were a variant of southen blues. One classic song, "Las Quejas de Zenaida," amusingly describes a relationship gone bad, and its final verse could be right out of a Patton, House, Brown, or Johnson song:

> *Ya me voy de este pueblo maldito.*
> *Donde quedan mis sueños dorados.*
> *Now I'm leaving this cursed town.*
> *Where my golden dreams remain.*

After the demonstration of his playing for his fellow musicians, Robert returned to his boarding house to prepare for the final day of recording. He may have wondered if it would be his last opportunity to leave his footprints on American music. Would his records be short-lived and soon forgotten in a few years? He was facing an important challenge. He had to make his Friday songs compare in quality and energy to his mainline Monday performances. He would have to prove that his creative abilities were, indeed, as strong or stronger than his previous two days of recording.

Robert's first recording of the final session was a surprising oddity for a Mississippi bluesman: "They're Red Hot." Stylistically the song is far more in keeping with the East Coast, Piedmont sound. What could have elicited such a unique sound from this Deltas bluesman? Since Robert was getting paid by the number of songs he recorded it was to his advantage to offer Law as many pieces as he could. Highly skilled in adapting melodies or even complete songs from other artists, the picturesque setting in which Robert

Alamo Plaza, San Antonio, Texas, 1930s. *Bruce Conforth*

found himself probably served as rich fodder for a new composition. Almost certainly the song was his response to having hot tamales for lunch while sitting around Alamo Plaza. For two consecutive days Robert, local well-to-do hanger-on Buster Wharton, and pianist Black Boy Shine bought their lunch in that plaza from Mexican street vendors.

Robert combined a hokum melody in the song with suggestive lyrics creating an up-tempo happy tale about a woman selling hot tamales.[11] "Hokum" was a term that primarily applied to happy, suggestive ditties with double meanings. Not only was it a different style of song for a Delta bluesman, it was an example of how Robert could vary his repertoire however he needed. Lyrically the song was also different for Robert, since most of its lines could be found in dozens of other blues and folk songs. "I got a gal, say she's long and tall. She sleeps in the kitchen with her feets in the hall" was used by Will Shade in 1934 in "Take Your Fingers Off It." That Robert borrowed a line from Will Shade should come as no surprise—the Memphis Jug Band leader recalled playing with Johnson in a band in West Memphis.[12] But Robert borrowed lines for "They're Red Hot" from many other artists as well. Buddy Boy Hawkins in "How Come Mama Blues" (1929), the Birmingham Jug Band in "Giving It Away" (1930), and Bill Wilbur's 1935 "Greyhound Blues" all included "She got two for a nickel, got four for a dime. Would sell you more, but they ain't none of mine." Walter Taylor in "Thirty Eight and Four" (1930) and Sleepy John Estes's 1935 "Stop That Thing" used the lyrics: "You know the monkey, now the baboon playin' in the grass. Well the monkey stuck his finger in that old Good Gulf Gas." The rest of Robert's lines seem likely to have also come from either other blues or oral tradition:

> *I got a letter from a girl in the room*
> *Now, she got somethin' good she got to bring home soon, now.*
> *The billy goat back in a bumblebee nest*
> *Ever since that he can't take his rest.*
> *You know Grandma left and now Grandpa too*
> *Well I wonder what in the world we chillum gon' do.*

In fact, the only original lyrics in the piece are probably the refrain: "Hot tamales and they're red hot, yes, she got 'em for sale."

The guitar arrangement to "They're Red Hot" featured rhythm chords played in a fashion normally used by jazz or swing band musicians. But as different as "They're Red Hot" was from Robert's other tunes, Law was willing to record whatever he offered. Law left it up to Satherly to decide what songs were placed on which sides of a 78-rpm record, or which were even released.

When he continued recording, Robert depicted his intense sexual conflicts with women on "Dead Shrimp Blues." Robert painted a masterful image of a young man whose woman has left him for another man: "I got dead shrimp here. Someone's fishin' in my pond." Robert's line "The hole where I used to fish, you got me posted out" was a southern expression for landowners who posted signs warning against trespassing on private property. But his most poignant plea was simply, "I couldn't do nothin' baby, till I got unwound." The lyrics of "Dead Shrimp Blues" have puzzled most blues scholars. Struck by the obscurity of the song and its reference to shrimp, it's been posited that this could have been a reference to shrimp as slang for prostitute.[13] The answer, however, may be much simpler than anyone imagined.

Just as "They're Red Hot" was almost certainly based on Robert's Alamo Plaza lunches, it might not be necessary to look any further for the reference in "Dead Shrimp Blues" than Robert's trip to the Jolly Roger Hunting and Fishing Club. Redfish Point is located on the outermost tip of Copano Bay, a natural nursery for shrimp. In fact, it is called Redfish Point because the crustaceans are so plentiful that they draw in schools of redfish. Whatever Robert meant metaphorically by the reference to shrimp is still unknown, but it's highly likely that this is where his inspiration came from.

Robert waited until that day's session to cut what has become known as one of his signature masterpieces: "Cross Road Blues." Interestingly, no one who knew Robert from this period recalled him performing the song. When the recording was played for Elizabeth Moore she was surprised and said that she never heard anything like it from him.[14]

"Cross Road Blues," now often called "Crossroad(s)," featured a first verse that actually contained a plea for salvation, not a deal with the devil: "I went to the crossroad and fell down on my knees, asked the Lord above have mercy, save poor Bob, if you please." The song continued with references to the "sun's going down, boys" before Robert named his best musical friend back in Robinsonville, Willie Brown: "You can run, you can run, tell my friend poor Willie Brown."

Not once in that song did Robert say he had gone to the crossroad to sell his soul to the devil. Never once in any song did he make such a statement. Actually, as Reverend Booker Miller of Greenwood noted, "There weren't many paved roads in them days. When you wanted to go to town, you walked down the dirt road from your house, 'til you come to where it crossed the [dirt] road goin' to town. Then you waited for somebody to come by and give you a ride."[15] Asked how Robert traveled to jukes, Elizabeth Moore explained: "He catch a bus or get somebody to come get him. He didn't have no car."[16] Miller further noted that a musician had a "much better chance of being picked up" than the average hitchhiker. "When somebody saw you with a guitar, they'd pick you up a lot quicker," Miller explained. "A guitar picker stood out more than anyone else."[17] Other transportation included small trains called "Pea Vines," or locals, that ran for short distances but left only once a day. Buses always traveled on Highways 49, 51, and 61 through the Delta, but if you lived on a plantation, you either hitchhiked, caught a bus, or hopped a freight train.

In "Cross Road Blues" Robert sings and plays with a sense of urgency. The sound is intense, and whatever caused him to fall down on his knees at the crossroad was a powerful influence. Only one other prewar blues had ever mentioned crossroads: Charley Patton's 1929 "Joe Kirby," which cited a specific crossroads. But it has none of the angst of Robert's lyric. Patton sang: "Well, I was standin' at Clack's crossroad, biddin' my rider goodbye. It [the train] blowed for the crossroad, Lord, she started to fly." In Robert's "Cross Road Blues," however, one cannot help but acknowledge the black mythical belief associated with that spot. Virtually every collection of black folklore contains legends about the crossroads, a syncretic blending of African and Anglo folklore. Hyatt collected numerous variations on the crossroads story; the most iconic in its relation to the blues was this:

If you want to know how to play a banjo or a guitar or do magic tricks, you have to sell yourself to the devil. You have to go to the cemetery nine mornings and get some of the dirt and bring it back with you and put it in a little bottle, then go to some fork of the road and each morning sit there and try to play that guitar. Don't care what you see come there, don't get 'fraid and run away. Just stay there for nine mornings and on the ninth morning there will come some rider riding at lightning speed in the form of the devil. You stay there then still playing your guitar and when he has passed you can play any tune you want to play or do any magic trick you want to do because you have sold yourself to the devil.[18]

Although the folklore is clear, we have no way of knowing what Robert meant by the song. He never mentioned a deal, the devil, or any other supernatural element. So why is his song so unique, and why does he sing it with such urgency?

Both versions of his song begin with Johnson kneeling at a crossroads to ask God's mercy, while the second verse tells of his failed attempts to hitch a ride. In the third and fourth verses, Robert shows concern, if not outright fear, at being stranded as darkness approaches. Finally, he implores the listener to run and tell his friend Willie Brown that "I'm sinkin' down."

Despite many blues fans and even some scholars attempting to link this song to some Satanic or Faustian bargain, it contains not a single reference in that regard. The devil, Legba, hoodoo, nor any reference to any supernatural being or event are mentioned. However, the belief in the ability to make a deal at a crossroads was so prevalent in the southern black community that Robert must have known of it. But the song could also be about protest and social commentary. The second verse included "the sun goin' down now, boy, dark gon' catch me here." This could be a reference to the sundown laws, or curfews, that were widely in place during racial segregation in the South. Signs in those rural regions advised "Nigger, don't let the sun set on you here." Robert may have been expressing a real fear of trumped up vagrancy charges or even lynching. It has been argued that the fifth verse in the second take captures the essence of the song: "left alone, abandoned, or mistreated, [Robert] stands at the crossroad, looking this way or that for his woman."[19] But what did Robert really mean? The passion in his voice indicates how seriously he took his lyrics. What he really meant, however, was known only to him.

Following this recording, Robert reached back to hearing House and Brown in country jukes in Robinsonville and their influence on him, for "Walkin' Blues" was a direct reworking of House's "My Black Mama" that featured the same bottleneck styling. "Last Fair Deal Gone Down" highlighted his Hattiesburg connection and featured damping on the bass strings with his right palm with the bottleneck added. It was a throwback to the type of work song Robert had first sung for Willie Moore shortly after they met around 1928. In it he emphasized the hardships of working on a railroad track gang, and dealing with a "captain so mean, good Lord." This was a common reference to the white boss man who towered over his black crew moving steel rails to and from a roadbed. His location was the "Gulfport Island Road," or the Gulfport and Ship Island that had been formed in 1900. It ran daily from Gulfport north to Hattiesburg, where it met the New Orleans and Northeastern (Southern) and then on to Jackson. It was the kind of heavy work that Robert avoided when he came to Hazlehurst in 1930 while Ike Zimmerman worked six days a week clearing a roadway for paving Highway 51. In fact, he could have learned it from Zimmerman, for it consisted of an A, A, A, B lyric format more often found in work songs than the A, A, B form of Johnson's usual blues formula.

"Preachin' the Blues," subtitled "Up Jumped the Devil," was Robert's rendition of House's "Preaching the Blues" from 1930. House had sung with intense conviction on his recording, and it seems Robert tried to duplicate his performance. His playing was masterful, and despite not possessing the powerful, overwhelming voice of House, Robert's emotions were still riveting. He urged himself on—"Help me, you gonna help me?"—as if he were talking to someone else in the room, creating a crescendo of emotions as he played.

Robert's last song, "If I Had Possession over Judgment Day," was musically borrowed from Hambone Willie Newbern's "Roll and Tumble Blues," but where Newbern sang about lost love, Robert sang about sex and power, combining his own fears of them with the fantasy of controlling them. It was another song that was never issued in the 1930s.

Robert finished his recordings on Friday, November 27, though Law's recording sessions lasted until Sunday, November 30. Robert stayed in San Antonio until all the recording was done just in case he was asked to provide another few songs. That Sunday afternoon Tony Garza, a shipping clerk for the company, took Robert, along with recording engineer Vincent Liebler, to a cockfight. Mexicans had brought the Sunday afternoon blood sport to San Antonio, and although officially outlawed, it was still embraced as one of that town's gambling operations.[20]

Robert Johnson left San Antonio with a nice roll of cash for his sixteen songs, the most he ever made as a professional bluesman. According to Don Law he was paid about twenty-five dollars per song. The companies paid what a musician would accept. Since a record deal meant name recognition back home, most bluesmen accepted what money a company offered them. And Robert was an untested unknown. "They [the musicians] didn't trust the companies to pay them royalties," Speir recalled. "They wanted cash when they got through recording."[21] During the 1920s, when companies were more prosperous, Speir had gotten as much as fifty dollars a song for some of his talent. But records in the 1930s sold for thirty-five cents on cut-rate labels (Okeh and Vocalion), but Columbia and Brunswick records ran anywhere from seventy-five cents to one dollar and fifty cents each. Columbia Masterwork records could command as much as two dollars each. "Getting on record was more important to a bluesman than the fee," Speir concluded. "When they had a record out, they could make more money playing on the streets and for parties."[22] Speir never saw Robert after his Texas sessions and said Oertle only told him later that he had taken Robert to Texas to record. Oertle died from a sudden heart attack in November 1941. Another voice from Robert's life had been silenced shortly after their connection.

Robert left San Antonio feeling he had attained his primary goal in life, just as he had told both Elizabeth Moore and Eula Mae Williams he would. At twenty-five he was now a recorded bluesman, a major feat when only three major companies controlled all recordings. If H. C. Speir's belief that Robert's music was perfect for the emerging jukebox market was correct then it might not be too long before his records began appearing on them. And they certainly would be offered in a variety of record stores throughout the South. And there were no hellhounds on his trail, just more of being a ramblin' professional bluesman who worked primarily on the weekends of his choice.

Arriving back in the Delta at the end of 1936, Robert temporarily moved back in with his mother and stepfather in Tunica. Perhaps the success of his returning from a recording session smoothed out the problems that Dusty Willis had with his stepson, for Robert seems to have stayed with them for a number of months without incident. While there he courted Willie Mae Holmes, the eighteen-year-old cousin of Honeyboy Edwards. Holmes was staying on a

Willie Mae Holmes Powell. © *Delta Haze Corporation*

farm run by Albert Creason, a sixty-three-year-old black man in Commerce, the same community Robert lived in as a youth on the Abbay and Leatherman plantation.

It was Robert's music, as usual, that introduced the couple. "He was on his way to make music somewhere that Saturday evening, and me and my girlfriend were sitting out on the porch, and he started talking with us, and that's how I got acquainted with him."[23] Robert saw Willie Mae as another available companion: a woman living with a much older man with whom she had no real connection. Soon Robert won Willie Mae's affection. She remembered him as being both handsome and loving. "He was a nice conditioned person. He was lovin' kind. He was a handsome boy. He was real young, and I was too. The cutest little brown thing you ever did see in your life. Oh, he was very handsome, he sure was. I was very much in love with him." Robert, of course, used his musical skills in his courtship. "Sit on the back porch: house was a shotgun house, facing the levee. And we'd be out on the back porch sittin' on the steps and he'd pick his box for me."[24]

They started courting in December 1936, and six months later, in June 1937, Robert left for Dallas for his last recording sessions. He told Willie Mae that he was leaving to go make more records, and two of the songs he sang for her before he left were "Stones in My Passway" and "I'm a Steady Rollin' Man," the two songs he would begin his Dallas recording sessions with. He asked her to come along with him, but she declined. Without her company, Robert vowed to put her in a song. "He said he was gonna [write a song about me]."[25] That song, of course, became "Love in Vain," the penultimate song of his recording career. Robert Johnson had kept his promise.

Another kind hearted woman had passed through his life.

I LEFT WITH MY HEAD CUT

Robert Johnson, waiting for his recordings to be released, fell back into his old, familiar patterns: he courted at least one woman, Willie Mae Holmes; he went back and forth between his mother's home in Robinsonville and his Memphis stepfamily; he traveled to his musical haunts in Helena; and he played guitar whenever and wherever he could.

While Robert was busy performing in Mississippi, Tennessee, or Arkansas, in New York Art Satherly was scheduling the first release from Robert's November San Antonio sessions for the March 1937 Vocalion record catalog. Typically the company would issue one recording a month by a new artist, and Satherly placed "Kind Hearted Woman Blues" and "Terraplane Blues" on opposite sides of a single disc using the time-honored policy of placing a slow song with an up-tempo one. That coupling was released on both Vocalion 03416, for thirty-five cents, and ARC's (American Recording Company) other labels, which were sold through dime stores for twenty-five cents.

"Terraplane Blues" was his major seller and may have sold as many as ten thousand copies, the amount Speir said designated a hit. More copies have been found of that record than any other Robert Johnson release. But the release Satherly chose for April, "I Believe I'll Dust My Broom" backed with "Dead Shrimp Blues," also sold well and had an initial pressing of at least five thousand copies. Vocalion later released it on the Conqueror label for sale through the Sears Roebuck catalog for rural dwellers who had no access to a record store. Only best sellers from the catalog were issued on Conqueror and surprisingly "Terraplane Blues," the assumed best seller, was not.

In May, Robert's best two-sided record from a Delta standpoint, with both sides showcasing his slide guitar talents, was offered to the public: "Cross Road Blues" and "Ramblin' on My Mind." Although neither song became a hit then, they were still widely heard in the Delta. Son House was considerably impressed when he heard Robert's recordings. "We heard a couple of his pieces come out on records. Believe the first one I heard was 'Terraplane Blues.' Jesus, it was good! We all admired it. Said, 'That boy is really going places.'"[1] Elizabeth Moore heard the records too, and Robert's use of Willie Brown's name in "Cross Road Blues" didn't surprise her. She had seen the two together many times at jukes. "He used to go around, sit and play with Willie Brown lots of days at Robinsonville. See, they had a colored juke just up the railroad north a little piece outta town. Some big dances or another, he'd be in there and Willie Brown knowed his blues—what he's playing. He played right there with Willie." After hearing "Cross Road Blues" she asked Brown, whom she called "old cat," if he had heard the record. "I say, 'Hey old cat, have you heard your name in Robert's record?' He say, 'Naw, girl. I ain't heard no record with my name in it.' I say, 'Well Robert done got your name right there.' He say, 'Well you know, I told Robert the only way I'd know he ever made a record like me, was to put my name in one of 'em.' I say, 'Sure nuff, Robert done made a record and your name right there in it.'"[2]

In just three months—March, April, and May of 1937—Robert had six of his songs released. The successes of these recordings gave Robert a sense of himself as a legitimate musician. In whatever manner Robert had presented himself before his recordings were released, he was now more sure of himself as a professional musician than ever before. That self-assurance might explain why an Arkansas piano player wanted to have his friend try to take Robert down a few pegs. The unrecorded Johnny Shines ended up becoming the victim of this scheme.

Shines was working in nearby Hughes, Arkansas, with a piano player, Jerry Hooks, who called himself M&O.[3] "I was playing in Hughes in a place called Doc Pickens," Shines remembered. "An old piano player called M&O, he was playing there, and I was playing with him, and he was telling me about this guy in Helena. He was supposed to be tough. But you know the guys had an act of cutting heads. You know, you hit up on a guy that's supposed to be good, you supposed to beat him playing, well this is what M&O expected [me to do]. Evidently he had some kind of bone to pick with Robert as a musician. At the time I was young, strong, playing hard, singing loud, and he thought I could outdo Robert Johnson. He [M&O] wanted me to go to Helena and cut Robert's head, outdo him and steal his crowd away from him; pull his crowd away from him. In other words, I make all the money; he makes nothing. That's what they call 'head cutting.'"[4] But when Shines and Hooks hopped a freight train and went to Helena to musically confront Johnson, he quickly realized it was his head that would be cut.

"I went to Helena," Shines recalled, "and I heard some of his records, a couple of his records, and that changed my mind about cutting his head because I knew how that was going, and it went like I thought it was going. I left with my head cut."[5] When they finally met and played together, Robert left Shines with his mouth open and his pockets empty. One of the most time-consuming tasks in writing a biography of Robert Johnson was attaching dates to people, places, and events. Johnny Shines, while being a very accurate informant concerning what Johnson was like and what he did—he traveled more with Johnson than any other musician or person—was off on dating his years (easily understandable since he was trying to recall, even in his first interviews, thirty years in the past). Most of his claims were that he met Johnson in 1934 or '35, but according to his own stories it was actually early 1937. If this recollection of him hearing Johnson's recordings before or at the time of meeting him is true, and there is no reason to doubt it, their meeting had to have taken place after Johnson's records were released in March 1937. If it was in March, the songs Shines would have heard were "Kind Hearted Woman Blues," in which Johnson, uncharacteristic for most Delta bluesmen, played largely out of the first position and included a guitar break, and "Terraplane Blues," in which Johnson first makes use of a signature slide guitar riff. If their meeting occurred in April, then Shines would have also had a chance to hear "I Believe I'll Dust My Broom," with both another signature slide riff and its hard-driving boogie beat, and "Dead Shrimp Blues," with its complex bass against melody picking. All four songs would have sounded different than the usual recordings coming out of the Delta and probably would have seemed quite imposing to Shines.

Ordinarily this would have been the end of their association, but their meeting proved to be propitious for both men: Shines found a mentor, and Robert, usually a loner, found a traveling companion who just wouldn't leave him alone. Robert was now able to take the role that Son House and Ike Zimmerman had played for him, and it provided him with a partner upon whom he could, when he wanted or needed it, depend on for company and support. Shines quickly became a Johnson acolyte, learning from and traveling with him when he could, helping him out of scrapes, and introducing

Johnny Shines. *Christopher Smith*

him to other musicians. "I met a man who could beat me playing. And that was the man I was looking for: someone who could beat me playing because I wanted to advance. And Robert was the man, I was trying to get up his pant leg, you know? But he was one of the greatest in my eyesights: he was the master. Robert was doing some of the things I wanted to do. Things that I never heard a guitar player do."[6] Once Shines found his master he was determined not to leave Robert until he had learned all he could from him. Robert simply couldn't shake Shines from his path. No matter where he went, Shines wanted to go with him. "The fact of it was that I was the bad penny. I stayed on Robert's heels, and at that time I would follow anyone who had a riff, or a chord that I wanted until I got it, if they were friendly at all."[7]

By most accounts Robert really was that much of a better guitarist than many of his known contemporaries, for Shines was not the only musician who admired his playing: Robert Lockwood was equally effusive. "Didn't nobody else play it like that. Guitar players didn't know how to play that way. Guitar players had another guitar player with him to play the chords and the other one played the melody. Robert was playing it all. Hacksaw Harney. He was the only one that I knew [who could also play like that]."[8] Henry Townsend also considered Robert to be a master after hearing him perform in Saint Louis. "But to me he was such a good musician! I thought he was great; matter of fact, my ambition was to keep in touch with him as much as I could because I felt like I could learn quite a bit. I was excited because to me he was a rare type of executor of music. Yes, he was that far advanced to me."[9] Another time he recalled more about Robert's playing style: "Oh Robert was doing, I think you'll find on his recordings, some real close up stuff of Lonnie Johnson. And the chords that he would make some, he would do all the sevenths, the ninths, and what have you, and he'd make it fit. Robert woulda left people shaking their heads."[10]

Although Robert's recordings didn't make much of an impact outside of a specific circle in Mississippi, anyone who saw him live at that time felt as though they were in the presence of a master talent. Even in the 1960s when blues guitarist and one of his musical contemporaries Ishmon Bracey heard Robert's recording of "Dead Shrimp Blues," he insisted that one guitarist could not play that way. "I know there is [two guitars on that recording]. See he can't carry that bass and tempo all at the same time like that."[11]

But Robert's playing was about more than just being able to play the bass, melody, and chords at the same time. What made him unique was his total approach to the guitar. Perhaps it was from the jazzy orchestras Robert heard in Memphis, or the piano players in Hattiesburg from whom he most likely adapted his boogie bass pattern, but Robert was determined to treat the guitar as an entirely different instrument than the one his peers played. As Robert Lockwood observed: "The mysterious quality was that he played guitar like you played the piano. See that's the way he played, and that's real difficult. People all over the world wants to do that. I knew what Robert was playing was rare because other guitar players didn't have it. You always seen two guitar players together, and one would back the other up. But Robert didn't need nobody to back him up. That's what attracted my attention, 'cause I never knew there was gonna be a time when you could put a piano in a case and walk away with it, you know. I didn't have no dream that was ever gonna happen."[12]

Virtually all the younger musicians who heard him knew that they were hearing something unique. Johnny Shines agreed that it was Robert's ability to imitate what was done by piano players that truly made his playing so special. "Anything I've heard a fellow do on the piano he could do it on the guitar. And he did it! It was a sound you had to stop and listen to. And that's the sound a lot of people are looking for today. Me, myself, I'm still looking for it."[13] On another occasion Shines stated: "To me, he was just as great as Charlie Parker. The man did everything they did—whatsoever you did on a horn or on a piano, he figured he could do it on a guitar, and he did it. . . . Whatever you wanted him to play, he'd play it. I never seen him look for a chord. I know many chords he never heard of, because he couldn't read music, but he could make them."[14] Shines did not know, of course, that Johnson did have school music training as a child in Memphis. This would not necessarily have taught him to read music, but it probably gave him a better theoretical perspective toward music, no matter how elementary, than his contemporaries were aware of. Shines remembers: "Ninths, diminisheds, augmenteds, sevenths, tenths, thirteenths, all that stuff. He made 'em and he made 'em in the right place!"[15]

But there was something else besides talent and hard work that helped Robert change the way blues guitar was approached: he apparently had a eidetic memory. One of the keys to being a successful traveling musician was the ability to play whatever songs people requested. This usually meant performing a lot of standards as well as the latest hits of the day, and this never seemed to be a problem for Robert. Whatever song was asked of him he was always able to perform a version of it, if not a true note-for-note rendition. His ability to do so never failed to amaze those around him. "Robert was a man who could sit and talk to you like I'm talking to you now, and be listening to the radio at the same time," Shines explained. "And whenever he got ready he'd play whatever he heard on that radio. Note for note, chord for chord, whether he knew the chord he was making, I don't think he knew it, but they just fell on his fingers, you know? He did it. He played it and sing it. Whenever he got ready. He didn't have to go for it a second time. I had to go for it a third time. But he didn't. He could hear it one time and do it. In other words I think he had a photographic memory, he was way before his time or something like that."[16] Once, when Shines and Robert were sitting in a house in Arkansas with the windows open, a radio in the house next door was playing swing band music. Robert shocked Shines that night by playing several of the pieces that they both heard.[17]

Since Robert never spoke about his family or background, none of his musical acquaintances had any idea that he had received music lessons in school in Memphis, that his older stepbrother Charles had given him some lessons on the guitar and piano, that he literally got beatings for devoting his time to music instead of field work, that he had apprenticed with Ike Zimmerman, one of Mississippi's finest guitarists, nor that he might have had an eidetic memory for music. To them he was just a natural genius. They had no idea of the hours, months, and years he had devoted to learning his craft. Instead, his contemporaries attributed his abilities to some unseen talent that none of them possessed. "He had a built in computer," Shines said. "Everything he heard was there. All he had to do was punch the button. . . . Any kind he heard: Polka, Irish, Jewish, well, like 'Stardust,' 'Danny Boy,' 'Willow Weep for Me.' He'd play and put the hat down and people'd put money in it."[18]

This ability went beyond simply memorizing blues songs, too. "Robert could play anything. He could play in the style of Lonnie Johnson, Blind Blake, Blind Boy Fuller, Blind Willie McTell, all those guys. And the country singer—Jimmie Rodgers. Robert used to play a hell of a lot of his tunes, man. Robert was good at ragtime, pop tunes, waltz numbers—shoot, a polka hound, man. Robert just picked songs out of the air. A whole lot of them things nobody else played with a slide, he played them with a slide. It was just natural to him."[19] Henry Townsend was similarly impressed with Robert's prowess for just picking songs out of the air. "He didn't ask nobody, How does it go? He just listened and done it. That was it."[20]

Given Robert's seemingly effortless abilities, it's understandable that some people attributed his skills to supernatural forces. How else could one man be so good at so many different styles of playing? And Robert, as protective of his playing techniques as he was, was certainly not going to reveal any of his secrets to anyone. Townsend recalled, "When I first met Robert he would run from me when I would start watching him play. He didn't appreciate that at all. None whatsoever. I don't know how he did Honeyboy but he didn't allow me to see him play, he'd turn his back on me. And if I got around in front of him on that side he'd turn his back on me. I didn't get in front of him no more 'cause he'd walk off."[21] While Robert's secrecy could be interpreted as simply not wanting to share his techniques, it also complemented his view of his songs as fixed compositions. Both stemmed from an acute self-awareness and protectiveness of his identity as a performer.

Robert and Shines's first encounter was short, only about three weeks, but it was long enough to forge a good enough relationship that they would meet and travel together again. It was also enough time for Shines to notice particulars of Robert's personality, including one behavior that Eula Mae Williams had noticed a few years earlier. Robert wouldn't say goodbye; whenever he was ready to go he just left quickly without any notice. "Well, Robert was a loner," Shines bemoaned. "He didn't care for the company of other people too much. You know he didn't want people to get too close to him. And, uh, he would leave ya. . . . We was staying here in town [Helena] . . . and I looked around for Robert and Robert was gone."[22] As much as people tried to get to know him, something about Robert prevented him from sharing himself with anyone. Whether he was ashamed of his illegitimacy, still too hurt from Virginia's death, and pained by his inability to create a life with Virgie and Claud, he never opened himself up to anyone. "Robert never talked about himself that much. He never talked about himself, his home life or anything like that to me," said Johnny Shines, the man with whom Robert would spend more time than anyone else.[23] "I didn't know he had relatives. He never mentioned his people."[24]

Robert's secretive nature did nothing to eliminate any rumors that were developing about him, and it certainly didn't help him win many close friends. But the one thing Robert *would* talk about was music. Shines said Robert admired few musicians, but that he highly respected another pair of Johnsons—Lonnie and perhaps

Tommy. "As far as musicians he liked, he only mentioned the Johnsons, Lonnie Johnson and some other Johnson who was a good guitarist at that time. He often talked about Lonnie Johnson," Shines said. "He admired his music so much that he would tell people he was one of the Johnson boys from Texas. He'd give people the impression that he was from Texas and was related to Lonnie Johnson."[25]

But Robert didn't have to be Lonnie Johnson. His records would soon be sold side-by-side with those of his hero throughout the South.

❧ 14 ❧

GOTTA KEEP MOVIN', BLUES FALLIN' DOWN LIKE HAIL

With the release of his songs, Robert became a proud young musician. He had a name now and had little trouble getting playing jobs in the centers that knew his music. And then there were the women. Although he never lacked for company before, women actively wanted to be with him now: he didn't need to pursue them, especially not in a place like Memphis, where his recordings were easily heard on jukeboxes, people's Victrolas, and on the radio. Robert was a local star.

In New York, Art Satherly realized that Robert had produced good sellers for Depression days. A company began to break even on its costs when a record sold five hundred copies, and Robert's first records had more than done so. Wanting to quickly capitalize on that market, Satherly instructed Law to find Robert for another session. Robert had given Law his family's address on Georgia Street in Memphis, and Johnny Shines confirmed that that was how he was found for his Dallas recording sessions.[1] Robert received notification asking him to come to Dallas in June for the new session, during which the company would also be recording more selections by Western swing and Mexican groups. When Robert accepted by collect telegram, Law wired him a one-way ticket that was uncash-able. Sending money, even to a known quantity like Robert, was frowned upon by record companies. Money could be spent and the artist could end up a no-show, but a ticket could only be used for one thing.

Elated by the opportunity to make more records, Robert bragged to anyone who would listen that he was going back to Texas to make more hits. That included Shines, with whom Robert reconnected in Memphis, giving him the exciting news and asking Shines to go with him. "I met [Robert] again in Memphis. That was my home and I wanted to be anywhere but there. So Robert was telling me about how he had to go to Dallas to make some records, and I told him 'Let's go,' but he had a ticket and I didn't."[2]

Normally Robert would have traveled south from Memphis into the Delta and visited the rest of his kin throughout Mississippi, but Shines was afraid of that state because of its intense racism. Since Robert's train ticket would have taken him through Misssis-sippi, they decided instead to hitch and hop trains together through Arkansas as long as they could, and then Robert would use his ticket to go the remaining way. Shines was partly raised in Arkansas, and Robert had lived in Helena, so they made that town their first stop on their southwestern journey. From there they headed west to Little Rock and Hot Springs (about which Robert had already sang on record), then down to Highway 67 that took them all the way to Texarkana. Sitting on the border of Arkansas and Texas, Shines told Robert to use his ticket to finish his trip into Dallas and that he would remain behind playing whatever small towns he could find work in. He would meet Robert in a week or so in Red Water, Texas, only a dozen miles from Texarkana. The two musical partners sepa-rated and, in something of a coincidence, Robert arrived in Dallas during another celebratory week. The only two times he recorded—in San Antonio and Dallas—were each around a holiday. The year before, when he was in San Antonio, the state was celebrating the end of the Texas Centennial Year and Thanksgiving week. In Dallas, the African American community was enjoying several weeks of revelry surrounding Juneteenth.

That celebration recognized the abolition of slavery in Texas in June 1865. It also became known as Black Independence Day or Freedom Day, since it also marked the final official emancipation of slaves in the South. The 1937 activities in Dallas were especially extravagant and featured at least one nationally recognized black entertainer, Bill "Bojangles" Robinson. Both the *Dallas Express* and the *Houston Informer* advised black Texans throughout the state that Dallas was the place to be. The *Houston Informer* even ran a headline saying everyone should "Be in Dallas June 'Teenth."[3]

A 1937 ad for Dallas Juneteenth Celebration.
Dallas Express/ Bruce Conforth

Robert arrived on Friday, June 18, and found boarding in the section of Dallas known as Central Track, an area that went north from Elm Street (marking the section known as Deep Ellum) to the black community known as Freedmantown or Old North Dallas. Founded adjacent to Dallas proper after the Civil War, Freedmantown was an African American enclave where many black businesses and residences were located, and by the 1930s it was a thriving community that provided some respite from the harsh vagrancy laws that targeted freed blacks. Deep Ellum, originally developed as a low-scale commercial district with pawnshops and secondhand stores was, like Chicago's Maxwell Street and Memphis's Beale Street, populated by Anglos and Eastern European Jews who sold their goods to both blacks and whites. While Deep Ellum and Central Track were more racially mixed, most of Dallas was segregated and under heavy influence of the Ku Klux Klan.[4] The pronunciation "Ellum" or "Elem" was a kind of syncretism of the pronunciation used by Jewish inhabitants and rural blacks who also populated the area. During the 1910s and 1920s blues musicians, including Blind Lemon Jefferson, Huddie "Lead Belly" Ledbetter, and Blind Willie Johnson, played on the sidewalks for tips, and barrelhouse blues pianists such as Alex Moore performed in cafes and houses of ill-repute sometimes along Central Track. Ella B. Moore's Park Theatre hosted variety shows and the city blues of Bessie Smith and Lillian Glinn, among others. Years before Robert came to Dallas, Blind Lemon Jefferson had been discovered by Paramount's J. Mayo Williams and brought to Chicago to record.

Because of its early heyday, Deep Ellum received more notoriety than Central Track, even though many consider them to be parts of the same neighborhood. Businesses on Central Avenue (Central Track) spread from the H&TC (Houston and Texas Central Railroad) tracks south to Main Street and even onto Elm Street (Deep Ellum). But in spite of this commonality, Deep Ellum became the

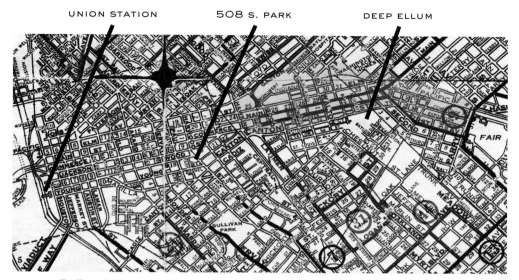

Dallas, 1937. *Bruce Conforth*

focus of much romanticizing and misunderstanding. The WPA Federal Writer's Project created *The WPA Dallas Guide and History* (unpublished as a book until five decades later) that was full of faulty, but colorful, information. It, along with the works of other authors, painted Deep Ellum as a place in which all manner of culture, both legal and illegal, could be found. Street prophets proclaiming the second coming allegedly mingled with hoodoo practitioners, pickpockets, and legitimate business owners. There, it was stated, you could find the goods to add to one's appearance: clothiers, barbershops, and tattoo parlors. If you were in need of something more personal it boasted drugstores, prostitutes, and drug dealers. If you were short of money there was no dearth of pawnshops and loan offices. For sport there were domino and pool halls. And when you needed privacy there were many walk-up hotels that rented rooms by the hour, day, or week. Finally, it was claimed, if you ran afoul of the many scam artists, card sharks, or crap shooters who frequented its streets there were also the local gun shops.[5]

While only portions of this perception had validity, it *was* true that because of the more tolerant racial atmosphere and the musical culture, white string bands became influenced by black music and even sung about Deep Ellum. The hillbilly Shelton Brothers played on Dallas radio stations and had a major hit for Decca Records in 1936 with their "Deep Ellum Blues."

> *When you go down in Deep Ellum, put your money in your*
>   *shoes,*
> *'Cause them women in Deep Ellum, sure take it 'way from*
>   *you.*
> *Oh, sweet mama, daddy got them Deep Ellum Blues.*

Both Lead Belly and Blind Lemon Jefferson were known to perform the traditional song "Take a Whiff on Me" that addressed these deeds:

> *Walked up Ellum an' I come down Main,*
> *Tryin' to bum a nickel jes' to buy cocaine.*
> *Ho, Ho, baby, take a whiff on me.*

Although Jefferson sang about Deep Ellum, he never recorded "Take a Whiff on Me." Much of Jefferson's repertoire was rooted in oral tradition, and the songs he recorded were largely based on his experiences in East Texas. In Dallas, Jefferson performed at the corner Elm Street and Central Avenue in front of R. T. Ashford's "shine parlor" and record store. Located at 408 North Central Avenue, Ashford's business catered to African Americans, many of whom worked in downtown Dallas. The young pianist Sammy Price brought Jefferson to Ashford's attention. Like H. C. Speir, in the 1920s and early '30s Ashford sent numerous musicians to Paramount, Victor, and Brunswick/Vocalion. Of these, Lemon Jefferson was unquestionably his most successful find.

Gypsy Tea Room. *Dallas Public Library*

By the 1930s, however, Deep Ellum was changing and the black population was being pushed toward Central Avenue and even further north. By the time Robert arrived, Deep Ellum had become largely a collection of pawnshops and secondhand stores. There were no nightclubs in which to hear the blues, and Central Track would have been where he was able to get lodging and food and to prepare himself for his Saturday recording session. The makeshift

Vocalion recording studio was located on the third floor of 508 Park Avenue, about ten blocks away from Deep Ellum.

Central Track, and what was left of the culture of Deep Ellum must have seemed to Robert quite similar to the Beale Street environs he had known in Memphis. The daytime hustling and the nighttime partying were old friends of his. As he walked along North Central Avenue, the familiar smells of collard greens, chitlins, pork chops, barbecued beef, catfish, and beer must have filled the air. And also like Beale Street, the black section of Dallas had practitioners of hoodoo who sold the local handmade tobys—mojo bags—and conjures juju doctors. Although flawed in some respects, the WPA Writer's Project documentation of these practices was testimony to the prevalence that these beliefs were important not only in providing additional context to the currency of such beliefs during Robert's life and culture but could help explain several references he made in his lyrics during the Dallas sessions.[6]

The songs Robert recorded during those days in Dallas were very different in style, tone, and message than his San Antonio recordings. Robert had changed a great deal over the last eight months. When he entered the 508 Park Avenue studio that Saturday morning he was equipped with songs that were even more autobiographical and introspective than those of his San Antonio sessions. His entrance, however, would have been uncomfortably familiar to his sessions at the Gunter Hotel in San Antonio the year before. Like the whites-only hotel where he was required to enter through the rear of the building, the extreme racism of Dallas would have again required him avoid the front, and public, entrance.

An imposing Zigzag Moderne building, 508 Park was built in 1929 as the Vitagraph/Warner Brothers Exchange Building. The first floor was devoted to film vaults from which Vitaphone (short subjects and cartoons), First National Pictures (contemporary comedies, dramas and crimes), and Warner Brother Pictures (motion pictures and musicals) were stored and distributed. The second floor housed offices, and the third floor (ultimately used as a make-shift recording studio) was open storage. The building also housed accommodations for executives and visiting movie stars.[7] Remnants of recording efforts on the third floor could still recently be seen from the outline of an enclosure on the floor and rusty nails on window cornices used to hang heavy burlap to deaden the sound.[8]

Robert still relied on the four musical styles he favored: the open-tuned bottleneck style dependent upon a signature riff and preva-lent on pieces such as "Terraplane Blues" and "Cross Road Blues"; the standard-tuned straight blues such as "Kind Hearted Woman Blues" and "Dead Shrimp Blues"; the boogie bass beat songs such as "I Believe I'll Dust My Broom" and "Sweet Home Chicago"; and his hokum and East Coast–style pieces such as "They're Red Hot." But in Dallas he fit these musical styles with a new type of lyrics.

The first day of recording, Thursday June 17, featured Al Dexter and Luke Owens. Friday's session laid down recordings by a group called the Hi-Flyers and several others by Roy Newan and His Boys. Saturdays work began with the Crystal Springs Ramblers, a West-ern swing band featuring great piano, saxophone, and fiddle, and a thumping bass fiddle style with a break, a technique that spawned rockabilly music in the early 1950s. The band was named after the Crystal Springs Palace west of Fort Worth that had been the stomp-ing grounds for Milton Brown and His Brownies. Robert recorded after them and was followed by Zeke Williams and His Rambling Cowboys.

The Light Crust Doughboys, formed in 1933 to advertise Light Crust Flour, opened Sunday's session and recorded eight sides. By 1937 some of the best musicians in the history of Western swing were members of this ensemble: Kenneth Pitts and Clifford Gross on fiddles, Dick Reinhart and Muryel Campbell on guitars, and Ramon DeArman was on bass with John "Knocky" Parker on

piano. Marvin "Smokey" Montgomery played tenor banjo. Clifford
Cross and Muryel Campbell followed the Doughboys, then it was
Robert's turn again.

In 1959, Montgomery, the longtime leader of the Dallas-based
Doughboys, was interviewed during an annual Jimmy Rodgers Festival in Meridian, the blue yodeler's hometown. Montgomery had
known members of the Ramblers personally. He had either played
with or knew the musicians for a large number of Western swing
bands that had recorded either in Dallas or San Antonio for Law or
his rivals Decca and Bluebird.[9]

Although Montgomery had no recollections of Robert being in
the studio, he did remember seeing a blues musician at the session.
And he remembered important contextual information about the
sessions: they recorded in the rear of the third floor of the building where a massive number of newly pressed records were kept
in boxes after being shipped in from pressing plants. The studio
conditions in Dallas were vastly different than the comfort of the
Gunter Hotel in San Antonio. "They had cleared out a little place
up there in the back of the building," Montgomery recalled, "and
the recording machine was set up in a little booth. We got in front
of those record boxes and gathered around one mike to record. They
had another mike on the piano and the engineer had his equipment
in that little booth."[10]

The weekend sessions gave the artists a distinct advantage over
those held on weekdays. Usually there was too much noise from
street traffic during the week for a suitable recording environment,
unless the sessions were held at night. The weekend sessions were
somewhat quieter. But the building was a warehouse with few windows, and since it was June in Texas, the temperature soared. Montgomery remembered the stifling heat in the building. "This was
kind of a storage place as far as I could tell, and it was a pretty big
building. We were right out in the middle of it, but it seemed like

they had some boxes around the side of us or something to keep us from wandering off in any other part of the place when we was playing. The air-conditioning was a big chunk of ice with a fan blowing over it, but then when they got ready to take a cut they had to turn the fans off [since] the humming of the fans was too much to be on record."[11] Although the washtubs full of ice and fans were placed around the recording area, turning them off during the actual recording ended up helping the musicians and everyone else very little, leaving them drenched in sweat.

Robert opened his new recording session with "Stones in My Passway," a uniquely personal introspection with an obvious double entendre:

> *I got three legs to truck on, boys,*
> *Please don't block my road.*
> *Been feelin' ashamed 'bout my rider*
> *I'm booked and I got to go.*

Robert often used the vernacular that was used daily by the Delta sharecroppers he played for. He sang countless expressions along the lines of his "rider" (the woman he was having sex with) or "makin' a spread," and "quiverin' down" (for intercourse). But what makes the lyrics in "Stones in My Passway" of particular interest is Robert's very direct reference to hoodoo practice:

> *I got stones in my passway and my road seems dark as night.*
> *My enemies have betrayed me, have overtaken poor Bob at last*
> *And there's one thing certain, they have stones all in my pass*
> *You laid a passway for me now, what are you trying to do*

There is no question that he was singing about hoodoo practice. Foot-track magic, a distinctly African form of laying down tricks,

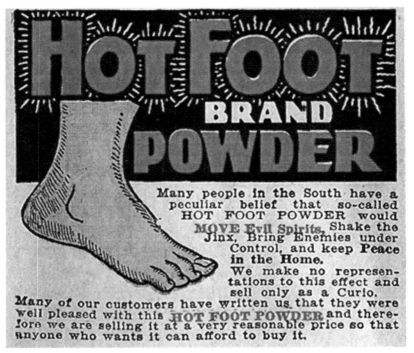

Vintage Hot Foot Powder ad. *Bruce Conforth*

is accomplished when an arrangment of objects (in Robert's lyrics, stones), called a "mess," is laid out in a pattern, line, cross mark, or crossroads symbol. The mess is positioned where the intended victim will walk over it, and is intended to hurt or poison the victim through the feet. The intent is physical harm, unlike much other magic that affects love, fortunes, or luck.[12] Robert's lyrics do claim that the passway stones did affect his health: "I have pains in my heart, they have taken my appetite."

Robert's second song, "I'm a Steady Rollin' Man," also had a double meaning. Primarily, he indicated that he was a good provider and worked hard "both night and day" for his woman. He stressed, "I have been a hard workin' man for many long years, I know." But the other meaning was fully sexual: "rollin'" was slang for performing consistently in bed. This seems in direct opposition to his failure to perform in songs like "Dead Shrimp Blues" and perhaps even in "Phonograph Blues." But those songs were from some seven months earlier. Since that time Robert's records had been released, he was becoming more of a known musician in the black community, and his access to women had become much easier. It shouldn't be a surprise, therefore, that he bragged about the women he had and could keep with his sexual prowess.

Robert had one more song to record that day before he headed out to the Dallas Juneteenth celebrations. He finished his Saturday session with another personal narration, "From Four Until Late." Robert began by singing about one of his old hangouts, Gulfport on the Mississippi Coast, where the Gulf and Ship Island Railroad began its journey to Jackson. Located in Harrison County, Gulfport was a busy port where fruit from the Caribbean arrived to be shipped all over the country. It also offered bonded whiskey for sale, unlike the rest of Mississippi, which was supposedly dry. Until liquor became legal in the state on a local county-option basis, Gulfport and Biloxi, the adjacent city, were among the most wide open places in the state.

The song became more autobiographical when he lyrically painted a travelogue: "From Memphis to Norfolk," where his nephew Louis was stationed in the US Navy, "is a thirty-six hour ride." The song was also one of the few times that he did not rhyme the last word of the third line with the last word of the first two lines in his variations of the standard twelve-bar blues phrasing. Melodically, Robert took the tune from the "Four o'Clock Blues" that Memphis bandleader Johnny Dunn had recorded in 1922. This seems to be more evidence of how important Memphis was to him as a child and as an adult. It is also evidence that Robert was no stranger to the East Coast, where he had relatives in both North and South Carolina and family members there who mentioned him visiting. Robert also employed a theme recently recorded by Charley

Jordan for Decca in March of that year under his pseudonym of Uncle Skipper, titled "Chiffarobe Blues." The Saint Louis musician did four verses comparing a woman to having "dresser drawers" that a man rambles through. Robert similarly sang: "A woman is just like a dresser / Some man always ramblin' through her drawers." Apparently he had heard Jordan's June release and was borrowing lyrics his contemporaries were having success with.

As Robert finished his session and was packing his guitar after his day's musical production, Zeke Williams and His Ramblin' Cowboys were waiting to take the microphone. He walked out of the studio with money in his pocket.

Reported in local newspapers as the largest Juneteenth celebration ever held in Dallas with parades, dances, and suppers with music, bootleg whiskey in fruit jars, and homebrew that was sometimes referred to as "Sister-Get-You-Ready," black Dallas was ready to offer Robert anything he wanted, including lots of women.[13] That year's festival was the biggest in Dallas history and featured four parades in that single weekend. The famous, and highly paid, black dancer and entertainer Bill "Bojangles" Robinson was performing free in Fair Park and there would be even larger crowds of people than for the regular festival. Robert strutted, or trucked, his way to the waiting audience, eager to play his music and impress and find one of those "Saturday night women [who] love to ape and clown." This time he didn't lack a nickel.

The lyrics that Robert sang the next day would be deeper and darker than any he had previously recorded. Some historians refer to these songs as his "devil connection." Perhaps he was remembering all the dark crossroads in his life: his mother's abandonment of him when he was just an infant, being uprooted again and taken from the city to the plantation, the beatings he got for not wanting to work in the fields, the deaths of Virginia and their unborn child and being blamed for them because of his playing the devil's music, the loss of Virgie and Claud for the same reason, and a whole host of other personal disappointments. When he reentered the makeshift studio, Robert's recordings projected distinct fears.

This was notable especially in his first song, "Hell Hound on My Trail." It is so different from his other compositions that it is often singled out as Robert's masterpiece, his most intense performance. The melody was borrowed from Skip James's 1931 Paramount recording "Devil Got My Woman," but Robert seemed entranced, in a fearful, unexplainable mindset. Either he was suffering from deep lingering fears and trauma from the tragedies in his life, or he was a master at projecting himself into a performance and selling a song. Placing the number in the same open E minor tuning that James had used for his recording—and which Robert had learned from Johnnie Temple—he tuned his guitar a full tone higher than James, causing him to strain to reach his singing notes. The musical and lyrical tension this created for the listener seems almost unbearable. And Robert seemed either unsure of his playing or overwhelmed by the song itself, for he muffed one guitar riff (early in the second verse) before he found the right notes. As an accomplished guitarist that was unusual for him.

The strange qualities of "Hell Hound" began with its first verse, "I got to keep moving, I got to keep moving, blues fallin' down like hail . . . and the days keep on worryin' me: there's a hellhound on my trail."

Robert never mentioned either hellhounds or the devil in succeeding verses. Only once before had a known blues musician sung about hellhounds: Oklahoma bluesman "Funny Paper" Smith, who also used the nickname "Howlin' Wolf" before Chester Burnett appropriated it. In 1931 Smith seemed to use the hellhound reference to describe something less demonic: "I often get blue and start howlin' and *the hellhound gets on my trail*. I'm that wolf that digs a hole and stick my nose down in the ground." Smith, in all likelihood, was using his "wolf" association to speak about white law enforcement officers. Robert, on the other hand, presented a more ambiguous, and even mysterious, meaning when he used the term.

Whatever Robert's hellhounds were, one can sense a certain angst in this song. It's not a happy piece, and it includes another distinct reference to hoodoo magic: the use of hot foot powder. Like his song "Stones in My Passway," the reference to hot foot powder refers to foot traffic magic. It's not unlike a hunter laying down a snare for his prey. Foot traffic magic is perhaps among the oldest forms of hoodoo practice, along with Goofer Dust, Graveyard Dirt, and Crossing Powder. Such magic seems to be of African origin and predates the nineteenth century. It's used precisely the way Robert spoke about it in his song: once sprinkled across someone's path, the victim must lead a life of restlessness and rambling.[14]

As in "Stones in My Passway" and possibly "Dust My Broom," Robert was being specific about hoodoo practice and how it worked. Add the eerie cry in his voice, more haunting than James's falsetto, and "Hell Hound" became one of his most noted performances. Of all his songs, "Hell Hound" has the most evocative imagery. Almost surrealist in its approach, the song paints visions and sound pictures. Robert emulates "the leaves tremblin' on the tree" by playing his slide in a shimmering single note vibrato. The effect is haunting.

His next songs, "Malted Milk" and "Drunken Hearted Man," appeared to center around an alcoholic theme, but perhaps only the latter truly does.

Most scholars have posited that "Malted Milk" referred to beer or malt liquor. However, when Robert was a child growing up in Memphis, Horlick's Malted Milk was a widely advertised and used product.

Since Memphis played such a huge role in his early life, Robert might have simply been taking a rather sugary, innocent approach to healing his blues in this song. The last verse of the song even

Horlick's Malted Milk ad. *Bruce Conforth*

depicts one of the most common childhood fears: "My doorknob keeps on turnin', It must be spooks around my bed. I have a warm, old feelin' and the hair risin' on my head." The influence of Lonnie Johnson, a major race artist since 1926 and Robert's musical idol, was obvious in his guitar playing on "Malted Milk." It was smooth and jazzlike, and in it Robert demonstrated his ability to play with a subtle touch.

"Drunken Hearted Man," conversely, was clearly about sorrows both caused by drink and being drowned by it. Vocalion chose not to release this song, one of five songs judged noncommercial for various reasons. Perhaps the song was too personal or autobiographical to be a commercial success. The complete recording, never publi-cally released, contains a hidden treasure: a sound check with Rob-ert playing a D major chord. Lyrically, Robert speaks of his mother and father: his father being absent and his mother doing the best she could. These events, he confesses, led to his alcoholism and womanizing. It's a sad song to hear and was about a life that Johnny Shines described in a 1966 interview. "Of course when he drank, and he was a heavy drinker, he was unpredictable. [He was] close to a split personality. You never knew what he was going to do or how he'd react to something. Sometimes he'd be the most mild man-nered, quiet person you'd ever meet; at other times, he would get so violent so suddenly, and you couldn't do nothin' with him. He was that changeable. [He was] different things to different people."[15] Yet Robert hadn't always been so unpredictable. Willie Moore had seen a different Robert in his younger years. "I ain't knowed him to get in no fights. He wudn't no clowny [arguing/bragging] person like that, you know. I never knowed Robert go out and get in no fights with nobody, [he didn't make] no fuss with that old guitar."[16] Obviously something had caused a change in Johnson's life and behavior in the years between the memories of Moore and Shines. Was it the loss of one wife and one potential wife and two children, all because he was accused of playing the devil's music? Was that the real crossroads in his life?

"Traveling Riverside Blues" was loosely based upon the 1929 "Rollin' and Tumblin'" bottleneck piece that was a huge hit in the Delta for "Hambone" Willie Newbern when it was released on the Okeh label. At his San Antonio session, Robert had used that same arrangement for "If I Had Possession over Judgment Day." In "Traveling Riverside Blues" Robert took the listener on a river-front tour of the Mississippi Delta. Reaching back for the localizing technique, Robert once again sang about his home territory: "I got women from Vicksburg, clean on in to Tennessee / but my Friars

Point rider jumps all over me." Robert also mentioned Rosedale, and all three locations lie along Highway 1, which ran beside the Mississippi River. But the lyrics also contained his exhortation: "You can squeeze my lemon, 'til the juice runs down my leg." That line was OK for juke house singing but it was unacceptable for Satherly, who, Speir said, "understood what they were singing better than any other recording director."[17] As a result, "Traveling" became the third unissued title from this session.

Another somewhat autobiographical song, "Stop Breakin' Down Blues," was probably about Robert's relationship with women, but his lyrics were laden with danger. "Now I give my baby the ninety-nine degree, she jumped up and threw a pistol down on me." The song's refrain had been recorded by Luke Jordan, a Virginia bluesman in 1927, and by the white guitarist Dick Justice in 1929: "Stop breaking down, please stop breakin' down. / The stuff I got / It's gonna bust your brains out baby, / ooh ooh, it'll make you lose your mind." Many believe this implied that he had access to cocaine, a familiar drug in the blues scene that the Memphis Jug Band had sung about in 1930 on their "Cocaine Habit Blues."

But Robert's bestseller from the session ended up being his 1938 release of "Little Queen of Spades" backed with "Me and the Devil Blues." More copies of that record and "Stop Breakin' Down" have been found in unsold store stocks—or by door knocking—than of his other Dallas recordings.

"Little Queen of Spades" was another reworking of the guitar style and pattern he created with "Kind Hearted Woman." His playing was concise and he took no new chances. This is not surprising, however, for throughout Robert's Dallas sessions his songs are even more compositionally constructed than his repertoire in San Antonio: it seems that every word, note, and nuance was planned.

This is particularly true of "Me and the Devil Blues." Even his added spoken asides in that song, "Now, babe, you know you ain't doin' me right" in the first line of the second verse, and "Baby, I don't care where you bury my body when I'm dead and gone" in the last verse, are identical in both of the existing takes. Robert's consistency reinforces his view that his songs were strict compositions, as inviolable as songs he heard on the radio.

Strong in its composition and execution, both lyrically and musically, "Me and the Devil Blues" has gained primary importance among those theorists who see it as evidence of Robert's alleged pact with the devil at the crossroads. His use of the devil theme seems, however, to be more of a nod to the many devil songs that preceded him than it is an admission of allegiance to the dark forces. Casey Bill Weldon's remake of Clara Smith's "Done Sold My Soul to the Devil," Lonnie Johnson singing about "making whoopee with the Devil," or Peetie Wheatstraw calling himself "the Devil's Son-in-Law" are only a few examples of earlier blues musicians mentioning the devil in their music or self-promotion. Certainly Robert was aware of these recordings and both the agency and humor they could bring to the artist and the song's performance. Almost always such songs were done with an element of humor. As other scholars have pointed out, black folklore is replete with the use of humor when addressing violence against its people. As Muddy Waters even said to Dave Van Ronk after hearing the latter perform "Hoochie Coochie Man": "But you know, that's supposed to be a funny song."[18] And when Robert sings the third verse, "I'm going to beat my woman until I get satisfied," the satisfaction to which he referred might have been sexual satisfaction, not a satisfaction from physically beating her. Although beating a woman was a fairly common theme in the blues, and that might have been what he meant, his pleasure may have come from other sources and not from the physical violence. There are literally dozens of blues, from Ma Rainey's 1927 "Slow Drivin' Moan" to Curly Weaver's 1928 "No No Blues" to Big Bill Broonzy's 1930 "I Can't Be Satisfied," in which the idea of being satisfied was related to sexual or romantic satisfaction. There seems little doubt that this is what Robert meant. Such a line probably amused most males in his audience, and rang somewhat true to the females. His final verse is something of a contradiction and doesn't entirely fit with the preceding verses. On the one hand he gives specific instructions as to how and why he should be buried by the highway side—"So my old evil spirit can get a Greyhound bus and ride"—yet he adds the spoken, "Baby I don't care where you bury me when I'm dead and gone." Why he should offer such a disparity in his lyric is a puzzle.

"Honeymoon Blues" was his eighth song, all eight requiring two or three performances. The transition between "Honeymoon Blues" and "Love in Vain" is of particular interest because just prior to the second song one can hear Robert say, in his normal street voice, "I wanna go on with that next one myself." His spoken words were not heard by the public until the 1991 centennial release of his complete recordings. If you listen carefully there seems to be no doubt those are his words, but that statement makes little sense out of context. Obviously Robert had been performing all his songs by himself, so he couldn't have been referring to playing solo. Was he referring to setting the time himself? Could he have been switching the order of the songs he had intended to record? Robert had just finished recording "Honeymoon Blues," in which he specifically called out to a woman named Betty Mae: "Betty Mae, Betty Mae, you shall be my wife someday, I wants a little sweet girl, that will do anything that I say." This is only the second time in any of his songs that he actually uses the name of a woman. It seems more than coincidental that in the very next song, "Love in Vain," he once again makes a specific reference to a woman by name, this time Willie Mae: "Ou hou ou ou ou, hoo, Willie Mae . . . All my love's in vain."

In "Honeymoon Blues," Johnson is deeply in love with Betty Mae but needs to depart, promising that he will return with a marriage license. In "Love in Vain" it is Willie Mae who is apparently leaving, and Johnson mourns the fact. At that time in the South the use of Mae as a middle name for a woman was fairly common, but in spite of that it seems extremely curious that in two successive songs, two of only three songs in which Robert actually uses a woman's name, he refers to the first as Betty Mae and the second as Willie Mae. Could he be referring to the same woman in his mind? Could he have recorded "Honeymoon Blues" and immediately realized he had made a pledge to Willie Mae to record a song about her and quickly wanted to "go on with the next one"? These are all conjectures and we'll never know, but these two songs, back to back, each mentioning a woman with the name Mae mediated by Robert's statement remain a minor mystery.

"Love In Vain" was based upon a melody used by the popular city blues singer Leroy Carr from his 1935 Bluebird release "When the Sun Goes Down." The song was so popular that both Memphis Minnie and Bumble Bee Slim covered it for the Vocalion and Decca labels. But Robert struggled with the verses to get the master that Law wanted. Its lyrics were similar to a May release by Black Ivory King (David Alexander) on Decca 7304. Recorded in February 1937 in Chicago, "The Flying Crow" heralded a streamlined passenger train on the Kansas City Southern that ran from Port Arthur, Texas, into Shreveport and then on to Kansas City. Robert's lyrics explained: "When the train it left the station, with two lights on behind / Well the blue light was my blues . . . and the red light was my mind." In contrast, Black Ivory King sang: "There she goes, there she goes, with two lights left behind (X2). One is my trouble, and other's my ramblin' mind."

Robert had been recording at least two takes of each song for a full day and had to be tired, and there is no sound of jocularity in his spoken words like one hears in the voices of Son House, Willie Brown, and Charlie Patton during their 1930 Grafton session.

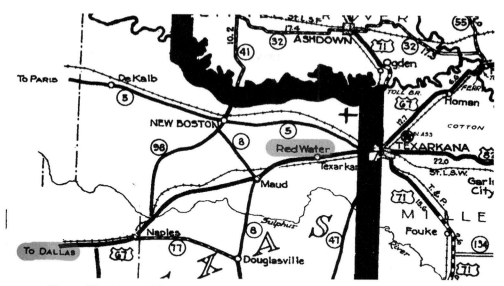

Map of Redwater, Texas. *Bruce Conforth*

Robert's voice is intent and direct: *this one is mine.* Both takes of "Love in Vain" are virtually identical, with only an eight-second difference in length between them. In both versions he croons sad lyrics about a love who's leaving, using a powerful image of a passenger train leaving the station with his lover onboard. His last verse was patterned after Leroy Carr's moaned vocables in "When the Sun Goes Down," but Robert added his loved one's name—Willie Mae—fulfilling his promise to put Willie Mae Powell's name on a record.

Robert ended his recording career with an old standard blues that dated back to pre-record folk tradition: "Milkcow's Calf Blues." Son House had included one of the lines in his 1930 recording of "My Black Mama Part 1": "Well if you see my milkcow, tell her to hurry home / I ain't had no milk since that cow been gone." Kokomo Arnold also recorded a more complete version of the song in 1934. It seems that Robert, not realizing this was to be his last recording opportunity, chose a song he probably heard as a child.

Robert completed ten songs that day, walked out of the Park Avenue third-floor studio, and sent a postcard to his half sister Carrie in Memphis:

> My dear sister,
> Hope you are okay. I will be home soon. Tell all hello. I haven't wrote Louis. Sorry, but haven't had time. Tell mother I wrote you. Yours truly. Robert Johnson.[19]

With another pocketful of cash, Robert began his trek out of Texas on Highway 67 to rejoin Johnny Shines, who had been waiting for Robert's return. The two met again, as planned, in Redwater, a small community of approximately 250 persons, twelve miles from Texarkana. It's directly on Highway 67, the most direct route for Robert to take to meet Shines. One day in late June Shines was playing on its streets, as he had been doing in Texarkana, when he saw a slim guitarist and recognized him as his friend, Robert Johnson, on his way back. "I caught him in a place called Red Water [*sic*], Texas. Robert had made his records."[20]

The two found playing jobs to stay in Texas for a while, and then they followed Highway 67 north to Little Rock, Arkansas. From there Robert continued on north and east and Shines headed to his mother's home near Hughes. It was early fall 1937. "We worked Texas until the cold weather began to set in, then we headed for the southern part of Texas. Robert and I came back into Arkansas as far as Little Rock. I can't recall just what happened, but my mother was in Arkansas not too far from Hughes and I ended up there. Robert went on, but I stayed in Hughes. We worked around there together, and most of the time individually. What I mean by that is that there were very few songs that Robert wanted to play with anyone, so we played mostly in turns. Hughes was a small town, but if anything was going on anywhere it was there. We made the paydays at Stuttgart, Cotton Plant, Snow Lake, and many other places, together and sometimes separately. If we were both in Hughes at the same time we shared the room, or whoever was there on Monday paid the rent."[21]

Soon Robert was returning regularly to Robinsonville to play for friends like Elizabeth Moore. The pride he exhibited after his San Antonio sessions was now built up even further by the fact that he had just returned from another session making more records. To Moore, his most memorable recordings were "Terraplane Blues" and "Kind Hearted Woman Blues," his first release from the San Antonio session.

The rural jukes Robert returned to had a very important function in his life: he made more money there than in towns such as Greenwood and Clarksdale where cafes had jukeboxes that could hold ten records of the latest race issues, including his own. The noise in a cafe made it difficult for an acoustic guitar player to be heard, and the owner didn't have to pay a live performer if he had a jukebox. The owner also got half of the take from the jukebox company. There was a second, perhaps even more important, reason for Robert to like country jukes: he had no competition on Saturday nights on the plantations. With his reputation, he could play on the streets on Saturdays for tips and to advertise where he would be playing that night for a dance. Because of his records, he would draw sharecroppers from miles around. They came in wagons, on mules, or in old beaten-up, run-down cars. The dances were held indoors, where old rusty black kerosene lamps provided dim lights, and the food was cooked over a wood-burning stove. In the summer, catfish and brim were fried in big, black-iron pans over a blazing wood fire in the backyard.

Robert had been in and out of big cities like Memphis and Saint Louis, where he faced competition from recorded guitar and piano players. But there were few, if any, pianos available for black musicians on plantations. And the women loved a guitar man who could sing to them personally. But their boyfriends and husbands hated it. That's what made the juke houses especially dangerous. Joe Callicott vibrantly recalled the dangers of playing in a juke and attracting the wrong women. "I say, look here honey, your man gonna get jealous. You gonna get me killed. When 'em women get to shakin' them fannies and start talkin' that trash to you, you gotta be careful," Callicott emphasized. "If you don't, you might get killed."[22]

But juking was Robert's life and livelihood. He couldn't seem to stay away from imminent dangers or dangerous women. He had no love for working in the cotton fields and the church had no appeal. All he could do was keep moving and try to outrun danger, both imaginary and real. He was moving toward his most impressive journey.

ᵍᵉ 15 ᵉᵍ

WHEN I LEAVE THIS TOWN I'M
GON' BID YOU FARE, FAREWELL

As Robert was taking advantage of his newly found renown among the Delta's black folks, one thousand miles away his reputation was being made in an entirely different way and to an entirely different audience. A Columbia record producer was reviewing his records for the first time—and, during his lifetime, probably the last.

John Henry Hammond II was born into privilege. The youngest child and only son of John Henry Hammond and Emily Vanderbilt Sloane he very early became a lover of black culture and music. Romantic anecdotes relate that Hammond acquired this love of black music from listening to his family's black maid sing gospel or blues songs, but by his own admission he actually acquired his taste for jazz during a 1923 trip to London when he was thirteen years old, where he heard the great jazz clarinetist Sidney Bechet. Upon his return to America he began buying race records from stores in Harlem.[1] He disappointed his family by dropping out of Yale to move to Greenwich Village to listen to, write about, and produce black musicians. Hammond seemed to have a great ear and eye for talent, and among his musical successes were introducing Benny Goodman to Fletcher Henderson, as well as convincing the former (his future brother-in-law) to integrate his band. Hammond also produced some of Bessie Smith's last records, and in 1933 he "discovered" Billie Holiday. He also wrote for numerous music magazines, and his word was highly respected.

Although distinctly involved in left-wing circles, Hammond was initially protective of his family name when he wrote a column for the March 1937 issue of the Communist magazine *New Masses*. Using the pseudonym Henry Johnson, in the article he included a short albeit glowing review of Robert's records. It read,

> Before closing, we cannot help but call your attention to the greatest Negro blues singer who has cropped up in recent years, Robert Johnson. Recording them in deepest Mississippi, Vocalion has certainly done right by us in the tunes "Last Fair Deal Gone Down" and "Terraplane Blues," to mention only two of the four sides already released, sung to his own guitar accompaniment. Johnson makes Leadbelly sound like an accomplished poseur.[2]

Before closing, we cannot help but call your attention to the greatest Negro blues singer who has cropped up in recent years, Robert Johnson. Recording them in deepest Mississippi, Vocalion has certainly done right by us in the tunes "Last Fair Deal Gone Down" and "Terraplane Blues," to mention only two of the four sides already released, sung to his own guitar accompaniment. Johnson makes Leadbelly sound like an accomplished poseur.

HENRY JOHNSON.

Ever since John Lomax had introduced Lead Belly to left-wing, East Coast society in 1933 the songster had been a darling novelty of a truly exotic savage who could be both charming and entertaining at their concerts or affairs. He was either heralded as the greatest

Negro songster to be recorded, or vilified as thieving and dangerous. He was considered many things, but of all of them he was certainly considered authentic. For Hammond, even writing under an assumed name, to call Lead Belly a "poseur" and to champion another musician in his place was almost heresy. But Hammond wasn't finished mentioning Robert in print. In the July issue of the same magazine Hammond (this time using his own name) again praised Robert: "Hot Springs' star is still Robert Johnson who has turned out to be a worker on a Robinsville [*sic*], Miss., plantation."[3]

It was these two musical comments that began the Robert Johnson myth among white scholars, musicologists, folklorists, and the public. Whether Hammond knew the inaccuracies he was reporting—that the recordings were *not* made in deepest Mississippi or that Robert was *not* a plantation worker from Hot Springs—didn't matter. His few published lines created a mythic Robert Johnson for a white public.

Even unaware of the reviews, however, Robert knew that there was something special about the home of John Henry Hammond II and *New Masses*, New York City. Charley Patton had recorded there, and the nearly seven million inhabitants necessitated hundreds of clubs and speakeasys, radio stations and theaters, professional sports and arts venues. In less than three months the prospects of money and fame would draw Robert to the city's streets.

While Shines went to Hughes, Robert continued his rambling into Memphis and then north to Saint Louis, where he met Henry Townsend, a long-standing professional musician who had started his recording career in 1929. Townsend's earliest years had been spent in Shelby, Mississippi, and then near Lula, listening to the local blues musicians. During the 1930s he recorded with musicians Roosevelt Sykes, John Lee "Sonny Boy" Williamson, Robert Nighthawk, and Mississippi-born Big Joe Williams and Walter Davis. With Robert's recordings only recently released, Townsend was unaware of his abilities and had no knowledge of Robert as a musician of any note: "his name didn't mean anything to me." He recalled, "How I really came across Robert, I was playing at one of the fellow's homes, it was, we called it a speakeasy, but it was just a big house that had plenty of room, and I was doing work for him more or less weekends, Thursday, Friday, and Saturday. So one of the Saturdays I came over there, he had hired Robert Johnson and I thought at that time maybe he's got rid of me but he wouldn't let me leave, he said, 'No, I want both of you.' He was only giving me, I think it was two dollars, and everything, all the drinks and all that was two dollars was my compesary [*sic*] there, as much as I ever got from him. I don't know what he was paying Robert. But anyway, we got together, and Robert was somewhat a shy guy, but when it come to his playing . . . You had to get his confidence before he would let you see all the works that he done. I was only with him a couple of weeks, or maybe a little less, and I only got about two of his chords, because he was secret with it."[4]

Robert, because of his newfound recording fame, became even more guarded of his playing techniques. Never again would he teach someone to play his style the way he had to Robert Lockwood. He was no longer a "meat-barreler," as Speirs had described: he was a recording artist, with the emphasis on the last word. His songs, his tunings, his playing style were all his: he owned them.

After playing with, and impressing, Townsend and the other Saint Louis musicians, as well as whatever women he could seduce with his music, Robert worked his way back down to West Memphis and Memphis, to Robinsonville (where he played at a juke called Perry Place), Friars Point (the Blue and White Juke), and into Helena. Eventually he made his way to Hughes and met back up with Shines. "One night I had come in from a joint to where I was staying at and the lady I was renting the room from told me, she says, 'There's a young man in there. He says he knows you.' She

John Henry Hammond II. *Jason Hammond*

was a young lady and I said, 'Yeah? What does he look like?' So she described him to me and I knew who it was. 'And Johnny, he sings like a bird.' I said, 'Oh, that's Robert.' He had told her that he knew me and he was in my room, in the bed. I went in and woke him up. And that was when we took off, going north."[5]

Although Robert had learned to drink when his boyhood friends were still playing children's games, his alcoholic consumption may have surpassed that of his contemporaries. Henry Townsend recalled his excesses: "Oh, he would drink. At that time I don't know if you would consider that heavy drinking or not because I guess everybody was lushing so hard then until you couldn't distinguish who was the worst!"[6] According to Shines and others who knew him then Robert drank "more often than not," with his main drinks being Ten High, Dixie Dew, Old Taylor, or Old Grand Dad (all bourbons or corn whiskeys). Shines had to rescue him from more than a few scraps that were caused by his love for bourbon. Robert and whiskey resulted in a brew that brought out the worst of his traits. Though even when sober he would rail against God and the church, when he was drunk his vitriol against religion reached new heights. His words were more than enough to convince even the most skeptical listener that his blues really were the devil's music. And, most unfortunately, especially for any companion of his such as Shines, he got nasty and wanted to fight with anyone he had a notion to attack. "If Robert wasn't drinking he wasn't really wild, but once he got a few drinks in him it didn't make him any difference what he did. He wasn't able to take care of himself when he started drinking. As a matter of fact he wasn't man enough to take care of himself when he wasn't drinking. He couldn't punch hisself out of a wet paper sack. He just wasn't able to maneuver and take care of himself for some reason. I've seen many people with the same build that he had that were much more capable of taking care of themselves than he was. He wasn't a scrapper or a fighter, but he tried, and he'd get the hell beat out of *you* if you didn't watch out. 'Cause he'd jump on a gang of guys just as quick as he would one and if you went to defend him, why, naturally you'd get it. . . . It's a wonder my head isn't as big as a garbage can, you know, the way he used to get my head knocked in. 'Cause he'd mess with people, mess with people's wives and things like that, women, he didn't have no respect for nobody. When he got to drinking. [It was very seldom that] he wasn't drinking too heavy."[7]

Robert really did see the road as his home and was always in quest of something new. "You could wake Robert up, you could quit playing at 2 o'clock and wake Robert up at three-thirty and say 'I hear a train making up, what you wanna do, catch it?' 'Yeah, let's catch it,' [he'd say]. He wouldn't exchange no words with you; he's just ready to go. Robert was one of the first hippies. But Robert was the cleanest hippie you'd ever see in your life. Robert could take a pair of pants, and press 'em, and roll 'em up and put 'em into a paper bag. He'd carry 'em for a week, and take those pants and shake 'em out, and it'd be straight."[8]

Unattached or attached, married or divorced, young or old, thin or heavy, women were Robert's main pursuit. In spite of their care, however, he always ended up abandoning them, re-creating what had happened to him during his formative years with his mother, Julia. Shines attempted to explain his behavior. "Since Robert was the particular person that he was, you would have to say that his love life was very slack or open. You see, no woman really had an iron hand on Robert at any time. When his time came to go, he just went. I never could see how a man could be quite so neutral. I have seen him treated so royally that you would think he would never depart from this kindhearted woman that would do anything in the world for him. But how wrong can you be?" And unfortunately, Robert was often too forward. "Even men's wives were fair game for him."[9] Robert's reckless behavior with "that type of woman," which Son House had warned him about seven years earlier, led him down a trail of heartbreak.

When the two musicians reached a small Arkansas town, Robert once again repeated his pattern of chasing a married woman. "We were having quite a time in this little town where people gathered every night to gamble, drink, and dance, or whatever employed their minds to do for their pleasure. We were playing regularly in this get-together joint every night and this specific night Robert saw this girl and wanted to meet her. He found another girl who knew her, and got this girl to introduce them. Robert didn't lose any time, even though she told him she was married. Robert would not let her out of his sight the rest of the night. And when we left there a couple of days later she was with us, and she stayed for quite a while. Her name was Louise, and she was everything that Robert wanted: she could sing, dance, drink and fight like hell. Oh, yes, she could play a little guitar too. She and Robert used to get on until she hit him on the head with a hot stove eye."[10]

Sometimes, however, Robert allowed a woman to penetrate his defensive exterior. "I only know two women who might have been near as close, and they were Shakey Horton's sister and Robert Lockwood Jr.'s mother. I have heard Bob talk more about Shakey's sister than anyone else. Robert's mother must have meant quite a bit to him too, because he called her his wife. I am sure that you've noticed that I call these ladies 'girls,' but that is just a figure of speech, because there was only one girl in the bunch, and that was Horton's sister. She was in her early teens, but the rest were thirty and older. Robert spent a lot of time getting the attention of girls without knowing it himself, and he spent the rest of the time trying to get away from them." Regardless of the consequences, Robert never stopped pursuing women. "Women, to Robert, were like motel or hotel rooms: even if he used them he repeatedly left them where he found them. Robert was like a sailor—with one exception: a sailor has a girl in every port but Robert had a woman in every town. Heaven help him, he was not discriminating—probably a bit like Christ. He loved them all—the old, young, fat, thin, and the short. They were all alike to Robert. . . . Did Robert really love? Yes, like a hobo loves a train—off one and on another."[11]

As Robert had learned as a boy on his stepfather's farm, the end of picking season (September through December) was when all the musicians would descend on the plantations to try to win over some of that year's farming profits (if there were any). He knew, therefore, that these were the best months for a traveling musician in the South since there was more available money and less labor for the workers to do, which meant more frolicking. West Memphis was a particularly good place to make money at this time, and toward the end of 1937 Shines and Robert were living there in a boarding house. Built around the lumber industry, West Memphis had a population of under one thousand but had a significant black nightlife. Eighth Street was known as "Little Chicago" and was as famous for its clubs as was Memphis's Beale Street.

West Memphis was a wide-open town and Robert had no trouble connecting with several local women. "We were in West Memphis, Arkansas, playing for a fellow called 'City.' There was a girl not more than a midget in height and size who also lived in this boarding house that we all took for granted because she was always running errands for us as well as anyone else in the neighborhood. When she would make a run for us, the change that was left, we would give it to her because we thought she was just a very nice girl. One day we missed Robert and thought he was on Eighth Street with a girl that he gave quite a bit of attention to. We were satisfied with this explanation until the girl we thought he was with came over with food for Robert, and the rest of us too, but when she didn't find Robert we had to make a quick guess as to where he was regardless of what we really thought. So we said he was in Memphis, but she wanted no part of this and was getting quite angry. So somebody had to find him." Knowing Robert's habits, Shines guessed where Robert had gone. "Well, I knew this little girl was up and around early and she might know where Robert was—and she did. One guess, and I bet you are right! He was there in her bed. She

West Memphis boarding houses. *Margaret Elizabeth Woolfolk*

only had one room and since it would have looked kind of foolish to ask her to go out of her room so I could talk to Robert, I told her what happened, and she was very broad-minded about the whole thing. She in turn told Robert a way to get out of the hotel without being seen, and it worked. After that Robert used this exit quite often, but he was not always coming from the little girl's room!"[12]

These boarding houses were flimsy contraptions with walls so thin you could hear a conversation in the next room. Such a ramshackle structure was an imminent fire hazard and when a blaze finally occurred Shines saw another previously unknown side of Robert's character and talents. "We was in West Memphis and we was staying at a fellow's place called Hunt. Robert and I went out to get something to eat, little drink, we looked up and we saw a fire. Robert said, 'That looks like Hunt's place.' I said, 'Yeah, it is!' Our guitars were in there. When we got there the place was burned on down to the ground. Our guitars were in there. So we started up [Highway 61] walking. And I didn't know Robert knew how to blow a harmonica. I never knew he knew anything about a harmonica at all. Robert had a harmonica in his pocket. He reached in his pocket and got his harmonica out and started blowing it. We blocked up Highway 61. He blowin' harmonica and I'm singing, and then he was singing and blowing, pattin' our hands and dancing. And we made enough money then on the highway, the highway patrolmen had to come and direct the traffic, 'cause people blocked the highway up. And we made enough money right then on the highway that when we got to Steele, Missouri, we bought two brand new guitars. Kept going."[13]

Reportedly Shines bought a new Stella and Robert bought a Kalamazoo KG-14. Such guitars sold new for $9.95 and $14.50, respectively. Eventually they found themselves back in Memphis in early 1938, and they separated for a brief period. But a violent act brought them together again for their most far-reaching trip.

Sometime during this period of separation, Robert apparently decided to take another photo of himself. Much speculation has been given as to when this dime store photo was taken. Some have insisted that it was taken in San Antonio, while others want to place the location in cities that can then lay claim to this important part of cultural history. The simple fact is that we do not know where it was taken, but we can estimate when it was done. Since it is generally agreed upon that the guitar Robert is holding is a Kalamazoo KG-14, and since that guitar did not become available until 1936, the photo had to be taken after that. The only record of a boarding house fire in West Memphis occurred on December 11, 1937. Since Shines remembers Robert purchasing a Kalamazoo after the boarding house fire, but has no recollection of Robert taking such a photo, it was probably done during their brief separation.

The photo is interesting for several reasons. First, it is Robert posing himself. This is Robert Johnson as he imagined himself to be, as he wanted others to see him. Second, it is no longer a photo of a young optimistic guitarist, but rather seems to portray a road-seasoned veteran who projects the journeys, both good and bad, of his life. He holds an unlit cigarette in his mouth, perhaps to indicate a certain worldliness or toughness. He no longer wears a suit, but is in a plain shirt and suspenders. He holds his guitar in a manner not very playable, but rather to show off his chording and long fingers. He stares directly at the camera with a rather stoic intent. This is Robert Johnson the blues musician.

Once Shines reunited with Robert their last adventure together would take shape. As Shines remembered, "My cousin, Calvin Frazier, had gotten in a little mix-up in Arkansas in which his brother was killed. And his arm was broken in two places. But he killed a couple of the guys that was shooting at him and his brother. He went to the John Gaston hospital and he was arrested in the John Gaston hospital, but they never did carry him to jail. They told him, 'Don't leave town.' He didn't leave town, so he had a magistrate's hearing, we went down to this hearing, and they told him, 'Frazier, we understand what your problem was and everything. We never had no trouble with you Fraziers, and neither you Shineses, not here. Suppose you just get up and walk out of here right now and we didn't know where you went. We couldn't tell nobody where you went if you walked out of here. Because if that man over in Arkansas gets you back over there, then he gonna give you a lotta trouble because one of those guys was one of his pets. They told him everything that happened on that farm. He was one of his pets, and you killed him. He wants you pretty bad, but he's not going to take the expense of trying to get you from outside the United States. Suppose you just got up and walked on out of the United States somewhere. We couldn't tell him where you went or anything like that. 'Cause we don't know where you're going. All we know is you're gonna leave here.' So we got up and walked out. We went on up in Canada."[14]

The three men—Johnny Shines, Robert Johnson, and Calvin Frazier—quickly headed north with the ultimate intention of reaching Canada. Hopping freight trains, hitchhiking, or just walking, the trio made their way toward Chicago. Along the way they learned more about how Robert operated as a musician. For

Robert Johnson, dime store photo. © *Delta Haze Corporation*

Robert, the rules for making money were specific, and he was adamant how he wanted it done. First: find the right place to play. "Just try to find out where the Black neighborhood was. Walk up and down the railroad track and just watch to see which side the Black kids are on. Whichever side we find the Black kids on, that's the side we go, 'cause that was the Black side. All the towns was segregated then—whites on one side of the tracks, Blacks on the other one."[15] Second: divide up the work. Robert didn't like playing with another musician on the streets because it would reduce the amount of money each could make. "Robert's motto was this: 'You make your money and I'll make mine. You play on this corner, I'll play on the next corner.' If we was together and made a quarter we'd have twelve and a half cents a piece. But if I was on this corner

Calvin Frazier. *Blues Archive at the University of Mississippi Libraries*

and he was on that corner and each of us made a quarter we'd have twenty-five cents a piece."[16]

As usual, even on the extented trip together Robert revealed little about his personal life. Shines remembered him being distant yet focused. "Well, I don't know if he had a personality. He had an approach. You know. He was a musician and he approached you as a musician. With song and play. If he liked you he liked you, if he didn't he didn't. He didn't pretend that he liked you. He didn't talk very much. He thought all the time."[17]

Robert didn't have to talk much about himself because his music revealed him as a vulnerable, deeply feeling man. And that's what allowed him to have such success with the women. Shines recalls Robert making an audience cry through his passionate playing: "Things like that often happened. And I think Robert would cry just as hard as anyone. It was things like this, it seems to me, that made Robert want to be by himself, and he would soon be by himself. The thing that was different, I think, was that Robert would do his crying on the inside. Yes, his crying was on the inside."[18]

Playing blues came with powerful moral condemnation, as Johnny Shines remembered: "A lot of black people, if they heard a young man even whistling the blues, they wouldn't allow him in their house, their yard, stop him at the gate. 'Go away, you're the devil.' They was afraid he'd bring a curse on them."[19] Robert may not have made a deal at the crossroads, but he was familiar enough with his own pain and with hoodoo beliefs that, having been rebuked several times for playing the devil's music, it would have been hard for him to completely dismiss ideas about the devil. And if you really thought that there was evil in your life, then why not spend it drinking, womanizing, and rambling? After all, for Robert, no place could ever truly be home. Many people confirmed his tendency to vanish quickly, to be in someone's company one minute and the next be gone, which explains why he didn't hesitate to leave

Memphis with Shines and Frazier. The trio of musicians thought they were leaving the Jim Crow South behind as they headed north, but the Depression and the Great Migration of blacks out of the South to northern industrial centers had created a new form of racism.

The group traveled north out of Memphis on Highway 51 until they hit Wickliffe, Kentucky, on the Mississippi River. There they had their first on-the-road romantic encounter. "[We] met some girls that I liked very much. They were a dance team that had never been no place and wanted to be seen and heard. I should have said a song-and-dance team of four people. They could really go to town, and I wanted to take them with us when we left and had it all arranged, but Bob, he would slip from one girl to the other until he had them all fighting among themselves. Now he was ready to give them the slip, and we did. It seems to me that where there were no women around, that's where Robert would find the woman he liked best; and he had to have her or go to hell trying to get her. And he got her."[20]

From Wickliffe they crossed the Mississippi River into Missouri and followed Highway 55 north to Saint Louis. There they met two well-known blues musicians: the much-recorded "Devil's Son-in-Law, the High Sheriff from Hell" Peetie Wheatstraw, and Blind Teddy Darby. Shines recalled them as "people you couldn't forget because of their type of music. I liked Teddy Darby's songs and I thought he was a pretty good player. And Peetie Wheatstraw, I thought he was great. We hit Saint Louis on that trip but we didn't stay there too long."[21]

From Saint Louis they continued north until they reached Decatur, Illinois, where they were hired to play for a white square dance. Their performances for white audiences in the North exposed them to a new type of racism that they hadn't seen in the South. Shines recalled their surprise at another event in Illinois. "We was in

Illinois and we stopped at this café and a fellow asked us to come in and play a piece or two and we played, and he hired us to play. And I didn't know, I know I didn't ever see any black people in there, but I didn't know it was a town where there wasn't any black people, none whatsoever. And every once in a while we'd see somebody try to peep in through the curtain, or over the curtain, get up on top of the car hood try to peep in over the curtain. So finally a fellow told us, 'This man was making a bunch of money off y'all, ain't he?' And I said 'How's that?' 'He's got people paying seventy-five cents a piece or something like that just to come in and see you all. Black people.' Well he didn't say black people, he said 'you niggers.' So I told Robert about it and we left the guy. He was payin' us good money to be there, but we didn't want to be there exhibited as niggers, you know? I didn't feel as though I should've been exhibited as that. An attraction. The music with most people was very effective. They liked the music. Even though they didn't like the faces doing the music."[22]

Eventually they arrived in the Windy City. Although the Harlem Renaissance of the 1920s gained much greater attention, Chicago was undergoing its own aesthetic flowering in the arts in the 1930s. The Great Migration brought thousands of southern blacks to northen cities such as Chicago, Detroit, Cleveland, and Pittsburgh, where manufacturing was booming. There they developed an urban culture that influenced all manner of the arts. By this time Chicago had already become a home for recording and performing music, and the new migrants quickly made their presence felt. The South Side of Chicago soon became known as the "Black Belt" or "Black Ghetto" and the more racist "Darkie Town." The new spirit of racial pride caused many blacks to resent these names until James J. Gentry, a theater editor for the *Chicago Bee,* suggested that the word Bronzeville should be used to identify the community. Most Chicago blacks loved the idea.

In addition to a cultural renaissance, Chicago was undergoing a musical shift largely spearheaded by Lester Melrose, who worked for several record labels simultaneously in the 1930s, including RCA Victor, Bluebird, Columbia, and Okeh. Melrose, along with J. Mayo Williams of Decca, helped found the sound known as the Chicago blues. Most of his recordings were made with a small group of session musicians and had a similar sound. The Chicago blues of the 1930s was largely full-band arrangements, ensemble playing with a rhythm section. The arrangements appealed to the increasingly urbanized black record-buying audience. Among the artists he recorded were Big Bill Broonzy, Sonny Boy Williamson, Memphis Minnie, Roosevelt Sykes, Lonnie Johnson, Big Joe Williams, and Washboard Sam.

Maxwell Street on the South Side flourished as the main center for these bluesmen. In the 1880s, Eastern European Jews had become the dominant ethnic group in the neighborhood, which remained predominantly Jewish until the 1920s. During this period the open-air pushcart market made the neighborhood famous. After 1920, most of the residents were blacks who came north in the Great Migration, although most businesses continued to be Jewish owned. In the 1930s and 1940s, when many black musicians came to Chicago from the segregated South, they brought with them their outdoor music. The area soon became well known for its street musicians, mostly playing the blues, but also gospel and other styles. Almost all of the musicians already in Chicago also played on Maxwell Street. Although there are no specific reports of such encounters, it seems likely that Robert, as a recording artist with at least one minor hit—"Terraplane Blues"—would have met Broonzy, Memphis Minnie, or some of the other local players while in Chicago.

From Chicago the trio headed east, bound ultimately for Canada, but stopped first in Detroit, just across the river from Windsor,

Ontario. The Black Bottom or Paradise Alley section of Detroit was the equivalent of Chicago's Bronzeville. Originally settled by Jewish immigrants, in the 1920s it began to be home for black migrants coming from the South looking for industrial jobs. The inexpensive, wood-framed houses that lined Hastings Street made suitable housing for the new black residents and soon the area rivaled New York's Harlem, Beale Street in Memphis, or Maxwell Street in Chicago for its entertainment, especially the blues. Bessie Smith performed on Hastings Street, Blind Blake named one of his songs after it, and other artists like Barbecue Bob (Robert Hicks), Victoria Spivey, and Bob Campbell all sang about Detroit in the 1920s and 30s.

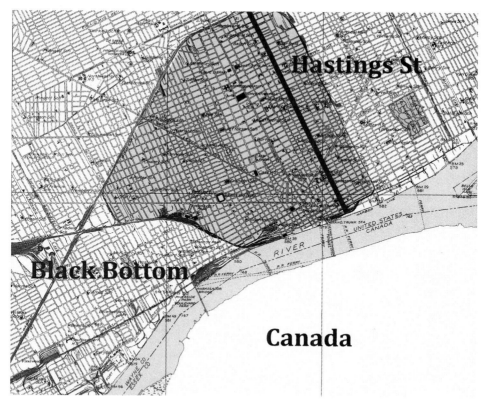

Map of Detroit's Black Bottom and Hastings Street. *Bruce Conforth*

Soon after arriving the trio met blues pianist Big Maceo Merriweather and performed with him in one or more of the clubs in which Merriweather played—The Post Club, Brown's Bar, and Crystal Bar, among others. But it was Robert's recordings that led to two of their most interesting musical performances in the area. The Reverend Clarence Leslie Morton Sr. hired Robert and Shines to perform on his Windsor-Chatham gospel radio show.[23] Morton was called to religious service as a child, and although a doctor's prognosis gave him only a few years to live, he apparently experienced several "divine interventions" and was healed. Never allowed to attend school, he nonetheless acquired, through what some claimed to be supernatural means, the ability to read and write. His religious convictions forced him to refuse to fight in the First World War and, although sentenced to prison for his refusal, he was freed by the passing of the conscientious objector law. This allowed him to return to religious practice. He created several Full Gospel, Pentecostal churches in Canada and preached on the streets of Windsor. In 1936 his ministry had become large enough that he became one of the earliest black preachers to have his own international radio program.[24]

Originally the show was broadcast only on radio station CFCO in Chatham, but by 1938 it was being aired on CKLW from Windsor and was also heard in Detroit. Morton was no stranger to the blues. Joe Stenson and Arkaner Campbell, the parents of his second wife, Mathilda Stenson, came from a "long line of guitar pickers and blues singers." Arkaner was possibly related to Bob Campbell who sang about Detroit.[25] Johnny Shines well remembered their performance at his church. "He was a preacher and he broadcasted out of Canada. Lots of people could pick him up back over there in Detroit and all over Canada. He was a sanctified preacher, and he wanted a lot of music with his outfit, you know. He had a pretty good-sized choir. Robert, Calvin, and myself, we go over there and play for him."[26] The trio played the gospel songs "Ship of Zion," "Stand by Me," "When the Saints Go Marchin' In," and "Just Over in Glory Land." The following week they played for a riverfront baptism for Reverand Morton at the mouth of the Detroit River.

Robert soon heard the road calling for him again. Frazier had relatives in Detroit and decided to stay there, while Shines and Robert left and headed for Buffalo, New York, where Shines recalled "there were several places we could play."[27] Whether they then stopped in New Jersey or went directly to New York City is unknown; however, Shines did recall that in Paterson or Newark, New Jersey, there were two or three places they played—speakeasies, taverns, houses. Both cities had large black populations and Harlem was only nineteen miles away. Finding work was easy since John Henry Hammond II had already praised Robert in his writings and his records were on local jukeboxes. "[We'd] hear 'em on jukeboxes," Shines remembered. "[Robert] was very proud of having it."[28]

Playing popular tunes, as well as anything else requested by the crowds, added to their popularity and marketability. And if they didn't know a particular song they just played the correct tempo for dancing. Shines commented that for waltzes "you could play anything just so long as you played it in cut-time, ¾ time. You could make up your numbers; you just had to set the right tempo."[29] This ability to fake their way through any genre provided varied opportunities. While in New York City they were asked to return to Newark to perform at an Italian wedding. As Shines noted, they already knew polkas and Jewish music, and for the wedding they played primarily tarantellas, adapting some of their own songs, a few standards, and some new ones to conform to the traditional 6/8 tarantella rhythm.[30]

Returning to New York City, Robert and Shines started seeing women in town, but Robert refused serious romance. He had a special goal on his mind: to appear on, and perhaps win, the *Major*

Bowes Amateur Hour. In order to pursue this dream he left Shines to seek his own fame.

Edward Bowes's show was broadcast on the CBS network during the 1930s and 1940s. Amateur winners of his program were invited to tour vaudeville theaters under the Major Bowes name. It became a launching pad for many famous artists. Frank Sinatra originally appeared on the show as part of the Hoboken Four quartet in 1935; and Maria Callas performed a piece from *Madame Butterfly* when she was only eleven. After Bowes's death the show reappared on television with host Ted Mack and was the forerunner of such popular television shows as *Star Search* in the 1970s, *American Idol,* and *The Voice.*

For Robert, as for thousands of other poor blacks from the South, the *Amateur Hour* looked like a one-way ticket to fame. He had already fulfilled one of his ambitions by becoming a recording artist; now he wanted to take an even larger step toward national success. But it was simply not to be. Over ten thousand people applied to be on the *Major Bowes* show every week, and only a few hundred were auditioned. We do not know

what happened, but it's likely that if Robert got the chance to audition, his listeners weren't interested.

Regardless, Harlem did provide myriad opportunities for Johnson and Shines. In 1938 the Harlem Renaissance was long past its peak, but the Apollo Theater had opened in 1934; in 1935 *Porgy and Bess* opened on Broadway with an all-black cast; Langston Hughes, Countee Cullen, Zora Neale Hurston, Claude McKay, and other black writers were publishing their written works, and black visual artists such as Aaron Douglas were exhibiting their own gallery shows. Paul Robeson was being featured in films and performances, and clubs like the Alhambra Ballroom, Clark Monroe's Uptown House, Barron's Club, the Theatrical Grill, and the Sugar Cane Club were among the many venues in Harlem that kept the nights jumping. There one could find such artists as Bessie Smith, Jelly Roll Morton, Frank Manning, Billie Holiday, Cab Calloway, Duke Ellington, Louis Armstrong, Ethel Waters, and Count Basie in residence. The great blues singer Victoria Spivey ("Black Snake Blues," "My Handy Man," "Dope Head Blues," etc.) was working in Broadway musicals and was appearing in the hit *Hellzapoppin'* when she ran into Robert in Harlem, as she later related to John Paul Hammond.[31] And Harlem wasn't just getting jazzier, it was also going electric.

Charlie Christian had begun using an electric guitar in 1936, and the instrument was becoming a standard in jazz ensembles. After meeting a local club musician on the streets of Harlem, Robert was invited to play the man's electric guitar. The musician saw Robert and Shines carrying acoustic guitars and wanted to turn them on to the latest technology. He took them to the club where his guitar and amplifier were set up and let Robert try his hand at playing it. Although he liked the volume, Robert told the guitarist and Shines he "couldn't make it talk" like he wanted.[32] The necessity of having to carry an amplifier to use with the guitar would also have seriously impaired Robert's wanderlust. And, of course, many of the jukes, plantations, parties, and picnics that he played had no electricity. Robert had no use for an electric guitar. He was happy with his small-bodied acoustic Kalamazoo.

With or without electricity, the music they performed in New York and New Jersey was still good enough to make them, by Shines's own admission, "good money." Their audiences appreciated their skills, and by this time the two musicians had been playing together so long that Shines said they "were really unloading."[33]

Robert showed merely a friendly interest in the women he was seeing, and no matter how they pleased him they weren't enough to keep him in New York. His plan to appear on the *Major Bowes* show had failed, almost certainly leaving him disappointed. Finally, the guitarists there were playing new instruments louder and faster than his songs called for. It was time to ramble again: destination Chicago.

Robert and Shines backtracked to Chicago only to have Robert disappear again. A befuddled Shines eventually heard that he was back in Saint Louis and found him again there, but as quickly as Shines found him Robert left for Blythesville, Arkansas. Then he went back to Memphis; on to Hughes, Arkansas; and finally to Helena, where Shines found him for the very last time. Their trip had lasted three months and it was turning to early spring 1938. It seemed like Robert was being driven faster than ever, but he still wanted Shines to come with him. "He was going over to Friars Point, and he wanted me to go with him, and I said, 'No, no. I don't want nothing in Mississippi. Nothing!' I wouldn't go to Mississippi with him. So he went there by hisself. It was open season on black people in Mississippi at that time. Kill 'em anywhere you see 'em. And hell, I didn't like that. So I went back in Arkansas."[34]

Robert went back to Memphis to visit his family, and then his mother in Robinsonville. After saying his final good-byes, he headed south. It was the last trip of his Delta rambling.

ᵅᶳ16ᶖᵒ

YOU MAY BURY MY BODY DOWN
BY THE HIGHWAY SIDE

In early 1938, CBS (Columbia Broadcasting System) purchased the ARC/Vocalion labels and immediately discontinued the five cheap twenty-five-cent labels that had featured releases by Robert Johnson. It kept its thirty-five-cent Vocalion label and issued Robert's recordings into early 1939. However, Robert was not called back to Texas for more recordings in 1938 because of poor sales from his 1937 session. He was deeply disappointed that none of his Dallas recordings met with the success of "Terraplane Blues" or any of the others from his San Antonio session. At Dallas he had produced some of his most memorable and arguably original recordings, but the music business, including the blues, was changing drastically and was quickly evolving into a city sound that no longer featured a solo guitarist but rather an ensemble that might feature an electric guitar. Robert was still able to continue his weekly performing out of Helena, Arkansas, and despite these changes his country blues style guitar was still popular on plantations as he went back and forth between the Mississippi and Arkansas Delta regions. Sometimes he went to towns where he had been previously popular along the Yazoo and Mississippi Valley Railroad (Yellow Dog), which ran from Clarksdale south to Yazoo City over two different routes. "I been down yonder on that old Mud Line," he told Elizabeth, referring to the rail line. "I sure had me a time down there."[1] Sometimes Robert mentioned performing in Lambert, a small town just northeast of Clarksdale, and other small towns where country dances were always staged on Saturday nights with a musician providing the music. He was primarily traveling alone now, not with Shines or Frazier. "Whenever he come into a place where I'd be playing, he always be by himself. Never saw him with anybody else. Strictly a lone wolf," Shines recalled. "The only thing he was ever close to was his guitar and he never let that go; took it with him everywhere."[2]

One Delta town that was easily accessible by car, bus, or train was Greenwood. One of the three largest towns in the Delta, in 1930 it had a population of just over eleven thousand. On its streets, Robert had no competition to match his skills or reputation. He had been to Greenwood many times before and, like many of the places he traveled to, he had extended family there. A relative, Jessie Dodds, whose family was from Hazlehurst and kin to Robert's stepfather, Charlie Dodds Spencer, lived on the nearby Star of the West plantation. Before he left Memphis, however, at the urging of his half sister Carrie, Robert went to see a doctor for stomach and chest pains. The doctor at the John Gaston Hospital there diagnosed him as having an ulcer and advised Robert to quit drinking, advice he was *not* going to follow. Concerned about his welfare, Carrie didn't want him to leave Memphis, but he left for Greenwood anyway.[3]

The seat of Leflore County, Greenwood, is on the eastern edge of the Mississippi Delta, 96 miles north of Jackson and 130 miles south of Memphis. It was a center of cotton planter culture and its two rail lines shortened transportation to cotton markets. Front Street, bordering the Yazoo River, was filled with cotton brokers and related businesses and was known as Cotton Row.

Howard Street, Greenwood, Mississippi, 1930s. *Bruce Conforth*

Baptist Town, where Robert stayed whenever he visited Greenwood, is one of the town's oldest black neighborhoods. It was settled in the 1800s as the cotton industry began to flourish. Robert could rent a room there for only three dollars a week: easy money for a Delta guitarist of his skill. Life there was undemanding for Robert. He played on the streets of Greenwood during the day, in local jukes in the evening, and when they closed, unless he had a better offer, he would play on one of the nearby plantations. There was no closing time for a juke at a plantation, especially on weekends. There was also no electricity in most plantation jukes, so kerosene lamps and barrels provided illumination and heat. In contrast, in Greenwood proper, he had to compete with loud volume recordings on jukeboxes—even his own records. Sometimes audiences didn't even believe that he was the same artist on those recordings. Honeyboy Edwards remembered a 1938 situation where such an event occured.

"When I first met him he was on Johnson Street near Main in Greenwood, playing right back on the alley. He was right outside of Emma Collins's—she kept a good-timing house and used to sell whiskey too. He was standing on a block and had a crowd of people back in the alley ganging around him. But they didn't know who he was! I didn't know at first either, and when I walked up I thought he was sounding a little like Kokomo Arnold. I walked up with my little old guitar, put mine on back and started listening. He was playing the blues so good.

"One woman, she was full of that old corn whiskey. She said, 'Mister, you play me "Terraplane Blues!"' She didn't know she was talking to the man who made it! She said, 'If you play me "Terraplane Blues," I'll give you a dime!' He said, 'Miss, that's my number.' 'Well, you play it then.' He started playing and they knew who he was then. He was playing and trembling and hollering. It was a little after noon and the people was coming out of the country, coming to town. He had the street blocked with all the people listening to him play.

"He was dressed nice, wearing a brown hat. He wore a hat most of the time broke down over that bad eye. I got acquainted with him when he finished playing. We started talking and I found out he was from around Robinsonville, had just been through Tunica. I asked him did he know my cousin there, Willie Mae Powell, and he said, 'That's my girlfriend!' And I said 'That's my first cousin!' So we started to laughing, chatting it up a bit and we kind of hooked up and started drinking and hanging around together. That's how I got attached with him. I met him and found out he was going with my cousin."[4]

The two men quickly became part of a Greenwood musical scene that centered around the home of Tommy and Ophelia McClennan. Although McClennan, nicknamed "Sugar," didn't start recording until the year after Robert died, he became one of the most successful down-home blues recording artists, with twenty singles for the Bluebird label (1939–1942). Among his most notable numbers were "Bottle It Up and Go," "Cross Cut Saw," "Travelin' Highway

David "Honeyboy" Edwards. *Bruce Conforth*

Man," and "New Highway No. 51 Blues." Also included in this musical scene were Robert Petway and Hound Dog Taylor. The men helped introduce Robert to many available, and some unavailable but willing, women, and true to his character, he soon started seeing several of them. As Johnny Shines said, "Sometimes he was too forward. Even men's wives were fair game for him."[5]

This stay in Greenwood was no exception. Soon Robert pursued the daughter of one of the sharecroppers on the Star of West plantation. The sharecropper was known only as "Tush Hog," and he and his family had come from Tunica County, where Robert was extremely well known and had extended family. Tush Hog was a common nickname for an individual who, in any situation or group, was shown respect as the ultimate authority. Such a person had a strong personality, and generally the physical ability to back it up. Plantation worker Rosie Eskridge said she never knew Tush Hog's last name and she asserted that "people didn't go round asking somebody their last name."[6]

Robert followed Tush Hog's daughter to the plantation store and juke house known as Three Forks, only a few hundred yards from the intersection of Highways 49 and 82 on the edge of the plantation. Eskridge recalled that Robert would "follow her out on Saturday nights. Tush Hog's baby girl. I don't know what the child's name was. We didn't even know [Robert] was on the place. He followed her out here."[7] However, at that juke Robert met a woman named Beatrice Davis, the wife of R. D. "Ralph" Davis, who also lived on the plantation.[8] Davis worked at the Three Forks store on weekends, doling out drinks to the patrons.

Robert once more went for the wrong woman, and the two found a mutual attraction and started seeing each other regularly. Beatrice had a sister living in Baptist Town near where Robert was staying, and every Monday she would tell her husband that she was going into Greenwood to see her sister. But this was merely an excuse for her to spend the afternoon having sex with Robert in his room.

Through mutual friends R. D. found out that the two were having an affair, and when he heard that Robert was hired to play a country-dance at the Three Forks juke on two successive weekends, he decided to act. On Saturday night, August 13, 1938, at around eleven, Davis gave the unknowing Beatrice a jar of corn liquor in which he had dissolved several mothballs. During a break from performing Robert drank from that bottle. The ingredient that Davis had surreptitiously slipped into the jar was a mostly colorless, odorless, tasteless poison known then as "passagreen" but now as naphthalin. Although it was a common way of poisoning people in the rural South, it was rarely, if ever, fatal. It was even used to remove troublesome drunks from bars or jukes because it would simply make them incapacitated. When Davis was found years later, he confessed that he "really didn't want to cause any trouble" because he genuinely meant it. If we are to believe his own admission, he really hadn't intended to kill Robert. Normally the concoction Davis prepared would have primarily caused confusion, nausea, vomiting, and other gastrointestinal distress. Nevertheless, any attempt to put a harmful substance in his drink must still be considered an act of violence.

But Robert, only a month earlier, had been diagnosed with an ulcer by a Memphis doctor, and was also suffering from esophageal varices, which caused the chest pains he experienced. The mixture Davis gave him, while not fatal, was strong enough to cause the ulcer and varices to hemorrhage.

There are several versions of the ensuing drama. Sonny Boy Williamson said that he knocked a bottle of un-bonded, already opened whiskey out of Robert's hand, or that Robert died in his arms in an ambulance on the way to a hospital in Jackson. Those stories are either exaggerations or outright lies. The most reliable account, corroborated by Rosie Eskridge, is that of Honeyboy Edwards, who explained exactly what happened that night. His narrative lacks the histrionics or romanticism of the falsehoods.

When I come back to the Delta, Robert was in Greenwood playing for this same man. And one Saturday a bunch of us

went out to Three Forks on an old flat-bottomed truck. We
was all high, ready to ball all night long. When we got there
Robert was sitting in a corner with his guitar under his arm.
He was sick. And the women jumped off the truck, come in,
and said to him, "Play me 'Terraplane Blues.'" "Play me 'Kind
Hearted Woman Blues'!" He said, "I'm sick." And they said,
"Have a drink of whiskey. Have another drink and you'll feel
alright."

But Robert had got poisoned. Robert was crazy about
whiskey and this man was mad about Robert going with his
wife. He had a friend lady give Robert a glass of whiskey that
had poison in it. People would do that. They poison you
rather than shoot you, get you in a smooth way. That way
people don't know what you done. All the folks kept on hollering "Play!" "Play!" "Play!" He tried to play once or twice
but couldn't and said, "I'm sick. I can't play." They took him
and laid him across a bed in the back room. And everything
got quiet then. Before day, some guy who had an old car carried him back to Greenwood, to his room in Baptist Town.[9]

The basic facts of Honeyboy's story are true. At first, the dosed
liquor only made Robert nauseous and confused. It incapacitated
him enough to prevent him from playing, and that's when he was
taken into a back room to try to recover. But the nausea became
worse and Robert's pain increased. Seeing that he was not improv-
ing, a few of the juke's patrons decided it to bring him back into
Baptist Town to sleep it off. Davis must have been satisfied that his
trick had taught Robert a lesson and that he had been forced to
leave Three Forks and Beatrice.

Once Robert was dropped off at his Baptist Town room he was
alone and languished in pain, his stomach cramping and the nausea
getting worse. He must have vomited, causing some of the varices

in his esophagus to rupture blood, for when he was visited the next day it was reported that he was howling and bleeding at the mouth. It's not uncommon for an esophageal hemorrhage to start as a preliminary bleed and then to stop, only to be followed by a larger, fatal attack soon after.

Robert languished for two days in his room with severe abdominal pains, vomiting, and bleeding from the mouth. Bleeding in the esophagus is extremely serious, with a death rate greater than 50 percent of cases, even with the attention of a doctor. Without medical attention there was little or no chance of survival. In 1938 Greenwood had a Colored Hospital where Robert could have been treated, but he was in no condition to go there himself, and no one else wanted to be implicated in what might have eventually been seen as murder. Even if he were taken to the hospital, there was little medical help to save his life: his loss of blood alone would have been fatal.

The night before Robert's death, either through his daughter's pleadings or the request of Robert's relative Jessie, Tush Hog went to Baptist Town and brought Robert back to his plantation house. Robert survived an excruciating night but had a major hemorrhage and died early Tuesday morning at Tush Hog's shack. Tush Hog knew that the plantation overseer had to be alerted, and he informed Luther Wade, his employer, that someone had died in his house, but since Robert wasn't one of Wade's workers, Wade only asked a few questions before deciding to bury the body.

That morning was a hot, torrid summer day and Wade walked to the Eskridges' house in search of Rosie's husband, Tom. "Mr. Wade come to our house up in the day," she remembered, explaining how she and Tom became involved in one of the blues's longest mysteries. "He told my husband, Tom, to go to [Little Zion Baptist, the church Wade used for burials for his sharecroppers] and dig that grave for that man who died that morning. He said the man didn't have no family on the place but he wanted to give him a Christian burial. . . . Wudn't no funeral. Put him in a box, little wood box, nailed it together and put it in the ground," she recalled. "His truck driver went over there [to the county barn], picked up the box, brought it back—put the body in it." Robert's body was wrapped in a white linen sheet and placed in the skinny wooden boxes that were used as coffins for indigents. "Brought it up here—slid it off and come on back. In them days they buried you the same day you died. Wudn't no way to keep a body like today. It would start smellin'." Because of the hot summer day, Eskridge took some cold water to her husband, who dug the grave by himself. "I couldn't see his head in the grave he dug. It must have been seven feet deep," she said. "He dug his grave with a sharpshooter," a small shovel used on plantations. "I took a fruit jar with some water up there for Tom."[10]

The digging was extremely laborious for the earth there is called Mississippi Gumbo—thick clay that can clot and stick like cement to your shoes or anything it touches. Tom Eskridge toiled in the heat but finally finished the grave. Even though Robert apparently never attended church during his blues career, Tom suggested that they find someone to read some words from the Bible before the burial. "My husband told the truck driver to go down there and get Reverend Starks. Reverend Starks come up here—he didn't have no church—and said a few words over him." Starks was a jackleg preacher—he had no formal training or ordination but rather made his living by providing spiritual services in exchange for food, drink, or trade. Eskridge paid no attention to the Bible verse nor had any particular thoughts about the man's burial without family members.

"It was a real hot day. It was in the summer and I wudn't doing nothing, so I walked up there with one of Tush Hog's daughters. He come in here with one of his daughters." But his daughter, Josephine, was "not the same one he come in here with. It was the other one. They both were married. They all come in here together.

They all left here together. Don't know where they went [or] when they left here. They didn't stay here but one year."[11] Traditionally, many sharecroppers farmed for one year on a planter's land and then moved on to another plantation for either more money or better working conditions after the fall harvest.

With little ceremony and brief formalities, Robert Johnson's life had come to an end, and he was buried under a large pecan tree in the small graveyard next to Little Zion Church on Money Road, a twenty-mile road that runs from Greenwood to Highway 8.

When Robert's half sister Carrie Spencer Harris heard of his death back in Memphis she was terribly distraught, "broken up, just torn apart," Annye Anderson recalls.[12] Carrie immediately decided to go to Greenwood with Julia and Dusty Willis and Robert's half sister Bessie Hines, with whom he and Virginia had lived in Bolivar County. She asked several of Robert's other friends to accompany them. One of them, Willie Coffee, was unable to attend but

Little Zion Church and cemetery, Greenwood, Mississippi.
Bruce Conforth

recalled some of the preparations for their trip. He noted that a number of Robert's friends from Commerce, Mississippi, went to Greenwood with Carrie. Coffee had just been the victim of a house fire, however, and did not have the clothes to accompany them.[13] Even by train, in 1938 the one-hundred-plus mile trip would have taken the better part of a day.

Once in Greenwood Carrie contacted the only local black undertaker, Paul McDonald, who had one of his embalmers, Fletcher Jones, exhume Robert's body, remove it from the pine box the county provided, and place it in a proper casket. He was reburied in the same spot with family members and a preacher in attendance.[14] Through McDonald's office, Carrie was able to obtain a copy of Robert's death certificate that had been filed on Thursday, August 18.

The certificate provided all correct family information: the name of his mother with her maiden name, Julia Major; the name of his biological father, Noah Johnson; the fact that he was born in Hazelhurst [sic], Mississippi; that he was "about 26" (actually twenty-seven) years old; and that he had been a musician for ten years (further evidence that he was performing before he met Son House in 1930). The cause of death was listed as "No Doctor," and the information was provided by one Jim Moore. The identity of Moore remained a mystery until Rosie Eskridge was interviewed. She confirmed that Moore had lived on the plantation for at least ten years. "Jim Moore farmed across the river, on the other side of the river. I knew him well. He lived here for years and years. He was a tall, light skinned man. Had a wife and one daughter. He left here years ago. That man's been dead for years."[15] Recently examined census records also confirm that Moore was indeed a resident of the plantation and lived there with his wife, Callie; daughter, Mildred; sons Alis and James; and six grandchildren. But most important, Moore's neighbor in 1938 was Jessie Dodds, Robert's relative.

Carrie had heard rumors that her half brother had been poisoned, and through McDonald she contacted the state's director of

STATE OF MISSISSIPPI

MISSISSIPPI STATE DEPARTMENT OF HEALTH
VITAL RECORDS

BUREAU OF VITAL STATISTICS   STANDARD CERTIFICATE OF DEATH   State File No. 13704

MISSISSIPPI STATE BOARD OF HEALTH

1. PLACE OF DEATH
County *Leflore*
Registered No.
Voting Precinct _____ or Village _____
or City *Greenwood (Outside)* _____ St., _____ Ward
(If death occurred in a hospital or institution, give its NAME instead of street and number)
Length of residence in city or town where death occurred _____ ds. How long in U. S., if of foreign birth? _____ yrs. _____ mos. _____ ds.

2. FULL NAME *Robert L. Johnson* (Write or Print Name Plainly)
(a) Residence: No. *Greenwood Miss.* St., _____ Ward
(Usual place of abode) (If nonresident give city or town and State)

PERSONAL AND STATISTICAL PARTICULARS

3. SEX *M*   4. COLOR OR RACE *B*   5. Single, Married, Widowed, or Divorced (write the word) *single*

5a. If married, widowed, or divorced
HUSBAND of (or) WIFE of

6. DATE OF BIRTH (month, day, and year)

7. AGE   Years *26*   Months   Days   If LESS than 1 day, __ hrs. or __ min.

8. Trade, profession, or particular kind of work done, as spinner, sawyer, bookkeeper, etc. *Musician*
9. Industry or business in which work was done, as silk mill, saw mill, bank, etc.
10. Date deceased last worked at this occupation (month and year) *July 1933*   11. Total time (years) spent in this occupation *10*
12. BIRTHPLACE (city or town) (State or country) *Hazlehurst Miss*
13. NAME *Nonald Johnson*
14. BIRTHPLACE (city or town) (State or country) *D K*
15. MAIDEN NAME *Julia Major*
16. BIRTHPLACE (city or town) (State or country) *miss*
17. INFORMANT (and Address) *Jim Moore*
18. BURIAL, CREMATION, OR REMOVAL
Place *Zion Church*   Date *8-17-1938*
19. UNDERTAKER (and Address) *Family*
20. FILED *8-18-38* 19__ *Cornelia J. Jordan* Registrar

MEDICAL CERTIFICATE OF DEATH

21. DATE OF DEATH (month, day, and year) *8-16-38*
22. I HEREBY CERTIFY, That I attended deceased from _____ 19__ to _____ 19__
I last saw h__ alive on _____ 19__. Death is said to have occurred on the date stated above, at _____
The principal cause of death and related causes of importance in order of onset were as follows: Date of onset

Contributory causes of importance not related to principal cause) *2-2 B*

no Doctor

Name of operation (if any was done) _____ Date of _____
What test confirmed diagnosis? _____
23. If death was due to external causes (violence) fill in also the following: Accident, suicide, or homicide? _____
Date of injury _____ 19__
Where did injury occur? _____
(Specify city or town, county, and State)
Specify whether injury occurred in industry, in home, or in public place _____
Manner of injury _____
Nature of injury _____
24. Was disease or injury in any way related to occupation of deceased? _____ If so, specify _____

(Signed) _____ M. D.
(Address) _____

THIS IS TO CERTIFY THAT THE ABOVE IS A TRUE AND CORRECT COPY OF THE CERTIFICATE ON FILE IN THIS OFFICE

F. E. Thompson Jr. MD
F. E. Thompson Jr. M.D. M.P.H.
STATE HEALTH OFFICER

JUL -9 96

Nita Cox Gunter
Nita Cox Gunter
STATE REGISTRAR

WARNING: A REPRODUCTION OF THIS DOCUMENT RENDERS IT VOID AND INVALID. DO NOT ACCEPT UNLESS EMBOSSED SEAL OF THE MISSISSIPPI STATE BOARD OF HEALTH IS PRESENT. IT IS ILLEGAL TO ALTER OR COUNTERFEIT THIS DOCUMENT.

Front of Robert Johnson's death certificate. *Mississippi State Board of Health*

health, Dr. R. W. Whitfield, asking him to investigate the possible murder. On the front side of the state document, Cornelia Jordan, the registrar who had signed Robert's death certificate, listed no cause of death—"no doctor" was present to rule on the cause. Under state law, a coroner's inquest must be conducted when such a death occurs. One had not been done. Dr. Whitfield ordered that Jordan investigate the death further. The results of her investigation were mailed to Carrie in Memphis on September 14, 1938. No files exist from that year to confirm whether or not the sheriff's office investigated, but Jordan's report on the back side of the certificate raised interesting questions.

> I talked with the white man on whose place the negro died and I also talked with a negro woman on the place. The plantation owner said this negro man, seemingly about 26 years old, came from near Tunica two or three weeks before he died to play a banjo at a negro dance given there on the plantation. He staid [sic] in the house with some of the negroes saying that he wanted to pick cotton. The white man did not have a doctor for this negro as he had not worked for him. He was buried in a homemade coffin furnished by the County. The plantation owner said it was his opinion that the negro died of syphilis.
>
> I am always glad to make investigations for you. C. Jordan

The white man Jordan spoke to was Wade. The woman could have been one of Tush Hog's daughters, Callie Moore, or even one of Robert's relatives. The information is surprisingly accurate. Robert was about twenty-six years old, he did come from near Tunica, and he had been there a few weeks to play (guitar, not banjo, but an understandable mistake) for dances on or near the plantations. Robert was not staying on the plantation, but the statement that

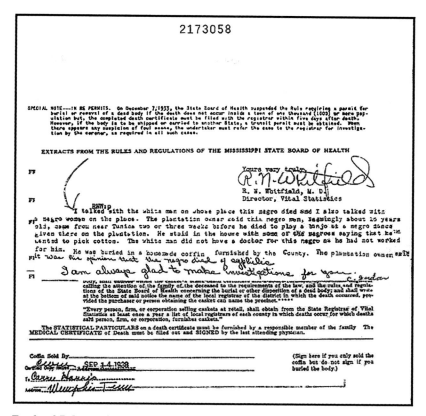

Back of Johnson's death certificate with notes.
Mississippi State Board of Health

he had been "in the house with some of the negroes saying that he wanted to pick cotton" was a convenient excuse as to why and how he died there.

Was this the beginning of at least a minor cover-up?

Since Robert died in such pain, vomiting blood, and experiencing other agonies, the proposition that he died of syphilis was impossible, but almost certainly Wade did not want to give any indication that foul play was involved. Did Wade believe Johnson had been murdered? It's impossible to tell. Obviously, he had contacted the county sheriff or Jordan directly. Was he completely forthcoming with his facts for the investigation? No. He only revealed enough information to absolve the plantation of any culpability in Robert's death. Was he entirely to blame for his omission or alteration of facts? Again, no. Wade was not present when Robert died, so he got his information from Tush Hog's family or Jim Moore. They knew the truth. Wade was only trying to whitewash the death.

Robert Leroy Johnson, the man, was gone.

His legend was just about to begin.

EPILOGUE

—◦—❧◦❧—◦—

LAST FAIR DEAL GOIN' DOWN

The legend of Robert Johnson began only a few months after his August 1938 death, at the historic Carnegie Hall "From Spirituals to Swing" concert. This groundbreaking show featured such band-leaders as Count Basie and Benny Goodman; singers Big Joe Turner and Helen Humes; pianists Meade Lux Lewis, Albert Ammons, and James P. Johnson; vocal groups Mitchell's Christian Singers and the Golden Gate Quartet, and many others. The concert was the brainchild of John Henry Hammond II, and his plan was to provide a musical journey through the history of black music, as well as presenting his favorite artists in a major venue, one usually reserved for the classical world.

In selecting artists to be featured at the show Hammond chose Robert Johnson to represent the Delta blues. It was natural for Hammond to want to include Robert: he had been championing him since his first records were released in 1937. He was certain he would be able to find and hire Robert to perform and give him his big break, and he had Robert's name included on the original promotional ad for the concert, printed in November of 1938, even though he had not yet had success in contacting Robert. When finally told of Robert's demise, Hammond would not be denied his great find. He wrote the following words for the December 13,

1938, issue of *New Masses* magazine, and then repeated them from the stage ten days later at the opening of the concert:

> It is tragic that an American audience could not have been found seven or eight years ago for a concert of this kind. Bessie Smith was still at the height of her career and Joe Smith, probably the greatest trumpet player American music ever knew would still have been around to play obligatos for her . . . [and] dozens of other artists could have been there in the flesh. But that audience as well as this one would not have been able to hear Robert Johnson sing and play the blues on his guitar, for at that time Johnson was just an unknown hand on a Robinsonville, Mississippi, plantation.
>
> Robert Johnson was going to be the big surprise of the evening for this audience at Carnegie Hall. I knew him only from his Vocalion blues records and from the tall, exciting tales the recording engineers and supervisors used to bring about him from the improvised studios in Dallas and San Antonio. I don't believe Johnson had ever worked as a professional musician anywhere, and it still knocks me over when I think of how lucky it is that a talent like his ever found its way onto phonograph records. [Tonight] we will have to be content with playing two of his records, the old *Walkin' Blues*, and the new, unreleased *Preachin' Blues*, because Robert Johnson died last week at the precise moment when Vocalion scouts finally reached him and told him that he was booked to appear at Carnegie Hall on December 23. He was in his middle twenties and nobody seems to know what caused his death.[1]

Although Hammond was a masterful manipulator of information, even he probably had little conception of how the words he spoke would lay the foundation for Robert Johnson's legendary, indeed mythic, status. What *is* certain, however, is that he consciously shaped that evening's image of Robert: from the recordings he chose to play to the information he provided about his life. By the time of the concert, fully twenty of Johnson's recordings had been released. Among those releases were Robert's only commercial hit, "Terraplane Blues" (selling a modest five to ten thousand copies), as well as those compositions that would become legendary and rank among the best known blues standards: "Cross Road Blues," "Sweet Home Chicago," "I Believe I'll Dust My Broom," "Hell Hound on My Trail," and others. Hammond was well aware of these recordings. Well-versed in Robert's recorded repertoire, Hammond still chose to play two of his lesser works at the opening of the concert.

"Walkin' Blues" and "Preachin' Blues" (subtitled "Up Jumped the Devil") were among Robert's most derivative pieces, compositions that owed a huge debt to one of Robert's mentors, Son House, who recorded songs by the same titles and with similar verses in 1930. Robert's versions are energetic and enthusiastic, but they were not nearly as adventurous or inventive as his compositions "Hell Hound on My Trail" or "Stones in My Passway," nor as commercial as "Terraplane Blues" or "Kind Hearted Woman Blues." Hammond chose "Walkin' Blues" and "Preachin' Blues," songs that Vocalion Records thought not even interesting enough to release until three years after they were recorded, one year after Robert's death (the two songs were actually released *after* the "From Spirituals to Swing" concert), partly to support his idea that Robert was more authentic than Lead Belly. Evidence of Hammond's notion of authenticity can be found in how Hammond described Robert's replacement—Big Bill Broonzy. Broonzy was already a well-established, *urban* recording artist, yet Hammond described him as a "primitive blues singer" who "shuffled" onstage. By the time the concert was held, however, Broonzy had been living in Chicago for eighteen years, had recorded over two hundred sides, and wore very fashionable suits. Hammond's use of "Walkin' Blues" and "Preachin' Blues" was due to his attraction to a more "primitive," and thus, to him, a more "authentic" blues sound. By selecting these two pieces to introduce Robert to the northern, white, liberal world Hammond created a very specific image of what constituted the true Delta blues as sung by "the greatest Negro blues singer who has cropped up in recent years . . . [who] . . . makes Leadbelly [*sic*] sound like an accomplished poseur."

Some of the errors in Hammond's various statements about Robert can be excused due to a legitimate lack of information, or misinterpretation of cultural context. When he stated that he didn't believe Robert worked as a professional musician and was, rather, a hand on a Mississippi plantation, he was probably thinking within the professional musical framework with which he was accustomed. Traveling from juke joint to tavern to house party might not have been what Hammond considered professional. How it might have surprised Hammond to learn that during his short lifetime Robert had played as far north as Canada, and had even been in his hometown of New York City and in New Jersey, traveling that great distance from the Delta! Robert was as professional as a Delta blues musician could be in the 1930s. Hammond also invented Robert's original mythic status with his claim that "Robert Johnson died last week at the precise moment when Vocalion scouts finally reached him and told him that he was booked to appear at Carnegie Hall on December 23." Although he certainly knew this was untrue, it made a terrifically romantic story. Hammond's praise of Robert's music and his concoction of a mysterious ethos surrounding him was enough to capture the interest of his friend and folk song collector Alan Lomax. Alan's father, John, had "discovered" Huddie "Lead Belly" Ledbetter in the early 1930s.

In 1942 Lomax, spurred by the interest in Robert that his friend Hammond had created, traveled to the Mississippi Delta in search

of any information about Robert Johnson he could find. In the
process, Lomax met Son House, Muddy Waters, and David "Honeyboy" Edwards. He recorded them all for the Library of Congress,
but he also added to Robert's myth by allegedly finding Johnson's
"mother." However, the woman who was supposedly introduced
to Lomax (we have no evidence that such a meeting actually took
place) told him, "Yessuh, I's Mary Johnson. And Robert, he my baby
son. But Little Robert, he dead." But Robert's mother's name was
Julia Ann Majors, so there are only several possibilities to explain
this anomaly. Either Lomax made the story up, or he was introduced to a woman who only claimed to be Robert's mother and
was duped.[2] Whether or not he actually met Robert's real mother,
Lomax added to the myth by insisting that he did and included the
following narrative he allegedly collected from her in his book *The
Land Where the Blues Began*:

> I'm mighty happy that someone came to ask about Little Rob-
> ert. He was a puny baby, but after he could set up, I never had
> no trouble with him. Always used to be listenin, listenin to the
> wind or the chickens cluckin in the backyard or me, when I
> be singin round the house. And he just love church, just love
> it. Don't care how long the meetin last, long as they sing every
> once in a while, Little Robert set on my lap and try to keep
> time, look like, or hold on to my skirt and sort of jig up and
> down and laugh and laugh. I never did have no trouble with
> him until he got big enough to be round bigger boys and off
> from home. Then he used to follow all these harp blowers,
> mandoleen and guitar pickers. Sometime he wouldn come
> home all night, and whippin never did him no good. First
> time there'd be somebody pickin another guitar, Little Robert
> follow um off. Look like he was just bent that way, and couldn
> help hisself. And they tell me he played the first guitar he pick
> up; never did have to study it, just knew it.

I used to cry over him, cause I knowed he was playin the devil's instruments, but Little Robert, he'd show me where I was wrong cause he'd sit home and take his little twenty-five cents harp and blow all these old fashioned church songs of mine till it was better than a meetin and I'd get happy and shout. He was knowed to be the best musicianer in Tunica County, but the more his name got about, the worse I felt, cause I knowed he was gonna git in trouble. Pretty soon he begun to leave home for a week at a time, but he always brought me some present back. Then he took off for a month at a time. Then he just stayed gone. I knowed something gonna happen to him. I felt it. And sure enough the word came for me to go to him. First time I ever been off from home, and the last time I'll go till the Lord call me. And, Lord have mercy, I found my little boy dyin. Some wicked girl or boyfriend had give him poison and wasn no doctor in the world could save him, so they say.

When I went in where he at, he layin up in bed with his guitar crost his breast. Soon's he saw me, he say, "Mama, you all I been waitin for. Here," he say, and he give me his guitar, "take and hang this on the wall, cause I done pass all that by. That what got me messed up, Mama. It's the devil's instrument, just like you said. And I don't want it no more." And he died while I was hangin his guitar on the wall. "I don't want it no more now, Mama, I done put all that by. I yo child now, Mama, and the Lord's. Yes—the Lord's child and don't belong to the devil no more." And he pass that way, with his mind on the angels. I know I'm gonna meet him over yonder, clothed in glory. My little Robert, the Lord's child.[3]

A romantic story to be sure—the prodigal son, a natural musician who played the devil's music, being saved on his death bed with his mother by his side—but one we now know to be full of factual inaccuracies. That Lomax published this book in 1993, well after enough facts were known about Robert to disprove Lomax's story, merely adds to the curious nature of the creation of Robert's myth.

Hammond's initial 1937 glorification of Robert's music, his mythic 1938 "From Spirituals to Swing" explanation of Robert's death, and Lomax's romantic fantasy about Johnson's mother all played into the construction of the mythic Robert Johnson. These tales were exacerbated by the well-intentioned but ill-informed suppositions about his life by writers like Charters, Welding, Cook, and others who attempted to define Robert by his lyrics or erroneous information. The exaggerated or concocted stories of Son House, Sonny Boy Williamson II (who claimed that Robert died in his arms on the way to a hospital), and many others who created tall tales to fill their interviewer's imagination led us further away from Robert Johnson the man and toward Robert Johnson the myth.

A vacant field just outside of Greenwood where Highways 49 and 82 meet is the location of the original Three Forks store and juke that was standing during Johnson's career. Honeyboy Edwards said it was destroyed by a tornado during World War II. Rosie Eskridge confirmed that event, as have numerous other Greenwood residents. Many of the towns that Robert Johnson frequented are completely gone: Penton, Clack, Its, and others. Those that still exist, such as Tutwiler or Friars Point, are only shadows of their former selves. The Delta plantations are gone except as historical landmarks. The only remaining element of the historical Delta that has prospered and grown is the story of Robert Johnson. The voices of those who knew him as a man and not a myth are, for the most part, forever stilled, yet their words are as poignant today as ever:

I thought a lot of him, I really did. Me and my brother we thought a lot about Robert. Sure did. He was friends with everybody. Robert was a nice fellow, he really was. He wasn't no way 'sumptuous or big-headed, stubborn, nothing. He liked to enjoy, he liked friends, he liked people.

—CHILDHOOD FRIEND WILLIE MASON

I remember everything about him. I remember he taught me how to play. I remember everything about him. He taught me how to make my living. —ROBERT LOCKWOOD

Robert Johnson is a parable. He was getting to be a very famous guy and all the girls and why is he dead? His fame killed him. —HENRY TOWNSEND

Since I been playing professionally, since I made my comeback, I look any day to walk up on Robert or Robert walk up on me. [I feel his presence] Many time. Many times.

—JOHNNY SHINES

APPENDIX I

RECORDING SESSIONS

Sequence of the sessions at which Robert Johnson recorded

1936—Gunter Hotel, Room 414, San Antonio, Texas:

Saturday, 11/21/36	W. Lee O'Daniel and His Hillbilly Boys
Sunday, 11/22/36	W. Lee O'Daniel and His Hillbilly Boys
Monday, 11/23/36	Robert Johnson
Tuesday, 11/24/36	Hermanas Barraza con guitarras
Wednesday, 11/25/36	The Chuck Wagon Gang
Thursday, 11/26/36	The Chuck Wagon Gang
	Robert Johnson
	Andres Berlanga y Francisco Montalvo y guitarras
Friday, 11/27/36	Robert Johnson
	Hermanas Barraza y Daniel Palomo con acompalimento de piano
	Hermanas Barraza con guitarras
	Al Dexter
Saturday, 11/28/36	Nothing recorded
Sunday, 11/29/36	Nothing recorded
Monday, 11/30/36	Eva Garza

1937—508 Park Avenue, Dallas, Texas

Thursday, 6/17/37	Al Dexter and Luke Owens
Friday, 6/18/37	The Hi-Flyers
	Roy Newman and His Boys
Saturday, 6/19/37	The Crystal Springs Ramblers
	Robert Johnson
	Zeke Williams and His Rambling Cowboys
Sunday, 6/20/37	The Light Crust Doughboys
	Clifford Gross and Muryel Campbell
	Robert Johnson
	Blue Ridge Playboys
	Donnell Lezah (personal record)
	John Boyd and His Southerners
	Bill Nettles and His Dixie Blueboys

APPENDIX II

─◆─

A ROBERT JOHNSON GENEAOLOGY

Julia Majors Lineage

Wiatt Majors (b. 1814 in Virginia) — Ann (?) (b. 1832 in Virginia)

> Gabriel b. 1850
> Anthony b. 1851
> William b. 1852
> Madison b. 1855
> Thomas b. 1857
> Amanda b. 1859
> Sylvester b. 1861
> Wyatt b. 1862
> Horace b. 1866
> Frank b. 1857
> John b. 1869

All listed as Mulattos in Townships 9 and 10, East of Railroad. Copiah, Mississippi

Gabriel marries Lucinda Brown (b. 1853) on September 12, 1868, in Hazlehurst

> Julia b. Oct. 1870
> James A. b. 1878

Jacob b. 1883
Charley b. 1890
Joseph b. 1892
Clara Belle b. 1902

Julia marries Charles Dodds (b. 1867) on February 2, 1889

Louise b. 1887
Harriet b. 1890
Bessie b. Oct. 1891
Willie M. b. Dec. 1894
Caroline b. 1895
Leroy b. 1896
John b. 1897
Melvin b. Oct. 1898
Codie M. b. 1900
Lilia S. b. 1903

Two children die in infancy.

Julia divorces Charles ca. 1920 and marries Will "Dusty" Willis in 1916

Charles Dodds Lineage

Charles Dodds (b. 1831 in North Carolina) — Harriet (?) (b. 1846)

Harry b. 1861
James b. 1862
Joseph b. 1865
Charles b. 1867
Ella b. 1868
Labritha b. 1870
John b. 1873

> William b. 1875
> Elizabeth b. 1877
> Aaron b. 1880

Living in Townships 1 and 2, East of Railroad, Copiah County
Charles marries Julia Majors on February 2, 1889

Noah Johnson Lineage:

Jack Johnson (b. 1850 in Louisiana) — Ann (?) (b. 1851 in South Carolina)

> Ella b. May 1876
> Lula b. 1881
> Noah b. Dec. 1884
> Willis b. Dec. 1887
> Olla b. Aug. 1888
> Maybel b. Mar. 1893

Living in Beat 2, Copiah County

Julia and Noah become parents of Robert Johnson, May 8, 1911

BIBLIOGRAPHY

Interviews

Austin, Henry, and Lilly Berry. Interview with Gayle Dean Wardlow. Tchula, Mississippi, [date].

Bracey, Ishmon. Interview with Gayle Dean Wardlow. Jackson, Mississippi, May 26, 1968.

Bracey, Ishmon, and Joe Callicott. Interview with Gayle Dean Wardlow. Hernando, Mississippi, December 30 and 31, 1967.

Cohn, Lawrence. Phone interview with Bruce Conforth. January 18, 2016.

Edwards, David "Honeyboy." Interview with Barry Lee Pearson, Blues Narrative Stage, "Robert Johnson Remembered," Smithsonian Folklife Festival. Washington, DC, 1991.

Edwards, David "Honeyboy." Interview with Bruce Conforth. Bloomington, Indiana, November 16, 1980.

Eskridge, Rosie. Interview with Gayle Dean Wardlow. Greenwood, Mississippi, June 2001.

Govenar, Alan. Telephone interview with Bruce Conforth. January 12, 2019.

Handwerker, Dan. Interview with Bruce Conforth. Memphis, Tennessee, May 7, 2015.

Hirsberg, Robert. Interview with Bruce Conforth. Friars Point, Mississippi, May 23, 2005.

Johnson, Ledell. Interview with Gayle Dean Wardlow. Jackson, Mississippi, 1969.

Lockwood, Robert. Interview with Robert Santelli, International Folk Alliance. 2000.

Lockwood, Robert. Interview with Worth Long, Blues Narrative Stage, "Robert Johnson Remembered," Smithsonian Folklife Festival. Washington, DC, 1991.

McCormick, Robert "Mack." Telephone interviews with Bruce Conforth. March 20, 2006, June 4, 2006, August 17, 2006, January 25, 2007, February 2, 2007, May 4, 2008, November 16, 2008, November 20, 2008, December 3, 2008.

Miller, Booker. Interviews with Gayle Dean Wardlow. Greenwood, Mississippi, 1968, 1969.

Moore, Willie, and Elizabeth Moore. Interviews with Gayle Dean Wardlow. Sumner and Mitchner Plantation, Tutwiler, Mississippi, May 1968; McManus Plantation, Sumner, Mississippi, November 1969, December 1969.

Mullan, Hayes. Interviews with Gayle Dean Wardlow. Tutwiler, Mississippi, July 29, 1967, August 12, 1967, May 18, 1968, September 13, 1968, November 30, 1968.

Shines, Johnny. Interview with Barry Lee Pearson, Blues Narrative Stage, "Robert Johnson Remembered," Smithsonian Folklife Festival. Washington, DC, 1991.

Shines, Johnny. Interview with Malcom Walls, Blues Narrative Stage, "Robert Johnson Remembered," Smithsonian Folklife Festival. Washington, DC, 1991.

Shines, Johnny. Interview with Worth Long, Blues Narrative Stage, "Robert Johnson Remembered," Smithsonian Folklife Festival. Washington, DC, 1991.

Speir, H. C.. Interviews with Gayle Dean Wardlow. Jackson, Mississippi, May 18, 1968, 1969, February 8, 1970.

Steps, Lula Mae, Reverend Frank Howard, and wife, Otis Hopkins, Charlie Mullin, and Willie Brown (from Arkansas). Interviews with Gayle Dean Wardlow. Pugh City, Mississippi, December 28, 1967.

Townsend, Henry. Interview with Barry Lee Pearson, Blues Narrative Stage, "Robert Johnson Remembered," Smithsonian Folklife Festival. Washington, DC, 1991.

Townsend, Henry. Interview with Worth Long, Blues Narrative Stage, "Robert Johnson Remembered," Smithsonian Folklife Festival. Washington, DC, 1991.

Watkins, Sammy, and Fred Morgan. Interviews with Gayle Dean Wardlow. Helena, Arkansas, May 26, 1968.

Williams, Eula Mae. Interview with Gayle Dean Wardlow, [date].

Zimmerman-Smith, Loretha, and James Smith. Interview with Bruce Conforth. Beauregard, Mississippi, May 2, 2007.

Books

Abernathy, Francis Edward, and Carolyn Fielder Satterwhite. Eds. *Juneteenth Texas: Essays in African-American Folklore*. Denton: University of North Texas Press, 1996.

Anderson, James D. *The Education of Blacks in the South, 1860–1935*. Chapel Hill: University of North Carolina Press, 1988.

Anderson, Jeffrey E. *Conjure in African American Society*. Baton Rouge: Louisiana State UP, 2007.

Barlow, William. *Looking Up at Down: The Emergence of Blues Culture.* Philadelphia: Temple UP, 1989.

Beaumont, Daniel E. *Preachin' the Blues: The Life and Times of Son House.* New York: Oxford UP, 2011.

Berlin, Ira. *Slaves Without Masters: The Negro in the Antebellum South.* New York: Pantheon, 1974.

Bullock, Henry Allen. *A History of Negro Education in the South from 1619 to the Present.* Cambridge, MA: Harvard University Press, 1967.

Bureau of Education. *The Public School System of Memphis, Tennessee. Report of a Survey Made under the Direction of the Commissioner of Education. Bulletin, 1919, No. 50. Part 1: I. An Industrial and Social Study of Memphis; II. School Organization, Supervision, and Finance; III. The Building Problem.* Bureau of Education, Department of the Interior, 1919.

Burma, John H. Ed. *Mexican-Americans in the United States: A Reader.* Cambridge, MA: Schenkman Publishing Company, 1970.

Calt, Stephen. *I'd Rather Be the Devil: Skip James and the Blues.* New York: Da Capo, 1994.

Calt, Stephen, and Gayle Wardlow. *King of the Delta Blues: The Life and Music of Charlie Patton.* Newton, NJ: Rock Chapel, 1988.

Charters, Samuel. *The Country Blues.* New York: Rinehart, 1959.

Charters, Samuel. *Robert Johnson.* New York: Oak Publications, 1972.

Cobb, James C. *The Most Southern Place on Earth: The Mississippi Delta and the Roots of Regional Identity.* New York: Oxford University Press, 1994.

Cochran, Robert. *Our Own Sweet Sounds: A Celebration of Popular Music in Arkansas.* Fayetteville: University of Arkansas, 1996.

Cochrane, Willard W. *Farm Prices, Myth and Reality.* Minneapolis: University of Minnesota Press, Minnesota Archive Editions edition, January 1, 1958.

Cohn, Lawrence. *Nothing but the Blues: The Music and the Musicians.* New York: Abbeville, 1993.

Cook, Bruce. *Listen to the Blues.* New York: Charles Scribner's Sons, 1973.

Davis, Francis. *The History of the Blues.* New York: Hyperion, 1995.

Davis, Rod. *American Voudou: Journey into a Hidden World.* Denton: University of North Texas Press, 1998.

de Lerma, Dominique-René. Ed. *Black Music in Our Culture: Curricular Ideas on the Subjects, Materials, and Problems.* Kent, OH: Kent State University Press, 1970.

DeSalvo, Debra. *The Language of the Blues.* New York: Billboard Books, 2006.

Dixon, Robert M. W., John Godrich, and Howard Rye. *Blues & Gospel Records: 1890–1943.* Oxford, UK: Clarendon, 1997.

Erikson, Erik H. *Identity and the Lifecycle.* New York: W. W. Norton, 1968.

Erikson, Erik H. *Identity, Youth, and Crisis.* New York: W. W. Norton, 1968.

Evans, David. *Ramblin' on My Mind: New Perspectives on the Blues*. Urbana: University of Illinois Press, 2008.

Finn, Julio. *The Bluesman: The Musical Heritage of Black Men and Women in the Americas*. New York: Interlink, 1992.

Gioia, Ted. *Delta Blues: The Life and Times of the Mississippi Masters Who Revolutionized American Music*. New York: W. W. Norton, 2008.

Govenar, Alan, and Jay Brakefield. *Deep Ellum: The Other Side of Dallas*. College Station: Texas A&M University Press, 2013.

Govenar, Alan, and Jay Brakefield. *The Dallas Music Scene 1920s–1960s*. Charleston, NC: Arcadia Publishing, 2014.

Graves, Tom. *Crossroads: The Life and Afterlife of Blues Legend Robert Johnson*. Spokane, WA: Demers Books, 2008.

Greenberg, Alan. *Love in Vain: A Vision of Robert Johnson*. New York: Da Capo, 1994.

Guralnick, Peter. *Searching for Robert Johnson*. New York: Dutton, 1989.

Harris, Sheldon. *Blues Who's Who: A Biographical Dictionary of Blues Singers*. New Rochelle, NY: Arlington House, 1979.

Hilliard, David Moss. *The Development of Public Education in Memphis Tennessee, 1848–1945*. Chicago: University of Chicago Press, 1946.

Hurston, Zora Neale. *Mules and Men*. New York: Harper and Row. 1990.

Hyatt, Harry Middleton. *Hoodoo, Conjuration, Witchcraft, Rootwork: Beliefs Accepted by Many Negroes and White Person, These Being Orally Recorded among Blacks and Whites*. St. Louis, MO: Western Publ., 1973.

Jenkins, Earnestine. *African Americans in Memphis*. Charleston, SC: Arcadia, 2009.

Jones, Lawrence A., and David Durand. *Mortgage Lending Experience in Agriculture*. Princeton, NJ: Princeton University Press, 1954.

Kail, Tony. *A Secret History of Memphis Voodoo*. Charleston, SC: History Press, 2017.

Keith, Michael C. *Radio Cultures: The Sound Medium in American Life*. New York: Peter Lang, 2008.

Komara, Edward M. *The Road to Robert Johnson: The Genesis and Evolution of Blues in the Delta from the Late 1800s through 1938*. Milwaukee, WI: Hal Leonard, 2007.

Lauterbach, Preston. *Beale Street Dynasty: Sex, Song, and the Struggle for the Soul of Memphis*. New York: W. W. Norton, 2015.

Laws of the state of Mississippi, passed at a called session of the Mississippi Legislature, held in Columbus, February and March, 1865. Meridian, MS: J.J. Shannon & Co., 1865.

Lawson, R. A. *Jim Crow's Counterculture: The Blues and Black Southerners, 1890–1945*. Baton Rouge: Louisiana State University Press, 2010.

Lee, George W. *Beale Street: Where the Blues Began*. College Park, MD: McGrath, 1934.

Lomax, Alan. *The Land Where the Blues Began*. New York: Pantheon, 1993.

MacAllister, John J. *Hospital and Medical Facilities in Mississippi*. Business Research Station, School of Business and State College, Mississippi, 1945.

Marcus, Greil. *Mystery Train: Images of America in Rock 'n' Roll Music*. New York: Dutton, 1975.

Mason, Kenneth. *African Americans and Race Relations in San Antonio, Texas, 1867–1937*. New York: Garland, 1998.

McKee, Margaret, and Fred Chisenhall. *Beale Black & Blue: Life and Music on Black America's Main Street*. Baton Rouge: Louisiana State University Press, 1981.

McLemore, Richard Aubrey. *A History of Mississippi*. Hattiesburg: University & College Press of Mississippi, 1973.

McPeek, Jan, and Naomi McPeek. *Merchants, Tradesmen and Manufaturers Financial Condition for Bolivar County, Mississippi 1921: Information Obtained from the January, 1921 R.G. Dun Mercantile Agency Reference Book*. Salem, OH: Aaron's Books, 2003.

McPeek, Jan, and Naomi McPeek. *Merchants, Tradesmen and Manufaturers Financial Condition for Coahoma County Mississippi 1921: Information Obtained from the January, 1921 R.G. Dun Mercantile Agency Reference Book*. Salem, OH: Aaron's Books, 2003.

McPeek, Jan, and Naomi McPeek. *Merchants, Tradesmen and Manufaturers Financial Condition for Copiah County, Mississippi 1921: Information Obtained from the January, 1921 R.G. Dun Mercantile Agency Reference Book*. Salem, OH: Aaron's Books, 2003.

McPeek, Jan, and Naomi McPeek. *Merchants, Tradesmen and Manufaturers Financial Condition for Leflore County Mississippi 1921: Information Obtained from the January, 1921 R.G. Dun Mercantile Agency Reference Book*. Salem, OH: Aaron's Books, 2003.

McPeek, Jan, and Naomi McPeek. *Merchants, Tradesmen and Manufaturers Financial Condition for Tunica and Quitman Counties Mississippi 1921: Information Obtained from the January, 1921 R.G. Dun Mercantile Agency Reference Book*. Salem, OH: Aaron's Books, 2003.

Nager, Larry. *Memphis Beat: The Life and Times of America's Musical Crossroads*. New York: St. Martin's Press, 1988.

Oakley, Giles. *The Devil's Music: A History of the Blues*. New York: Taplinger, 1977.

Obrecht, Jas. *Blues Guitar: The Men Who Made the Music: From the Pages of Guitar Player Magazine*. Milwaukee, WI: Hal Leonard, 1990.

Obrecht, Jas. *Early Blues: The First Stars of Blues Guitar*. Minneapolis: University of Minnesota Press, 2015.

Obrecht, Jas. *Rollin' and Tumblin': The Postwar Blues Guitarists*. San Francisco: Miller Freeman, 2000.

Oliver, Paul. *The Story of the Blues*. Philadelphia: Chilton Book, 1969.

Olsson, Bengt. *Memphis Blues and Jug Bands*. London: Studio Vista, 1970.

Palmer, Robert. *Deep Blues*. New York: Viking, 1981.

Payne, Darwin. *Dallas: An Illustrated History*. Woodland Hills, CA: Windsor, 1982.

Pearson, Barry Lee. *Jook Right On: Blues Stories and Blues Storytellers*. Knoxville: University of Tennessee, 2005.

Pearson, Barry Lee. *"Sounds so Good to Me": The Bluesman's Story*. Philadelphia: University of Pennsylvania, 1984.

Pearson, Barry Lee, and Bill McCulloch. *Robert Johnson: Lost and Found*. Urbana and Chicago: University of Illinois Press, 2003.

Powdermaker, Hortense. *After Freedom: A Cultural Study in the Deep South*. New York: Russell & Russell, 1968.

Puckett, Newbell Niles. *Folk Beliefs of the Southern Negro*. Chapel Hill: University of North Carolina Press, 1926.

Rubin, Dave. *Robert Johnson: The New Transcriptions*. Milwaukee, WI: Hal Leonard, 1999.

Schroeder, Patricia A. *Robert Johnson: Mythmaking and Contemporary American Culture*. Urbana and Chicago: University of Illinois Press, 2004.

Sharp, Timothy W. *Memphis Music: Before the Blues*. Charleston, SC: Arcadia, 2007.

Spencer, Jon Michael. *Blues and Evil*. Knoxville: University of Tennessee, 1993.

Wald, Elijah. *Escaping the Delta: Robert Johnson and the Invention of the Blues*. New York: Amistad, 2004.

Wardlow, Gayle Dean. *Chasin' That Devil Music*. San Francisco: Backbeat, 2001.

Woolfolk, Margaret Elizabeth. *A History of Crittenden County, Arkansas*. Greenville, SC: Southern Historical Press, 1991.

Writers' Project of the Works Projects Administration in the City of Dallas—1936–1942. *The WPA Dallas Guide and History*. Dallas, TX: UNT Digital Library.

Writers' Project of the Works Projects Administration in the City of Dallas—1936–1942. *Along the San Antonio River: City of San Antonio*. Dallas, TX: UNT Digital Library.

Writers' Project of the Works Projects Administration in the City of Dallas—1936–1942. *San Antonio: An Authoritative Guide to the City and its Environs*. Dallas, TX: UNT Digital Library.

Articles

Barnes, Bertrum, and Glen Wheeler. "A Lonely Fork in the Road." *Living Blues* 94 (November–December 1990): 27.

Calt, Stephen. "Robert Johnson Recapitulated." *Blues Unlimited* 86 (November 1971): 12–14.

Calt, Stephen, and Gayle Dean Wardlow. "Robert Johnson (1911–1938)." *78 Quarterly* 1, no. 4 (1989): 40.

Conforth, Bruce. "Ike Zimmerman: The X in Robert Johnson's Crossroads." *Living Blues* 194 (2008): 68.

Conforth, Bruce. "The Death of Robert Johnson's Wife." *Living Blues* 226 (2013): 5.

Conforth, Bruce. "The Business of Robert Johnson Fakery." *Living Blues* 241 (2016): 7.

Davis, Francis. "Blues Walking Like a Man: The Complicated Legacy of Robert Johnson." *Atlantic* 267, no. 4 (April 1991): 92.

Evans, David. "Ramblin' David Evans: Robert Johnson—Pact with the Devil." *Blues Review* 21 (February–March 1996); (Apr–May 1996); (June–July 1996).

Freeland, Tom. "He Would Go Out and Stay Out: Some Witnesses to the Short Life of Robert Johnson." *Living Blues* 150 (March–April 2000): 42.

Garon, Paul. "Robert Johnson: Perpetuation of a Myth." *Living Blues* 94 Special issue (November–December 1990): 34–36.

Gates, Henry Louis Jr. "Free Blacks Lived in the North, Right?" *Root* July 8, 2013, http://www.theroot.com/articles/history/2013/07/free_blacks_precivil_war_where_they_lived.

Guralnick, Peter. "Searching for Robert Johnson." *Living Blues* 53 (Summer–Autumn 1982): 27.

Gurza, Agustín. "The Blues and the Borderlands." *The Strachwitz Frontera Collection of Mexican and Mexican American Recordings*. http://frontera.library.ucla.edu/blog/2016/02/berlanga-y-montalvo-blues-and-borderlands.

Hammond, John. "Sight and Sound." *New Masses* 23 (June 8, 1937): 30.

House, Eddie James "Son." "I Can Make My Own Songs." *Sing Out!* 15, no. 3 (July 1965): 38.

Hurston, Zora. "Hoodoo in America." *Journal of American Folklore* 44.174 (1931): 317.

James, Steve. "Robert Johnson: The San Antonio Legacy." *Juke Blues* (Spring 1988): 26.

Johnson, Henry (pseudonym for John Henry Hammond II). "Sight and Sound." *New Masses* 22 (March 2, 1937): 27.

LaVere, Steve. "Robert Johnson's Census Records." *Living Blues* 203 (Summer 2009): 74.

LaVere, Steve. "Tying Up a Few Loose Ends." *Living Blues* 94 Special issue (November–December 1990): 31–33.

Lee, Peter. "The Fella Y'all Looking For, Did He Die a Natural Death?" *Living Blues* 94 Special issue (November–December 1990): 2.

Moser, Margaret. "The Girl Who Met Robert Johnson: Shirley Ratisseau, Living History." *Austin Chronicle*, August 3, 2012. http://www.austinchronicle.com/music/2012-08-03/the-girl-who-met-robert-johnson.

Obrecht, Jas. "Johnny Shines: The Complete 1989 Living Blues Interview." Jas Obrecht Music Archive, 2011. http://jasobrecht.com/johnny-shines-complete-living-blues-interview.

O'Neal, Jim. "Living Blues Interview: Houston Stackhouse" *Living Blues* 17 (Summer 1974): 20.

O'Neal, Jim. "A Traveler's Guide to the Crossroads." *Living Blues* 94 Special issue (November–December 1990): 21–24.

Pearson, Barry Lee. "CeDell Davis' Story and the Arkansas Delta Blues." *Arkansas Review: A Journal of Delta Studies* 33 (April 2002): 3–14.

Perls, Nick. "Son House Interview, Part One." *78 Quarterly* 1 (1967): 60.

Reed, Stephen B. "One hundred years of price change: the Consumer Price Index and the American inflation experience." *Monthly Labor Review* (April 2014), http://www.bls.gov/opub/mlr/2014/article/one-hundred-years-of-price-change-the-consumer-price-index-and-the-american-inflation-experience.htm.

Richard, Melissa J. "The Crossroads and the Myth of the Mississippi Delta Bluesman." *Interdisciplinary Humanities* 23 no. 2 (Fall 2006): 19.

Rubin, Dave. "Robert Johnson: The First Guitar Hero." *Living Blues* 94 Special issue (November–December 1990): 38–39.

Scherman, Tony. "Phantom of the Blues." *American Visions* 3, no. 3 (June 1988): 21.

Shines, Johnny. "The Robert Johnson I Knew." *American Folk Music Occasional* 2 (1970).

Sydnor, Charles S. "The Free Negro in Mississippi Before the Civil War." *American Historical Review* 32, no. 4 (July 1927): 769–788.

Waterman, Dick. "To Robert Johnson." *Living Blues* 94 Special issue (November–December 1990): 42–43.

Welding, Pete. "Ramblin' Johnny Shines." *Living Blues* 22 (July–August 1975): 23–32.

Welding, Pete. "Ramblin' Johnny Shines." *Living Blues* 23 (September–October 1975): 22–29.

Welding, Pete. "The Robert Johnson I Knew: An Interview with Henry Townsend." *Blues Unlimited* 64 (1969): 10–11.

Welding, Pete. "The Robert Johnson I Knew: An Interview with Henry
    Townsend." *Blues Unlimited* 65 (1969): 15.
Welding, Pete. "The Robert Johnson I Knew: An Interview with Henry
    Townsend." *Blues Unlimited* 66 (1969): 9.
Welding, Pete. "Hell Hound on His Trail: Robert Johnson." *Down Beat's
    Music '66* (1966).
Wilson, Charles Reagan. "Chinese in Mississippi: An Ethnic
    People in a Biracial Society." *Mississippi History Now.* November
    2002. http://mshistorynow.mdah.state.ms.us/articles/86/
    mississippi-chinese-an-ethnic-people-in-a-biracial-society.
Yronwode, Catherine. "Foot Track Magic." *Hoodoo in Theory and Practice.*
    http://www.luckymojo.com/foottrack.html

Multiple authors:

The Death of Robert Johnson. Special issue of *Living Blues* 94 (November—
    December 1990) This issue contains the articles "The Death of Robert
    Johnson," pp. 8–20 with contributors: Jim O'Neal, pp. 9–10, 13–15;
    Steve Brazier, pp. 10–11; Deacon Richard Johnson interview by Peter Lee
    transcribed by Ken Woodmansee, pp. 11–12; Queen Elizabeth inter-
    viewed by Jim O'Neal, Peter Lee, Patty Johnson, and Matthew Johnson,
    pp. 12–13; Bob Scott interviewed by Kenwoodmansee and Peter Lee, p.
    15; CeDell Davis interviewed by Chris Nesmith, p. 15; Memphis Slim
    interviewed by Jim O'Neal, pp. 15–16; James Banister interviewed by
    Jim O'Neal, p. 16; Johnny Shines interviewed by Matthew Johnson, pp.
    16–18; Honeyboy Edwards interviewed by Matthew Johnson, pp. 18–20.

Films and Video

Hunt, Chris, dir. *The Search for Robert Johnson.* Sony Music Entertainment, 2000.
Meyer, Peter, dir. *Can't You Hear the Wind Howl: The Life and Music of Robert
    Johnson.* Sweet Home Pictures, 1997.
Mugge, Robert, dir. *Hellhounds on My Trail: The Afterlife of Robert Johnson.*
    Mug Shot/Nonfiction, 1999.

Recordings

Dunn, Johnny. *Four O'Clock Blues.* Columbia A3729. September 1922.
Howell, Peg Leg Howell. *Low Down Rounder Blues.* Columbia 14320. April
    1928.
Johnson, Robert. *Robert Johnson, King of the Delta Blues Singers.* Columbia.
    1961.
Johnson, Robert D. *Robert Johnson, King of the Delta Blues Singers, Volume 2.*
    Recorded in 1937. CBS Records, 1967, vinyl.
Johnson, Robert. *Robert Johnson, the Complete Recordings.* Columbia, 1990,
    CD.

Johnson, Robert. *Robert Johnson, the Complete Original Masters: Centennial Edition*. Columbia, 2011, CD.

Smith, Bessie. *Blue Spirit Blues*. Columbia 14527, October 11, 1929.

Smith, Clara. *Done Sold My Soul to the Devil*. September 20, 1924. 140053 (Columbia-14039).

Smith, J. T. *Fool's Blues*. Vocalion 1674, April 1931.

Liner Notes

Brooks, Michael. "In Search of Robert Johnson 78s." *Robert Johnson: The Complete Original Masters Centennial Edition*. Sony Music Entertainment, 2011: 19.

Driggs, Frank. *Robert Johnson: King of the Delta Blues Singers*. Columbia, 1961.

Gioia, Ted. "100 Years of Robert Johnson." *Robert Johnson: The Complete Original Masters Centennial Edition*. Sony Music Entertainment, 2011: 3.

LaVere, Stephen C. *Robert Johnson: The Complete Recordings*. Sony Columbia, 1990.

LaVere, Stephen C. "An Ambition Realized." *Robert Johnson: The Complete Original Masters Centennial Edition*. Sony Music Entertainment, 2011: 6.

LaVere, Stephen C. "Art and Law Prevail." *Robert Johnson: The Complete Original Masters Centennial Edition*. Sony Music Entertainment, 2011: 14.

Waxman, John. *Robert Johnson: King of the Delta Blues Singers, vol. 2*. Columbia, 1970.

Census Records

Alabama

Alabama. Pine Level, Enumeration District #140, Montgomery County. 1870 U.S. census, population schedule. Digital images. Ancestry.com. http://www.ancestry.com: 2016.

Alabama. Pine Level, Enumeration District #140, Montgomery County. 1880 U.S. census, population schedule. Digital images. Ancestry.com. http://www.ancestry.com: 2016.

Alabama. Dublin (Precinct 14), Enumeration District #117, Montgomery County. 1900 U.S. census, population schedule. Digital images. Ancestry.com. http://www.ancestry.com: 2016.

Arkansas

Arkansas. Lucas Township, Enumeration District #61, Crittenden County. 1920 U.S. census, population schedule. Digital images. Ancestry.com http://www.ancestry.com: 2016.

Arkansas. Big Creek Township, Enumeration District #114, Lee County. 1920 U.S. census, population schedule. Digital images. Ancestry.com http://www.ancestry.com: 2016.

Arkansas. St. Francis Township, Second Ward, Enumeration District #54-21, Phillips County. 1930 U.S. census, population schedule. Digital images. Ancestry.com. http://www.ancestry.com: 2016.

Arkansas. St. Francis Township, Helena City, Enumeration District #54-21, Phillips County. 1930 U.S. census, population schedule. Digital images. Ancestry.com. http://www.ancestry.com: 2016.

Mississippi

Mississippi. Hazlehurst, Beat 1, Copiah County, 1870 U.S. census, population schedule. Digital images. Ancestry.com. http://www.ancestry.com: 2016.

Mississippi. Hazlehurst, Townships 1 and 2 east of RR, Copiah County, 1870 U.S. census, population schedule. Digital images. Ancestry.com. http://www.ancestry.com: 2016.

Mississippi. Hazlehurst, Townships 9 and 10 east of RR, Copiah County, 1870 U.S. census, population schedule. Digital images. Ancestry.com. http://www.ancestry.com: 2016.

Mississippi. Hazlehurst, Beat 1, Copiah County, 1880 U.S. census, population schedule. Digital images. Ancestry.com. http://www.ancestry.com: 2016.

Mississippi. Hazlehurst, Townships 1 and 2 east of RR, Copiah County, 1880 U.S. census, population schedule. Digital images. Ancestry.com. http://www.ancestry.com: 2016.

Mississippi. Beat 3, Copiah County, 1880 U.S. census, population schedule. Digital images. Ancestry.com. http://www.ancestry.com: 2016.

Mississippi. Hazlehurst, West Precinct, Part of Beat 1, Enumeration District #31, Copiah County. 1900 U.S. census, population schedule. Digital images. Ancestry.com. http://www.ancestry.com: 2016.

Mississippi. Hazlehurst, West Precinct, Part of Beat 1, Enumeration District #33, Copiah County. 1900 U.S. census, population schedule. Digital images. Ancestry.com. http://www.ancestry.com: 2016.

Mississippi. Part of Beat 2, Enumeration District #35, Copiah County. 1900 U.S. census, population schedule. Digital images. Ancestry.com. http://www.ancestry.com: 2016.

Mississippi. Hazlehurst, Beat 1, Enumeration District #45, Copiah County. 1910 U.S. census, population schedule. Digital images. Ancestry.com. http://www.ancestry.com: 2016.

Mississippi. Hazlehurst, Beat 1, Enumeration District #44, Copiah County. 1910 U.S. census, population schedule. Digital images. Ancestry.com. http://www.ancestry.com: 2016.

Mississippi. Commerce, Beat 1, Enumeration District #98, Tunica County. 1910 U.S. census, population schedule. Digital images. Ancestry.com.

http://www.ancestry.com: 2016.

Mississippi. Hazlehurst, Enumeration District #47, Copiah County. 1920
U.S. census, population schedule. Digital images. Ancestry.com. http://
www.ancestry.com: 2016.

Mississippi. Beat 3, Enumeration District #6-24, Bolivar County. 1930 U.S.
census, population schedule. Digital images. Ancestry.com. http://www.
ancestry.com: 2016.

Mississippi. Rosedale City, Enumeration District #6-8, Bolivar County. 1930
U.S. census, population schedule. Digital images. Ancestry.com. http://
www.ancestry.com: 2016.

Mississippi. Hazlehurst, Beat 3, Enumeration District #6-24, Copiah County.
1930 U.S. census, population schedule. Digital images. Ancestry.com.
http://www.ancestry.com: 2016.

Mississippi. Hazlehurst, Beat 3, Enumeration District #17-10, Copiah
County. 1930 U.S. census, population schedule. Digital images. Ancestry.
com. http://www.ancestry.com: 2016.

Mississippi. Beat 3, Enumeration District #17-10, DeSoto County. 1930
U.S. census, population schedule. Digital images. Ancestry.com. http://
www.ancestry.com: 2016.

Mississippi. Beat 4, Enumeration District #17-11, DeSoto County. 1930
U.S. census, population schedule. Digital images. Ancestry.com. http://
www.ancestry.com: 2016.

Mississippi. Beat 4, Enumeration District #42-27, Leflore County. 1940 U.S.
census, population schedule. Digital images. Ancestry.com. http://www.
ancestry.com: 2016.

Tennessee

Tennessee. Memphis (part of), Enumeration District #176, Shelby County.
1920 U.S. census, population schedule. Digital images. Ancestry.com.
http://www.ancestry.com: 2016.

Tennessee. Memphis (Ward 10), Enumeration District #9, Shelby County.
1940 U.S. census, population schedule. Digital images. Ancestry.com.
http://www.ancestry.com: 2016.

City Directories

R.L. Polk & Co., Memphis City Directory. 1908, 1909, 1910, 1911, 1912,
1913, 1914, 1915, 1916, 1917, 1918, 1919, 1920, 1921, 1922, 1923,
1924, 1925, 1926, 1927, 1928, 1929, 1930, 1931, 1932, 1933, 1934,
1935, 1936, 1937, 1938.

Digital Sanborn Maps 1867–1970
Helena (Phillips County), Arkansas, 1926–1950.
West Memphis (Crittenden County), Arkansas, 1938.
Clarksdale (Coahoma County), Mississippi, 1929–1948.
Friars Point, Mississippi, 1924–1936.
Greenwood (Leflore County), Mississippi, 1926–1948.
Hazlehurst (Copiah County), Mississippi, 1886, 1892, 1897, 1902, 1907,
    1913, 1925, 1925–43.
Rosedale (Bolivar County), Mississippi, 1924–1945.
Memphis (Shelby County), Tennessee, 1907, 1927, 1907–51.
Dallas (Dallas County), Texas, 1921–1952.
San Antonio (Bexar County), Texas, 1911–1951.

Vital Records
Death Certificates
Death certificate for Virginia Johnson, April 10, 1930. File No. 7664,
    Mississippi State Board of Health. Certified copy in possession of authors.
Death certificate for Robert L. Johnson, August 16, 1938. File No. 13704,
    Mississippi State Board of Health. Certified copy in possession of authors.
Death certificate for Charlie Dodds Spencer, November 28, 1940. File No.
    28840, Tennessee State Board of Health. Certified copy in possession of
    authors.
Death certificate for Mollie Spencer, March 12, 1942. File No. C427,
    Tennessee State Board of Health. Certified copy in possession of authors.
Death record for Isaiah Zimmerman, August 3, 1967. *Social Security Death
    Index, 1935–2014*. Digital images. Ancestry.com. http://www.ancestry.
    com: 2016.

Marriage Licenses
C. C. Dodds and Julia Majors, February 2, 1889. Mississippi. Hazlehurst,
    City of. Copiah County. Marriage Certificates. Recorder of Deeds, City of
    Hazlehurst.
Noah Johnson and Mary Nelson, December 2, 1904. Mississippi. Hazlehurst,
    City of. Copiah County. Marriage Certificates. Recorder of Deeds, City of
    Hazlehurst.
Robert Johnson and Virginia Travis, February 16, 1929. Mississippi. Tunica,
    City of. Tunica County. Marriage Certificates. Recorder of Deeds, City of
    Hazlehurst.
Robert Johnson and Callie Craft, May 4, 1931. Mississippi. Hazlehurst, City
    of. Copiah County. Marriage Certificates. Recorder of Deeds, City of
    Hazlehurst.

NOTES

Introduction

1 Samuel Charters, *The Country Blues* (New York: Rinehart, 1959).

2 Charters, *Country Blues*, 207–210.

3 Robert Johnson, *Robert Johnson: King of the Delta Blues Singers* (New York: Columbia Records, 1961).

4 Frank Driggs, Liner notes, *Robert Johnson: King of the Delta Blues Singers* (New York: Columbia Records, 1961).

5 Pete Welding, Liner notes, *Robert Johnson: King of the Delta Blues Singers, Vol II* (New York: Columbia Records, 1970).

6 Samuel Charters, *Robert Johnson* (New York: Oak Publications, 1972).

7 Bruce Cook, *Listen to the Blues* (New York: Charles Scribner's Sons, 1973).

8 Peter Guralnick, "Searching for Robert Johnson," *Living Blues* 53 (Summer-Autumn, 1982).

9 Peter Guralnick, *Searching for Robert Johnson"* (New York: Dutton, 1989).

10 "The Death of Robert Johnson," *Living Blues* 94, special issue (November/December, 1990).

11 Lawrence Cohn, e-mail to Bruce Conforth, January 4, 2016.

12 Stephen LaVere, Liner notes, Robert Johnson, *The Complete Recordings* (New York: Columbia Records, 1990).

13 *The Search for Robert Johnson*, directed by Chris Hunt (1992; Sony Music Entertainment, 2000) DVD.

14 Barry Lee Pearson and Bill McCulloch, *Robert Johnson: Lost and Found* (Urbana: University of Illinois Press, 2003).

15 Elijah Wald, *Escaping the Delta: Robert Johnson and the Invention of the Blues* (New York: Amistad, 2004).

16 Tom Graves, *Crossroads: The Life and Afterlife of Blues Legend Robert Johnson* (Spokane, WA: Demers Books, 2008).

17 Steve LaVere, foreword to *Crossroads: The Life and Afterlife of Blues Legend Robert Johnson*, by Tom Graves (Spokane, Washington: Demers Books, 2008).

18 Graves's first chapter, "The Early Years," is only four pages long, does not at all discuss Johnson's childhood in Memphis (a very curious omission since Graves lives and teaches in that town), and devotes a full page and a half to the history of the diddley bow and Hawaiian music. In Graves's second chapter, "Johnson as a Young Man," Johnson's life from age ten to nineteen is covered in only three pages. Chapter 3, "The Walking Musician Years," is a scant seven pages that includes only one sentence about Ike Zimmerman (who Graves, following LaVere's lead, erroneously identifies as Ike Zinermon), the guitarist who may have been Johnson's greatest mentor. Chapter 4, "The Recording Years," is another short seven-page offering with its majority dealing with the mechanics of recording in the 1930s. Finally, chapter 5, "The Death of a Rising Star," is nine pages devoted to speculation about Johnson's murder.

19 Robert Johnson, *Robert Johnson, The Complete Original Masters: Centennial Edition* (Columbia: B00512ZFRU. 2011).

20 Dogfish Head Craft Brewery, *Hellhound on My Ale* (Rehoboth Beach, DE: 2011).

Chapter 1: Robert Johnson Is in Town

1 Hugh Jenkins (owner of Robert Johnson's birthplace and longtime friend of Rosa Redman), interview by Bruce Conforth, Hazlehurst, Mississippi, August 14, 2017.

2 Elizabeth Moore, interview with Gayle Dean Wardlow, Mitchner Plantation, May 18, 1968.

3 Robert Hirsberg (son of the original owners of Hirsberg's store in Friars Point, Mississippi), interview by Bruce Conforth, May 16, 2008.

Chapter 2: Before the Beginning

1 "Mississippi Black Codes" in *Laws of the State of Mississippi, Passed at a Called Session of the Mississippi Legislature, Held in Columbus, February and March, 1865* (Meridian, MS: J.J. Shannon & Co., 1865).

2 James C. Cobb, *The Most Southern Place on Earth: The Mississippi Delta and the Roots of Regional Identity* (New York: Oxford University Press, 1994).

3 According to the Gilder Lehrman Institute of American History, between 9.6 and 10.8 million Africans arrived in the Americas as a result of the slave trade. Over 90 percent of African slaves went directly to either the Caribbean or South America, while only 6 percent, or 600,000 to 650,000 Africans, were imported directly into North America. http://www.gilderlehrman.org/history-by-era/slavery-and-anti-slavery/resources/facts-about-slave-trade-and-slavery. Other sources such as the

Trans-Atlantic Slave Trade Database (http://www.slavevoyages.org/tast/index.faces) put the number of Africans coming directly to North America even lower, perhaps as low as 305,000.

4 Henry Louis Gates Jr., "Free Blacks Lived in the North, Right?," *The African Americans: Many Rivers to Cross*, PBS, 2013. http://www.pbs.org/wnet/african-americans-many-rivers-to-cross/history/free-blacks-lived-in-the-north-right.

5 Census records for the Dodds, Majors, and Johnson families are all from the US Department of Commerce United States Census.

6 Department of Commerce, Bureau of the Census, State: Mississippi; County: Copiah; Hazlehurst, Part of Beat One ; Enumeration District 33, Sheet 7, June 8, 1900.

7 LaVere, *Complete Recordings*, 5.

8 Randall Day, executive director of the Hazlehurst Area Chamber of Commerce, interview with Bruce Conforth, Hazlehurst, Mississippi, August 14, 2016.

9 R. L. Polk & Co. 1908 Memphis City Directory; Dan Handwerker, interview by Bruce Conforth, Memphis, TN, May 7, 2015.

10 Department of Commerce, Bureau of the Census, State: Mississippi; County: Copiah; Hazlehurst City; Enumeration District 45, Sheet 6-B, April 20, 1910.

11 Department of Commerce, Bureau of the Census, State: Mississippi; County: Copiah; Hazlehurst City; Enumeration District 44, Sheet 13-B, May 3, 1910.

12 Marriage license of Noah Johnson and Mary Nelson, December 14, 1904, Copiah County Courthouse, Hazlehurst, Mississippi.

Chapter 3: Memphis Days

1 As important as Robert's early life in Memphis was (it was crucial in shaping his musical and adult life), of the few works that have attempted to tell any portion of Robert Johnson's life story none have spent more than a few sentences on his childhood in Memphis. Some of this is undoubtedly due to the belief that there was no information to be had about this period in Johnson's life. Some of it is also due to the fact that apparently no one tried to put together information based upon contextual data: material that ends up revealing quite a bit about young Robert and the man he would become.

2 Robert "Mack" McCormick, *Search for Robert Johnson*, DVD.

3 Department of Commerce, Bureau of the Census, State: Tennessee; County: Shelby; Memphis, (Part of); Enumeration District 176, Sheet 2-A, January 3, 1920. This record was made after Julia Majors had taken

Robert back from the Spencer family, hence his absence. Charles's wife Mollie is erroneously identified as Mandy. This type of census error was common on these early records.

4 Preston Lauterbach, *Beale Street Dynasty: Sex, Song, and the Struggle for the Soul of Memphis* (New York: W. W. Norton, 2016), 121.

5 George W. Lee, *Beale Street: Where the Blues Began* (College Park, MD: McGrath Publishing Co., 1934), 82–83.

6 Lee, *Beale Street*, 79.

7 Lee, *Beale Street*, 80.

8 Larry Nager, *Memphis Beat: The Life and Times of America's Musical Cross-roads* (New York: St. Martin's, 1998), 24.

9 Bengt Olsson, *Memphis Blues and Jug Bands* (Studio Vista, 1970), 22.

10 Tony Kail, *A Secret History of Memphis Hoodoo: Rootworkers, Conjurers & Spirituals* (Charleston, SC: History Press, 2017) 29–30.

11 "Voudouism, African Fetich Worship Among the Memphis Negroes," *Memphis Daily Appeal*, date and author unknown, reprinted in Paschal Randolph's *Seership!* (1870), excerpted at www.southern-sprots.com.

12 R. L. Windum, *Can't You Hear the Wind Howl: The Life & Music of Robert Johnson*, directed by Peter Meyer (WinStar Home Entertainment, 1998), DVD.

13 R. L. Polk & Co. 1917 Memphis City Directory.

14 Gayle Dean Wardlow, *Chasin' That Devil Music* (San Francisco: Backbeat Books, 1998), 201.

15 *The Public School System of Memphis, Tennessee. A Report of a Survey Made under the Direction of the Commissioner of Education* (Washington, DC: Government Printing Office, 1920), 72.

16 LaVere, *Complete Recordings*, 5.

Chapter 4: Back to the Delta

1 Nikki Walker, "Horseshoe Lake, Arkansas," The Encyclopedia of Arkansas History and Culture (Little Rock, AR: Butler Center for Arkansas Studies, Central Arkansas Library System, 2018), http://www.encyclopediaofarkansas.net/encyclopedia/entry-detail.aspx?entryID=7164.

2 Nikki Walker, "Horseshoe Lake."

3 An incorrect age for Robert is not unusual. Ages reported on census records were highly unreliable. Julia's reported age and those of all her children were inconsistent from one census record to the next.

4 Margaret Elizabeth Woolfolk, *A History of Crittenden County, Arkansas* (Greenville, SC: Southern Historical Press, 1991), 83.

5 Tom Freeland, "'He Would Go Out and Stay Out'—Some Witnesses to the Short Life of Robert Johnson," *Living Blues* (March 2000): 44.

6 Lawrence A. Jones and David Durand, eds., *Mortgage Lending Experience in Agriculture* (Princeton, NJ: Princeton University Press, 1954), 95–96.
7 David "Honeyboy" Edwards, interview with Gayle Dean Wardlow, 1991.
8 Indian Creek school record 1924, Tunica County, Mississippi.
9 Guralnick, *Searching for Robert Johnson*, 12–13.
10 Guralnick, *Searching for Robert Johnson*, 13.
11 Windum, *Can't You Hear the Wind Howl*, DVD.
12 Freeland, "'He Would Go Out and Stay Out,'" 44.
13 Freeland, "'He Would Go Out and Stay Out,'" 44.
14 Freeland, "'He Would Go Out and Stay Out,'" 44.
15 Dr. Richard Taylor, email correspondence to Dr. Bruce Conforth, February 5, 2016.
16 Debra Devi, "Robert Johnson and the Myth of the Illiterate Bluesman," *Huffpost: Arts & Culture*, December 8, 2013, http://www.huffingtonpost.com/debra-devi/robert-johnson-and-the-my_b_1628118.html.
17 Israel "Wink" Clark, *Search for Robert Johnson*, DVD.
18 Pearson and McCulloch, *Robert Johnson*, 6.
19 R. L. Windum, *Can't You Hear the Wind Howl*, DVD.
20 Willie Mason, *Can't You Hear the Wind Howl*, DVD.
21 Freeland, "'He Would Go Out and Stay Out,'" 44.
22 Elizabeth Moore, interview by Gayle Dean Wardlow, Sumner, Mississippi, November 30, 1969.

Chapter 5: Musical Roots and Identity

1 Freeland, "'He Would Go Out and Stay Out,'" 44.
2 Israel "Wink" Clark, *Search for Robert Johnson*, DVD.
3 Israel "Wink Clark, *Can't You Hear the Wind Howl*, DVD.
4 Freeland, "'He Would Go Out and Stay Out,'" 45–46.
5 Jas Obrecht, "Robert Johnson Revisited," *Guitar Player*, September 1990, 63; Jas Obrecht, "Robert Johnson," *Blues Guitar*, September 1990, 4.
6 Freeland, "'He Would Go Out and Stay Out,'" 45.
7 Freeland, "'He Would Go Out and Stay Out,'" 46.
8 Willie Moore, interview by Gayle Dean Wardlow, Sumner, Mississippi, November 30, 1969.
9 Willie Moore, interview by Gayle Dean Wardlow, Sumner, Mississippi, November 30, 1969.
10 Elizabeth Moore, interview with Gayle Dean Wardlow, Mitchner Plantation, May 18, 1968.
11 Elizabeth Moore, interview with Gayle Dean Wardlow, Mitchner Plantation, May 18, 1968.

12 Elizabeth Moore, interview with Gayle Dean Wardlow, Mitchner Plantation, May 18, 1968.

13 Elizabeth Moore, interview with Gayle Dean Wardlow, Mitchner Plantation, May 18, 1968.

14 Elizabeth Moore, interview with Gayle Dean Wardlow, Mitchner Plantation, May 18, 1968.

15 Nat Richardson, *Search for Robert Johnson*, DVD.

16 Steve LaVere, Liner notes to *Robert Johnson: The Complete Original Masters Centennial Edition* (Columbia, 2011), 6.

17 Freeland, "'He Would Go Out and Stay Out,'" 45–46.

18 Wink Clark, *Search for Robert Johnson*, DVD.

19 Willie Moore, interview with Gayle Dean Wardlow, Mitchner Plantation, May 18, 1968.

20 Jan McPeek, Merchants, *Tradesmen and Manufacturers Financial Condition for Greenville, Mississippi 1921* (Salem, OH: Jan and Naomi McPeek, 2003). Information obtained from 1921 R.G. Dun Mercantile Agency Reference Book, University of Mississippi Libraries Mississippi Delta Archives, https://guides.lib.olemiss.edu/delta.

21 Charles Reagan Wilson, "Chinese in Mississippi: An Ethnic People in a Biracial Society," Mississippi History Now (November 2002), http://mshistorynow.mdah.state.ms.us/articles/86/mississippi-chinese-an-ethnic-people-in-a-biracial-society.

22 Willie Moore, interview with Gayle Dean Wardlow, McManus Plantation, Sumner, Mississippi, November 30, 1969. If Moore's recollection is correct then we have more evidence that Johnson had a guitar and was at least learning to play by early 1927, as the Mississippi levees broke in April of 1927.

23 Willie Moore, interview with Gayle Dean Wardlow, McManus Plantation, Sumner, Misssissippi, November 30, 1969.

24 Willie Moore, interview with Gayle Dean Wardlow, McManus Plantation, Sumner, Mississippi, November 30, 1969.

25 Willie Moore, interview with Gayle Dean Wardlow, McManus Plantation, Sumner, Mississippi, November 30, 1969.

26 Willie Moore, interview with Gayle Dean Wardlow, McManus Plantation, Sumner, Mississippi, November 30, 1969.

27 Willie Moore, interview with Gayle Dean Wardlow, McManus Plantation, Sumner, Mississippi, November 30, 1969.

28 Elizabeth Moore, interview with Gayle Dean Wardlow, Mitchner Plantation, May 18, 1968.

29 Elizabeth Moore, interview with Gayle Dean Wardlow, Mitchner Plantation, May 18, 1968.

30 Wink Clark, *Search for Robert Johnson*, DVD.

Chapter 6: Marriage, Death, and the Blues

Much of the information in this chapter was originally published in Bruce Conforth, "The Death of Robert Johnson's Wife—Virginia Travis," *Living Blues* 226, vol. 44, no 4 (August 2013).

 1 The information given on the Johnson-Travis record of marriage is misleading. Virginia apparently listed Lula Samuels as her mother, yet her death certificate identifies Mattie Barrett as her mother. Lula Samuels is listed on census records as Virginia's grandmother.
 2 Johnson-Travis marriage license, Tunica County courthouse, Tunica, Mississippi.
 3 "Commodity Data," US Bureau of Labor Statistics, https://www.bls.gov/data, Retrieved November 30, 2008; Willard W. Cochrane, "Farm Prices, Myth and Reality," US Bureau of Labor Statistics (1958), 15.
 4 Department of Commerce, Bureau of the Census, State, Mississippi; County, Bolivar; Beat 3 (part); Enumeration District 6-24, Sheet 4-B, April 12, 1930.
 5 Steve LaVere, "Robert Johnson's Census Records," *Living Blues* 203, vol. 40, no. 5 (2009), 75.
 6 LaVere, *Complete Recordings*, 7.
 7 Department of Commerce, Bureau of the Census, State, Mississippi; County, DeSoto; Beat 3 (part); Enumeration District 17-10, Sheet 3-A, April 7, 1930.
 8 Department of Commerce, Bureau of the Census, State, Mississippi; County, Bolivar; Beat 3 (part); Enumeration District 6-24, Sheet 4-B, April 11, 1930.
 9 Department of Commerce, Bureau of the Census, State, Mississippi; County, Bolivar; Rosedale City; Enumeration District 6-8, Sheet 21-A, April 12, 1930.
 10 LaVere, "Robert Johnson's Census Records," 75; Pearson and McCulloch, *Robert Johnson*, 56; Obrecht, "Robert Johnson Revisited," 63: "For many plantation blacks, blues was 'devil's music' and strictly taboo."
 11 Jas Obrecht, "Johnny Shines: The Complete 1989 *Living Blues* Interview," http://jasobrecht.com/johnny-shines-complete-living-blues-interview; Henry Townsend, *Can't You Hear the Wind Howl*, DVD.
 12 Jim O'Neal, "The Death of Robert Johnson," *Living Blues* no. 94 (November/December 1990), 15.

Chapter 7: The Music Begins

 1 Jas Obrecht, "Robert Johnson," *Blues Guitar*, September 1990, 4.
 2 Willie Moore, interview by Gayle Dean Wardlow, Sumner, Mississippi, November 30, 1969.

3 Willie Moore, interview by Gayle Dean Wardlow, Sumner, Mississippi, November 30, 1969.

4 Elizabeth Moore, interview with Gayle Dean Wardlow, Mitchner Plantation, May 18, 1968.

5 Julius Lester, "I Can Make My Own Songs: An Interview with Son House," *Sing Out!* vol. 15, no. 3 (July 1965), 41.

6 Lester, "My Own Songs," 41.

7 Nick Perls, "Son House Interview, Part One," *78 Quarterly* vol. 1 (1967), 60.

8 Freeland, "'He Would Go Out and Stay Out,'" 46.

9 H. C. Speir, interview with Gayle Dean Wardlow, Pearl, Mississippi, April 10, 1964.

Chapter 8: Here Comes That Guitar Man

1 Freeland, "'He Would Go Out and Stay Out,'" 47.

2 All direct quotes from Loretha Zimmerman in chapter 8 are from her interview with Bruce Conforth, Beauregard, Mississippi, May 15, 2007.

3 Henry Townsend, *Can't You Hear the Wind Howl*, DVD; Loretha Zimmerman, interview by Bruce Conforth, Beauregard, Mississippi, May 15, 2007.
   The name Zimmerman has been presented in different manners: Zinneman, Zinnerman, Zinman, Zinermon, Zinemon. He is mentioned as Zinnerman in Pearson and McCulloch, 7; in Palmer as Zinneman, 113; in Schroeder as Zinermon, 22 This last spelling is based upon Schroeder's assertion that blues researcher Steven LaVere "uncovered a document with his signature from the cemetery where he buried his wife and where he was buried a short time later. The signature on the document is spelled Zinermon." (Schroeder, 167 fn. 2). The accuracy of this evidence would seem to point to someone else signing the form (if it exists) since 1) Zimmerman's daughter was quite insistent that her father spelled the name with two Ms, as did she and the rest of her family, 2) Zimmerman was buried in California prior to his second wife's death, 3) on his funeral program Zimmerman's name is spelled as such, 4) his Social Security records spell the name Zimmerman, and 5) all census records going back to the early 1800s record the name as Zimmerman.
   Myriad blues fan websites make claims regarding Zimmerman. For instance, www.thunderstruck.org makes the claim that some contemporaries of Johnson thought that Zinnerman was actually the Devil, www.canadajoeblue.com calls Zinnerman a "dark and devilish looking man," artruch.wordpress.com claims that Zinnerman was "a shadowy figure," en.wikipedia.org calls Zinnerman a "mysterious figure," and bitterman.

journalspace.com even goes so far as to claim that "Robert Johnson made a deal with a rakish devil named Ike Zinnerman to learn how to play the blues."

4 Willie Mason, Wink Clark, and Johnny Shines, *Can't You Hear the Wind Howl*, DVD.

5 Personal experience of the author. When Conforth was visiting Son House in Detroit his wife would not let him play the blues in the house. He was only allowed to play spiritual songs.

6 Loretha Zimmerman, interview with Bruce Conforth, Beauregard, Mississippi, May 15, 2007.

7 Freeland, "'He Would Go Out and Stay Out,'" 47.

8 Freeland, "'He Would Go Out and Stay Out,'" 44.

9 Freeland, "'He Would Go Out and Stay Out,'" 47.

10 Freeland, "'He Would Go Out and Stay Out,'" 47.

11 The idea that Zimmerman believed that in order to learn the blues one had to play in a graveyard at midnight has been claimed widely in most sources discussing him.

12 James Zimmerman Smith, interview with Bruce Conforth, Beauregard, Mississippi, May 15, 2007.

13 James Zimmerman Smith, interview with Bruce Conforth, Beauregard, Mississippi, May 15, 2007.

14 Freeland, "'He Would Go Out and Stay Out,'" 47.

15 Eula Mae Williams, interview with Gayle Dean Wardlow, Hazlehurst, Mississippi, May 20, 1998.

16 Eula Mae Williams, interview with Gayle Dean Wardlow, Hazlehurst, Mississippi, May 20, 1998.

17 Freeland, "'He Would Go Out and Stay Out,'" 47.

18 Eula Mae Williams, interview with Gayle Dean Wardlow, Hazlehurst, Mississippi, May 20, 1998.

19 Freeland, "'He Would Go Out and Stay Out,'" 47.

20 Freeland, "'He Would Go Out and Stay Out,'" 47.

21 Freeland, "'He Would Go Out and Stay Out,'" 47.

22 Freeland, "'He Would Go Out and Stay Out,'" 47.

23 Freeland, "'He Would Go Out and Stay Out,'" 48.

24 Freeland, "'He Would Go Out and Stay Out,'" 48.

25 Freeland, "'He Would Go Out and Stay Out,'" 47.

Chapter 9: Ramblin' at the Crossroads

1 Loretha Zimmerman, interview with Bruce Conforth, Beauregard, Mississippi, May 15, 2007.

2 Lester, "My Own Songs," 42.

3 Lester, "My Own Songs," 42.

4 Daniel Beaumont, *Preachin' the Blues: The Life and Times of Son House* (New York: Oxford University Press, 2011), 44.

5 Julio Finn, *The Bluesman: The Musical Heritage of Black Men and Women in the Americas* (London: Quartet Books, 1986), 215; Pearson and McCulloch, *Robert Johnson*, 45, 49, 51.

6 Jeffrey E. Anderson, *Conjure in African American Society* (Baton Rouge: Louisiana State University Press, 2005), 11.

7 Niles Newbell Pucket, *Folk Beliefs of the Southern Negro* (Chapel Hill: University of North Carolina Press, 1926, reprinted by Patterson Smith, 1968).

8 Zora Neale Hurston, "Hoodoo in America," *Journal of American Folklore* 44 (1931): 317–417.

9 Zora Neale Hurston, *Mules and Men* (New York: Harper Perennial Modern Classics, 2008).

10 Harry Middleton Hyatt, *Hoodoo - Conjuration - Witchcraft - Rootwork* (Racine, WI: Western Publishing, 1974).

11 Hortense Powdermaker, *After Freedom: A Cultural Study in the Deep South* (New York: Viking Press, 1939), 286–287.

12 Willie Mae Powell, *Search for Robert Johnson*, DVD.

13 "Queen" Elizabeth, *Search for Robert Johnson*, DVD.

14 Dean, *Chasin' That Devil Music*, 197.

15 O'Neal, "Death of Robert Johnson," 12.

16 Henry Townsend, *Can't You Hear the Wind Howl*, DVD.

17 Barry Lee Pearson, *Sounds So Good to Me: The Bluesman's Story* (Philadelphia: University of Pennsylvania Press, 1984), 62.

18 Pearson, *Sounds So Good*, 63.

19 Pearson, *Sounds So Good*, 63.

20 Clara Smith, "Done Sold My Soul to the Devil," recorded September 20, 1924, 140053 Columbia-14039.

21 Peg Leg Howell, "Low Down Rounder Blues," recorded April 1928, Columbia-14320.

22 Bessie Smith, "Blue Spirit Blues," recorded October 11, 1929, Columbia-14527.

23 J. T. "Funny Paper" Smith, "Fool's Blues," recorded April 1931, Vocalion-1674.

24 Elizabeth Moore, interview with Gayle Dean Wardlow, Mitchner Plantation, May 18, 1968.

25 Joe Callicott, interview with Gayle Dean Wardlow, Hernando, Mississippi, December 30–31, 1967.

26 Pete Franklin, interview with Steven Calt, June 1971.

27 Joe Callicott, interview with Gayle Dean Wardlow, Hernando, Mississippi, December 30–31, 1967.

28 Tom Freeland, "Some Witnesses to the Short Life of Robert Johnson," *Living Blues* 31, no. 2 (March–April 2000): 42.

29 Freeland, "'He Would Go Out and Stay Out,'" 48.

30 Freeland, "'He Would Go Out and Stay Out,'" 44.

31 Freeland, "'He Would Go Out and Stay Out,'" 44.

32 Freeland, "'He Would Go Out and Stay Out,'" 48.

33 Johnnie Temple, interview with Gayle Dean Wardlow, Jackson, Mississippi, April 1965.

34 Johnnie Temple, interview with Gayle Dean Wardlow, Jackson, Mississippi, April 1965.

Chapter 10: Traveling Riverside Blues

1 Eula Mae Williams, interview with Gayle Dean Wardlow, Hazlehurst, Mississippi, May 20, 1998.

2 Freeland, "Some Witnesses," 48.

3 Willie Moore, interview with Gayle Dean Wardlow, Sumner, Mississippi, McManus Plantation, November 30, 1969.

4 Pete Welding, "Ramblin' Johnny Shines," *Living Blues* 22 (July–Aug., 1975): 27.

5 Welding, "Ramblin' Johnny Shines," 27.

6 Larry Hoffman, "Robert Lockwood, Jr.," in *Rollin' and Tumblin': The Postwar Blues Guitarists*, ed. by Jas Obrecht (Backbeat Books, 2000), 165.

7 Department of Commerce, Bureau of the Census, State, Arkansas; County, Lee; Big Creek Township; Enumeration District 114, Sheet 6-A, January 29, 1920.

8 Department of Commerce, Bureau of the Census, State, Arkansas; County, Phillips; Helena City; Enumeration District 54-21, Sheet 26-A, April 26, 1930.

9 Bruce Conforth was married to Lockwood's goddaughter and during their many conversations Lockwood admitted that he made dates up "just to mess with" the people interviewing him.

10 Robert Lockwood, International Folk Alliance interview with Robert Santelli, 2000, FP-2006-CT-0187.

11 Hoffman, "Robert Lockwood, Jr.," 165.

12 Hoffman, "Robert Lockwood, Jr.," 166.

13 Hoffman, "Robert Lockwood, Jr.," 166.

14 Hoffman, "Robert Lockwood, Jr.," 166–67.

15 Robert Lockwood, Blues Narrative Stage: "Robert Johnson Remembered" interview by Worth Long, Smithsonian Folklife Festival, 1991. Festival recordings tape FP-1991-DT-0033.

16 Hoffman, "Robert Lockwood, Jr.," 166–67; Robert Lockwood, *Can't You Hear the Wind Howl*, DVD.

17 Lockwood, "Robert Johnson Remembered."

18 Guralnick, *Searching for Robert Johnson*, 48.

Chapter 11: I'm Booked and Bound to Go

1 All H. C. Speir quotes in chapter 11 are from interview with Gayle Dean Wardlow, Pearl, Mississippi, April 10, 1964, unless otherwise noted.

2 Speir music contract papers, collection of Gayle Dean Wardlow.

3 Elizabeth Moore, interview with Gayle Dean Wardlow, Mitchner Plantation, May 18, 1968.

4 Freeland, "'He Would Go Out and Stay Out,'" 48.

5 Marie Oertle, interview with Mack McCormick, 1984. McCormick interviews with Steve Cushing, December 2010, January 2011, and March 2011, in *Pioneers of the Blues Revival* Rev. Ed. (Urbana, Chicago, and Springfield: University of Illinois Press, 2014); McCormick conversations with Bruce Conforth, December 2008; McCormick conversations with Gayle Dean Wardlow, June 2000.

6 H. C. Speir, interview with Gayle Dean Wardlow, Pearl, Mississippi, April 10, 1964

7 Label Copy. Notice of Coupling and Assignment. Combination No. 7-03-56, Release Date January 4, 1937, Perfect and Oriole Records SA-2580 (Kind Hearted Woman Blues) and SA 2586 (Terraplane Blues); Label Copy. Notice of Coupling and Assignment. Combination No. 7-04-60, Release Date February 10, 1937, Perfect and Oriole Records SA-2616 (32-20 Blues) and SA 2631 (Last Fair Deal Gone Down); Label Copy. Notice of Coupling and Assignment. Combination No. 7-04-81, Release Date March 10, 1937, Perfect and Romeo Records SA-2628 (Dead Shrimp Blues) and SA 2581 (I Believe I'll Dust My Broom); Label Copy. Notice of Coupling and Assignment. Combination No. 7-05-81, Release Date April 20, 1937, Perfect and Romeo Records SA-2629 (Cross Road Blues) and SA 2583 (Ramblin' On My Mind); Label Copy. Notice of Coupling and Assignment. Combination No. 7-07-57, Release Date June 1, 1937, Perfect and Romeo Records SA-2627 (They're Red Hot) and SA 2585 (Come On In My Kitchen); Label Copy. Notice of Coupling and Assignment. Combination No. 7-09-55, Release Date August 1, 1937, Perfect and Romeo Records DAL-379 (From Four Until Late) and DAL 294 (Hell Hound On My Trail); Label Copy. Notice of Coupling and Assignment. Combination No. 7-10-65, Release Date September 15, 1937, Perfect and Romeo Records DAL-403 (Milkcow's Calf Blues) and DAL 296 (Malted Milk);

Label Copy. Notice of Coupling and Assignment. Combination No. 7-12-67, Release Date November 15, 1937, Perfect Records DAL-377 (Stones In My Passway) and DAL 378 (I'm A Steady Rollin' Man). Collection of Lawrence Cohn. Used by permission.

8 Don Law Jr., *Can't You Hear the Wind Howl*, DVD.

9 The fact that Johnson's guitar was destroyed by the San Antonio police and that Law had to borrow one for him should help put an end to the claims of ownership of the Gibson L-1 that he's holding in the famous Hooks Brothers studio photograph. If that was actually Johnson's guitar, since the photo was taken in 1936 shortly before his recording in San Antonio, that would, in all likelihood, have been the guitar that he had with him when arrested for vagrancy. It would have been the guitar that was destroyed.

10 Don Law Jr., *Can't You Hear the Wind Howl*, DVD.

11 Elizabeth Moore, interview with Gayle Dean Wardlow, Mitchner Plantation, May 18, 1968.

12 Larry Cohn, phone interview with Bruce Conforth, June 12, 2014.

13 Frank Driggs, Original liner notes, *Robert Johnson: King of the Delta Blues Singers* (Sony Music Entertainment, 1961).

14 Don Law, Letter to Frank Driggs, April 10, 1961.

15 Patricia Schroeder, *Robert Johnson: Mythmaking and Contemporary American Culture* (Chicago: University of Illinois Press, 2004), 26–27; Jas Obrecht, "Robert Johnson," in *Blues Guitar: The Men Who Made the Music* (San Francsico: Miller Freeman, 1993), 12.

16 Johnny Shines, *Can't You Hear the Wind Howl*, DVD.

17 Hoffman, "Robert Lockwood, Jr.," 167.

Chapter 12: Kind Hearted Women

1 Pete Welding, "The Robert Johnson I Knew, Pt 2," *Blues Unlimited* 66, 1969, 15.

2 H. C. Speir, interview with Gayle Dean Wardlow, Pearl, Mississippi, April 10, 1964.

3 Dave Rubin, *Robert Johnson: The New Transcriptions* (Milwaukee, WI: Hal Leonard, 1999).

4 Hyatt, *Hoodoo*, 349.

5 Debra DeSalvo, *The Language of the Blues* (New York: Billboard Books, 2006), 64.

6 Johnny Shines, *Can't You Hear the Wind Howl*, DVD.

7 Johnny Shines, *Can't You Hear the Wind Howl*, DVD.

8 Elizabeth Moore, interview with Gayle Dean Wardlow, Mitchner Plantation, May 18, 1968.

9 Shirley Ratisseau, "The Girl Who Met Robert Johnson," *Austin Chronicle*, August 3, 2012.

10 Agustín Gurza, "Frontera Project: Berlanga y Montalvo: The Blues and the Borderlands," Strachwitz Frontera Collection of Mexican and Mexican American Recordings, February 11, 2015, http://frontera.library. ucla.edu/blog/2016/02/berlanga-y-montalvo-blues-and-borderlands.

11 LaVere, *Complete Recordings*, 24.

12 Robert Avant-Mier, "Heard It on the X," in *Radio Cultures: The Sound Medium in American Life*, ed. Michael C. Keith (New York: Peter Lang Publishing, 2008), 54.

13 Pearson and McCulloch, *Robert Johnson*, 25–26.

14 Elizabeth Moore, interview with Gayle Dean Wardlow, Mitchner Plantation, May 18, 1968.

15 Booker Miller, interview with Gayle Dean Wardlow, Greenwood, Mississippi, April 20, 1968.

16 Elizabeth Moore, interview with Gayle Dean Wardlow, Mitchner Plantation, May 18, 1968.

17 Booker Miller, interview with Gayle Dean Wardlow, Greenwood, Mississippi, April 20, 1968.

18 Hyatt, *Hoodoo*, 349.

19 Pearson and McCulloch, *Robert Johnson*, 77.

20 Timothy Matovina and Jesús F. de la Teja, eds., *Recollections of a Tejano Life: Antonio Menchaca in Texas History* (Austin: University of Texas Press, 2013).

21 H. C. Speir, interview with Gayle Dean Wardlow, Pearl, Mississippi, April 10, 1964.

22 H. C. Speir, interview with Gayle Dean Wardlow, Pearl, Mississippi, April 10, 1964.

23 Willie Mae Powell, *Search for Robert Johnson*, DVD.

24 Willie Mae Powell, *Can't You Hear the Wind Howl*, DVD.

25 Willie Mae Powell, *Search for Robert Johnson*, DVD.

Chapter 13: I Left with My Head Cut

1 Lester, "I Can Make My Own Songs," 41–42.

2 Elizabeth Moore, interview with Gayle Dean Wardlow, Mitchner Plantation, May 18, 1968.

3 Pete Welding, "Ramblin' Johnny Shines," *Living Blues* 22 (Jul.–Aug. 1975): 25.

4 Johnny Shines, Blues Narrative Stage: "Guitar Styles," Smithsonian Folklife Festival, 1991. Festival recordings tape FP-1991-DT-0048.

5 Johnny Shines, "The Robert Johnson I Knew," in *The American Folk*

Music Occasional, Chris Strachwitz and Pete Welding, eds., Vol. 2 (New York: Oak, 1970), 31.

6 Shines, "The Robert Johnson I Knew," 31.

7 Barry Lee Pearson, *Jook Right On: Blues Stories and Blues Storytellers* (Knoxville: University of Tennessee Press, 2005), 172.

8 Robert Lockwood, Blues Narrative Stage: "Guitar Styles," Smithsonian Folklife Festival, 1991. Festival recordings tape FP-1991-DT-0048.

9 Pete Welding, "The Robert Johnson I Knew: An Interview with Henry Townsend," *Down Beat* 35 (October 31, 1968): 18, 32, Reprinted in *Blues Unlimited* no. 64 (July 1969): 10.

10 Henry Townsend, Blues Narrative Stage: "Guitar Styles," Smithsonian Folklife Festival, 1991. Festival recordings tape FP-1991-DT-0048.

11 Ishmon Bracey, interview with Gayle Dean Wardlow, December 30 and 31, 1967, Hernando, Mississippi, Inventory #tta0182dd, track #7.

12 Robert Lockwood, interview by Robert Santelli, International Folk Alliance, 2000, FP-2006-CT-0187.

13 Johnny Shines, *Can't You Hear the Wind Howl*, DVD.

14 Obrecht, "Johnny Shines."

15 Johnny Shines, *Search for Robert Johnson*, DVD.

16 Shines, Blues Narrative Stage.

17 Shines, interview with Lawrence Cohn, May 1985.

18 Johnny Shines, *Can't You Hear the Wind Howl*, DVD.

19 Johnny Shines, "Remembering Robert Johnson," *American Folk Music Occasional 2*, Oak Publications, 1970.

20 Townsend, Blues Narrative Stage.

21 Shines, Blues Narrative Stage.

22 Johnny Shines, *Can't You Hear the Wind Howl*, DVD.

23 Johnny Shines, *Search for Robert Johnson*, DVD.

24 Guralnick, *Searching*, 26–27.

25 Welding, "Ramblin' Johnny Shines."

Chapter 14: Gotta Keep Movin', Blues Fallin' Down Like Hail

1 H. C. Speir, interview with Gayle Dean Wardlow, Pearl, Mississippi, April 10, 1964.

2 Shines, "The Robert Johnson I Knew," 31.

3 William H. Wiggins Jr., "Juneteenth: A Red Spot Day on the Texas Calendar," in *Juneteenth Texas: Essays in African-American Folklore*, eds. Francis Edward Abernathy and Carolyn Fielder Satterwhite (Denton: University of North Texas Press, 1996), 243.

4 Alan Govenar and Jay Brakefield, *Deep Ellum: The Other Side of Dallas* (College Station: Texas A&M University Press, 2013), 78.

5 Darwin Payne, "The Spirit of Enterprise," in *Dallas, An illustrated History* (Woodland Hills, CA: Windsor Publications, 1982), 157–185.

6 Writers' Program of the Work Projects Administration in the City of Dallas, 1936–1942, *The WPA Dallas Guide and History* (Denton, TX: UNT Digital Library, 1992), 296–297, http://digital.library.unt.edu/ark:/67531/metadc28336.

7 Alan Govenar and Jay Brakefield, *The Dallas Music Scene 1920s–1960s* (Charleston, NC: Arcadia Publishing, 2014), 47.

8 Alan Govenar, phone interview with Bruce Conforth, January 12, 2019.

9 Marvin "Smokey" Montgomery, interview with Gayle Dean Wardlow, June 10, 1959.

10 Marvin "Smokey" Montgomery, interview with Gayle Dean Wardlow, June 10, 1959.

11 Smokey Montgomery, *Can't You Hear The Wind Howl*, DVD.

12 Catherine Yronwode, "Foot Track Magic," in *Hoodoo in Theory and Practice*, http://www.luckymojo.com/foottrack.html.

13 Wiggins, "Juneteenth," 244.

14 Yronwode, "Foot Track Magic."

15 Welding, "Ramblin' Johnny Shines," 29.

16 Willie Moore, interview with Gayle Dean Wardlow, Mitchener Plantation, Mississippi, May 18, 1968.

17 H. C. Speir, interview with Gayle Dean Wardlow, Pearl, Mississippi, April 10, 1964.

18 Wald, *Escaping the Delta*, 177.

19 *Can't You Hear the Wind Howl*, DVD.

20 Shines, "The Robert Johnson I Knew," 31.

21 Shines, "The Robert Johnson I Knew," 31.

22 Joe Callicott, interview with Gayle Dean Wardlow, Hernando, Mississippi, December 30–31, 1967.

Chapter 15: When I Leave This Town I'm Gon' Bid You Fare, Farewell

1 John Henry Hammond II, "An Experience in Jazz History," in Dominique-René de Lerma, ed., *Black Music in Our Culture: Curricular Ideas on the Subjects, Materials, and Problems* (Kent, OH: Kent State University Press, 1970), 42–53.

2 Henry Johnson (John Henry Hammond II), *New Masses*, March 2, 1937, 29.

3 John Henry Hammond II, *New Masses*, July 1937, 31.

4 Townsend, Blues Narrative Stage.

5 Welding, "Ramblin' Johnny Shines," 29–30.

6 Welding, "The Robert Johnson I Knew," 32.

7 Shines, *Search for Robert Johnson*, DVD.

8 Shines, "The Robert Johnson I Knew," 32.

9 Shines, "The Robert Johnson I Knew," 32.

10 Shines, "The Robert Johnson I Knew," 33.

11 Shines, "The Robert Johnson I Knew," 33.

12 Shines, *Can't You Hear the Wind Howl*, DVD.

13 Shines, *Can't You Hear the Wind Howl*, DVD.

14 Shines, Blues Narrative Stage. This part of Shines's narrative helps corroborate the dates in question since the John Gaston Hospital in Memphis did not open until the second half of 1936. Since we have accounted for Johnson's whereabouts through the end of 1936 and into early 1937, the end of that year is the only possibility.

15 Obrecht, "Johnny Shines," 9.

16 Obrecht, "Johnny Shines," 8.

17 Shines, "The Robert Johnson I Knew," 32.

18 Shines, Blues Narrative Stage.

19 Shines, "The Robert Johnson I Knew," 33.

20 Welding, "Ramblin' Johnny Shines," 30.

21 Welding, "Ramblin' Johnny Shines," 30.

22 Shines, Blues Narrative Stage.

23 Until this current research the pastor's name was always believed to be *Moten* instead of *Morton*. It is probably for this reason that no previous information about him or this incident has ever been published, not unlike the mistaken spelling of Ike Zimmerman's name.

24 mtzion, "History," http://mtzionfgc.wikifoundry.com/page/History, January 10, 2008.

25 Paul McIntyre, *Black Pentecostal Music in Windsor*, Paper #15 (Ottawa: Canadian Centre for Folk Culture Studies, 1976), 20.

26 Obrecht, "Johnny Shines."

27 Welding, "Ramblin' Johnny Shines," 30.

28 Obrecht, "Johnny Shines."

29 Welding, "Ramblin' Johnny Shines," 29.

30 Shines interview with Lawrence Cohn, May 1985.

31 Victoria Spivey, discussion with John Paul Hammond, when he recorded for her record label in the 1960s.

32 McCormick letter and conversation to Bruce Conforth, March 23, 2006.

33 Shines, "The Robert Johnson I Knew," 32.

34 Shines, *Can't You Hear the Wind Howl*, DVD.

Chapter 16: You May Bury My Body Down by the Highway Side

1 Elizabeth Moore, interview with Gayle Dean Wardlow, Mitchner Plantation, May 18, 1968.

2 Welding, "Ramblin' Johnny Shines."

3 McCormick, letter and phone conversation with Conforth, February 12, 2007.

4 Honeyboy Edwards, *The World Don't Owe Me Nothing* (Chicago: Chicago Review Press, 1997), 99–100.

5 Shines, "The Robert Johnson I Knew," 32.

6 Rosie Eskridge, interview with Gayle Dean Wardlow, Greenwood, Mississippi, June 2001.

7 Rosie Eskridge, interview with Gayle Dean Wardlow, Greenwood, Mississippi, June 2001.

8 Cedell Davis claimed that the woman who gave Robert the poison was named "Craphouse Bea." According to Mack McCormick her real name was Beatrice Davis, the young wife of R. D. "Ralph" Davis.

9 Edwards, *The World Don't Owe*, 103–104.

10 Rosie Eskridge, interview with Gayle Dean Wardlow, Greenwood, Mississippi, June 2001.

11 Rosie Eskridge, interview with Gayle Dean Wardlow, Greenwood, Mississippi, June 2001.

12 Freeland, "'He Would Go Out and Stay Out,'" 40.

13 Willie Coffee, interview with LaVere, *Hellhounds on My Trail: The Afterlife of Robert Johnson* (WinStar TV & Video, 1999), DVD.

14 Mack McCormick, phone invterview with Bruce Conforth, May 14, 2008.

15 Rosie Eskridge, interview with Gayle Dean Wardlow, Greenwood, Mississippi, June 2001.

Epilogue: Last Fair Deal Goin' Down

1 John Henry Hammond II, "Jim Crow Blues," New Masses, December 13, 1938, 27–28.

2 Alan Lomax, *The Land Where the Blues Began* (New York: Pantheon, 1993), 14. A search of the Alan Lomax archives and his field notes for the 1942 trip reveals no information about his meeting Johnson's mother. To report a conversation with such specificity one would imagine that field notes were used, but none containing this dialogue exist. There is no evidence, therefore, to suggest that such an event actually took place.

3 Alan Lomax, *The Land Where the Blues Began* (New York: Pantheon, 1993), 14–15.

INDEX